THE HISTORY OF HOLLAND

Mark T. Hooker

The Greenwood Histories of the Modern Nations
Frank W. Thackeray and John E. Findling, Series Editors

Greenwood Press
Westport, Connecticut • London

THE
HISTORY OF
HOLLAND

Library of Congress Cataloging-in-Publication Data

Hooker, Mark T.
    The history of Holland / Mark T. Hooker.
       p.   cm. — (The Greenwood histories of the modern nations,
  ISSN 1096–2905)
    Includes bibliographical references and index.
    ISBN 0–313–30658–3 (alk. paper)
    1. Netherlands—History. I. Title. II. Series.
  DJ111.H66   1999
  949.2—dc21   98–51895

British Library Cataloguing in Publication Data is available.

Library of Congress Catalog Card Number: 98–51895
ISBN: 0–313–30658–3
ISSN: 1096–2905

First published in 1999

Greenwood Press, 88 Post Road West, Westport, CT 06881
An imprint of Greenwood Publishing Group, Inc.
www.greenwood.com

Printed in the United States of America

The paper used in this book complies with the
Permanent Paper Standard issued by the National
Information Standards Organization (Z39.48–1984).

10 9 8 7 6 5 4 3 2 1

My great thanks to
Anne Jacobs-Otten,
who read the manuscript and
made innumerable valuable suggestions

My appreciation to
Frank Thackeray and John Findling
for providing me the opportunity
to participate in this project

And my special thanks to
my wife, Stella—born and raised
in The Hague—who is the inspiration
for my interest in
Holland and things Dutch

Contents

Series Foreword

The Greenwood Histories of the Modern Nations series is intended to provide students and interested laypeople with up-to-date, concise, and analytical histories of many of the nations of the contemporary world. Not since the 1960s has there been a systematic attempt to publish a series of national histories, and, as series editors, we believe that this series will prove to be a valuable contribution to our understanding of other countries in our increasingly interdependent world.

Over thirty years ago, at the end of the 1960s, the Cold War was an accepted reality of global politics, the process of decolonization was still in progress, the idea of a unified Europe with a single currency was unheard of, the United States was mired in a war in Vietnam, and the economic boom of Asia was still years in the future. Richard Nixon was president of the United States, Mao Tse-tung (not yet Mao Zedong) ruled China, Leonid Brezhnev guided the Soviet Union, and Harold Wilson was prime minister of the United Kingdom. Authoritarian dictators still ruled most of Latin America, the Middle East was reeling in the wake of the Six-Day War, and Shah Reza Pahlavi was at the height of his power in Iran. Clearly, the past thirty years have been witness to a great deal of historical change, and it is to this change that this series is primarily addressed.

With the help of a distinguished advisory board, we have selected nations whose political, economic, and social affairs mark them as among the most important in the waning years of the twentieth century, and for each nation we have found an author who is recognized as specialist in the history of that nation. These authors have worked most cooperatively with us and with Greenwood Press to produce volumes that reflect current research on their nation and that are interesting and informative to their prospective readers.

The importance of a series such as this cannot be underestimated. As a superpower whose influence is felt all over the world, the United States can claim a "special" relationship with almost every other nation. Yet many Americans know very little about the histories of the nations with which the United States relates. How did they get to be the way they are? What kind of political systems have evolved there? What kind of influence do they have in their own region? What are the dominant political, religious, and cultural forces that move their leaders? These and many other questions are answered in the volumes of this series.

The authors who have contributed to this series have written comprehensive histories of their nations, dating back to prehistoric time in some cases. Each of them, however, has devoted a significant portion of the book to events of the past thirty years, because the modern era has contributed the most to contemporary issues that have an impact on U.S. policy. Authors have made an effort to be as up-to-date as possible so that readers can benefit from the most recent scholarship and a narrative that includes very recent events.

In addition to the historical narrative, each volume in this series contains an introductory overview of the country's geography, political institutions, economic structure, and cultural attributes. This is designed to give readers a picture of the nation as it exists in the contemporary world. Each volume also contains additional chapters that add interesting and useful detail to the historical narrative. One chapter is a thorough chronology of important historical events, making it easy for readers to follow the flow of a particular nation's history. Another chapter features biographical sketches of the nation's most important figures in order to humanize some of the individuals who have contributed to the historical development of their nation. Each volume also contains a comprehensive bibliography, so that those readers whose interest has been sparked may find out more about the nation and its history. Finally, there is a carefully prepared topic and person index.

Readers of these volumes will find them fascinating to read and useful in understanding the contemporary world and the nations that comprise it. As series editors, it is our hope that this series will contribute to a heightened sense of global understanding as we enter a new century.

Frank W. Thackeray and John E. Findling
Indiana University Southeast

Timeline of Historical Events

57 B.C.	Julius Caesar begins the conquest of the Belgian tribes
15 B.C.	Augustus designates the territory of the Belgian tribes Gallica Belgica
12 B.C.	The Frisians come under Roman dominion
A.D. 28	Frisian revolt against Rome
A.D. 48	The Romans build a castellum on an island in the Rhine at the present site of the city of Utrecht
A.D. 68–69	Batavian revolt against Rome
ca. A.D. 400	Fall of the Roman Empire in Western Europe
481	Clovis becomes king
486	Clovis captures the last Roman possession in Gaul
493	Clovis subjugates all the Salian tribes
506	Clovis defeats the Alemanni, a German tribe
511	Clovis dies and his empire is split between his sons

687	Pépin the Younger (steward of the Merovingian king) reunites the empire
689	Pépin defeats Radbod, king of the Frisians
695	Willibrord establishes a base for his evangelistic efforts among the Frisians at Utrecht
714	Radbod takes back the south of Friesland and expands his territory as far as Cologne
717	Karel Martel defeats Radbod
732	Karel Martel defeats the Muslims near Poitiers
751	Pépin III takes the Crown of the Frankish Empire in fact as well as in deed
800	Pope Leo II recognizes Charlemagne as the Holy Roman Emperor
843	The Treaty of Verdun divides Charlemagne's empire among his three grandsons
850–1007	The Viking invasions
1287	The Zuiderzee is formed by flooding from the sea
1356	Blijde Inkomst (Joyful Ingress; the Dutch equivalent of the Magna Carta) recognizes the rights of citizens
1419	Philip the Good, Count of Burgundy, ascends to power
1464	Philip creates the first States-General (central Parliament)
1477	The States-General is granted the "Great Privileges" charter
	Mary of Burgundy marries Maximilian I of the House of Hapsburg
1516	Charles V becomes king of Spain
1519	Charles V becomes Holy Roman Emperor
1532	The Council of State is instituted
1543	Charles V conquers Gelre, the last of the seventeen provinces
1555	Charles V abdicates in favor of Philip II
1559	Margaret of Parma becomes vicereine of the Netherlands
1564	Cardinal Granvelle recalled
1566	The "Compromis" of the lesser Dutch nobles

1567	Duke of Alva dispatched to the Netherlands
	Margaret abdicates
1568–1648	The Eighty Years' War for independence from Spain
1572	The *Watergeuzen* (Water Beggars) attack harbors in Holland and Zeeland
	The first free assembly of the States-General
1573	Duke of Alva replaced by Requeséns
1574	The siege of Leiden broken
1576	The Pacification of Ghent
1579	The Union of Atrecht restores Spanish rule in the south
	The Union of Utrecht declares de facto independence from Spain
1581	The Act of Abjuration officially declares independence from Spain
1584	William of Orange assassinated in Delft by a Roman Catholic fanatic
1588	The Spanish Armada
1598	Philip II dies
1602	The Verenigde Oostindische Compagnie (VOC; United East India Company) established
1609–1621	The Twelve Years' Truce in the Eighty Years' War
1621	The Westindische Compagnie (WIC; West India Company) established
1648	The Treaty of Westphalia (Münster) ends the Eighty Years' War: The seven northern provinces recognized as an independent state; the southern provinces remain under Spanish rule
1650	William II dies
1650–1672	The first Stadholderless Period
1652–1654	The first Anglo-Dutch War
1665–1667	The second Anglo-Dutch War
1672–1674	The third Anglo-Dutch War

1677	William III marries Mary, daughter of James II of England
1689	The Glorious Revolution proclaims William and Mary joint rulers of England
1702	William III dies childless, bringing an end to the direct line of the House of Orange
1702–1747	The second Stadholderless Period
1748	William IV proclaimed stadholder; the title is made hereditary
1780–1784	The fourth Anglo-Dutch War
1782	John Adams arrives in The Hague as the first U.S. ambassador
1791	The WIC is dissolved
1795–1806	The Batavian Republic: The Netherlands ruled by the Patriot Movement, whose leaders sympathize with France
1799	The charter for the VOC expires
1806–1810	Louis Bonaparte, brother of the emperor, rules as king of Holland
1810	The Kingdom of Holland incorporated into the French Empire
1813	The Dutch are liberated from the French, following the collapse of the Napoleonic Empire
	William I (of Orange-Nassau) crowned king of the Netherlands
1815–1830	Present-day Belgium and Holland united in the Kingdom of the Netherlands under William I by the Congress of Vienna
1830	The Belgian revolution
1839	The official separation of Belgium and Holland
1848	A new constitution marks the beginning of modern democracy
1872	The New Water Way canal opens
1914–1918	World War I: Belgium is a battlefield; Holland is neutral
1916	Extensive flooding north of Amsterdam
1917	Universal suffrage for men
1922	Universal suffrage for women
1932	The Afsluitdijk (the Barrier Dike) is completed
1940–1945	World War II: German occupation

1946–1949	Police actions in Indonesia
1948	Queen Wilhelmina abdicates in favor of her daughter Juliana
	Formation of the Benelux Customs Union
1948–1954	The Marshall Plan
1949	Indonesian independence
1953	Massive flooding in Zeeland
1957	The Treaty of Rome establishes the European Economic Community
1967	The formation of the European Community
1975	Surinam (formerly Dutch Guiana) obtains independence
1980	Queen Juliana abdicates in favor of her daughter Beatrix
1986	The four IJsselmeer/Zuiderzee polders officially become the twelfth province, named Flevoland
1992	Treaty of Maastricht sets Europe on the path to the Economic and Monetary Union (EMU)
1993	Formation of the European Union
1995	Massive flooding along the rivers in the south
	The safe haven of Srebrenica in Bosnia under the protection of Dutch peacekeeping troops falls on July 11
1999	The Euro becomes a currency as the European Central Bank is established on January 1
2002	The Euro becomes a circulating currency on January 1
	The current national currencies of the EMU member states are withdrawn from circulation on July 1
2003	Queen Beatrix turns sixty-five

Abbreviations

AAW	Algemene Arbeidsongeschiktheidswet (General Disabilities Pensions Act)
ABW	Algemene Bijstandswet (National Assistance Act)
AEX	Amsterdam Stock Exchange
AKW	Algemene Kinderbijslagwet (General Children's Benefit Act)
ANW	Algemene Nabestaandenwet (General Survivors' Pensions Act)
AOV	Algemeen Ouderen Verbond (General Federation of Seniors)
AOW	Algemene Ouderdomswet (General Old Age Pensions Act)
AVRO	Algemene Vereeniging Radio Omroep (General Association of Broadcast Radio)
AWBZ	Algemene Wet Bijzondere Ziektekosten (General Act on Exceptional Medical Costs)
BTW	Belasting op de Toegevoegde Waarde (value-added tax)
CDA	Christen-Democratisch Appel (Christian Democratic Appeal coalition)
CPN	Communistische Partij Nederland (Dutch Communist Party)

D'66   Democraten '66 (Democrats 1966)

ECB   European Central Bank

EEC   European Economic Community

EMU   Economic and Monetary Union

EU   European Union

EUF   Energy Use Factor

GDP   gross domestic groduct

GNP   gross national product

IKV   Interkerkelijk Vredesberaad (Interfaith Peace Consultative Com-
                mittee)

IMF   International Monetary Fund

KRO   Katholieke Radio Omroep (Catholic Broadcast Radio)

KVP   Katholieke Volkspartij (Catholic People's Party)

NATO   North Atlantic Treaty Organization

NCRV   Nederlandsche Christelijke Radio Vereeniging (Dutch Christian
                Radio Associaton)

NDT   Netherlands Dance Theater

NRC   *Nieuwe Rotterdamse Courant* (New Rotterdam Courier)

OECD   Organization for Economic Cooperation and Development

PC   personal computer

PPR   Politieke Partij Radikalen (Radical Party)

PvdA   Partij van de Arbeid (Labor Party)

REB   Regulerende Energie Belasting (Energy Regulation Tax)

SFOR   Stablization Force

TEU   twenty-feet equivalent units

UNTSO   United Nations Truce Supervision Organization

USIS   United States Information Service

VARA   Vereeniging van Arbeiders Radio Amateurs (Association of Labor
                Radio Amateurs)

VOC   Verenigde Oostindische Compagnie (United East India Company)

VPRO	Vrijzinnig Protestantse Radio Omroep (Liberal Protestant Broadcast Radio)
VUT	Vervroegde Uittreding (Early Retirement)
VVD	Volkspartij voor Vrijheid en Democratie (People's Party for Freedom and Democracy)
WAO	Wet op de Arbeidsongeschiktheidsverzekering (Disability Benefits Act)
WIC	Westindische Compagnie (West India Company)
WULBZ	Wet Uitbreiding Loondoorbetaling bij Ziekte (Act on Expanding Continuing Salary Payments during Illness)
WW	Werkeloosheidswet (Unemployment Benefits Act)
ZFW	Ziekenfondswet (Health Insurance Act)

Part I

The Contemporary Nation: An Overview

1

Geography

The official name of Holland is the Kingdom of the Netherlands. It is a constitutional monarchy about the size of the states of Massachusetts and Connecticut put together. Dutch purists insist that Holland is only the name of two of the country's twelve provinces (North and South Holland), but the names Holland and the Netherlands are used almost interchangeably in most contexts. Just listen to Dutch fans rooting for the national team at a soccer match. They are rooting for Holland, not the Netherlands: "Hup—Holland—Hup!"

The English word "Dutch" really comes from the German word *deutsch*, which means German. The English originally used it for all Germanic people, but toward the end of the sixteenth century, because they came into contact and conflict with Hollanders more often than with the other Germans, the use of the word "Dutch" came to be limited to Hollanders—except in Pennsylvania.

The Pennsylvania Dutch are not really from Holland at all but are from Germany and Switzerland. Their name also has its origin in the word *deutsch*. They are the descendants of German and Swiss immigrants who settled in Pennsylvania in the seventeenth and eighteenth centuries. The largest Dutch (Hollander) communities in America are in Michigan. Holland, Michigan, is the home of the Dutch Village, the Holland Museum, the Dutch Winter Fest, and the Tulip Time Festival. Queen Beatrix stopped there on her trip to the United States in 1982.

LANGUAGE

Dutch is a Germanic language. It is spoken by approximately 16 million people in the Netherlands and 5 million in northern Belgium. (Southern Belgium is French speaking.) Dutch distinguishes itself from German by major differences in pronunciation, vocabulary, and grammar. Knowing one helps you learn the other, but they are not mutually intelligible.

The Dutch spoken in the Netherlands differentiates itself from Flemish—the Dutch spoken in Belgium—by differences in pronunciation and vocabulary that approximate the differences between American and British English. Within the Netherlands, there are also a number of regional dialects that are so strong as to be almost incomprehensible to Dutch speakers from outside the area. Televised interviews with someone who has a strong Limburg accent are subtitled so that everyone watching can understand what is being said.

Dutch is not the only language spoken in the Netherlands. The province of Friesland is officially bilingual. All documentation must be prepared in both Frisian and Dutch. Frisian competes with Dutch in Friesland just as Welsh and Irish (Gaelic) compete with English in Wales and Ireland. Frisian is also still spoken in the areas of northern Germany that border on the province of Groningen. Approximately 400,000 people speak it. Frisian vocabulary is much closer to English than to Dutch. This underscores the fact that the Angles and the Saxons of England came from the same group of German tribes as the Frisians: the Ingaevones. Frisian is subtitled on Dutch television, just like English, German, French, or any other foreign language would be.

In this present age, it is hard to imagine any use for Dutch outside the Netherlands and Belgium. Unless you are willing to put a lot of effort into learning Dutch, there is no real need to learn more than a few courtesy phrases. Three-quarters of the population speak English, and those who do speak it very well. English is taught beginning in the fifth grade. English-language movies and television programs are shown in the original language with Dutch subtitles. The language of pop music is English, and fans are motivated to understand the lyrics. Universities regularly present courses taught in English.

In the seventeenth century, however, the Republic of the United Netherlands was one of the great economic, cultural, and scientific powers of the world. Many Dutch scientists were world renowned, such as Hermann Boerhaave (1668–1738), the founder of the modern clinical method of teaching medicine; Hugo de Groot (1583–1645), the founder of international law; and Christiaan Huygens (1629–1695), the inventor of the pendulum clock. Dutch universities attracted large numbers of foreign students. This all led to Dutch being much better known outside the Netherlands than it is currently.

The influence of Dutch can still be seen today in the Russian language, where many of the nautical terms are of Dutch origin. This is because the Russian czar Peter the Great (1672–1725) studied shipbuilding in Zaandam in the seventeenth century. When he returned to Russia, the Dutch words that were part of his skills and experience as a shipbuilder went with him.

For centuries, after 1641, when Shogun (1623–1651) Tokugawa Iemitsu (1604–1651) expelled all the foreigners from Japan, the Dutch were the only Europeans who had access to the country. Dutch merchants were the only source of Western goods and ideas entering the country, and Dutch was the only European language spoken there. Many Japanese medical and nautical terms are Dutch in origin, as are words like *biiru* (beer), *koohi* (coffee), and *uotaa* (water). In present-day Japan, Dutch is still taught in a number of universities as a part of Indonesian studies. This seemingly incongruent combination of Dutch and Indonesian studies is explained by the fact that Indonesia used to be a Dutch colony. Much of the material written about Indonesia in the Dutch period is written in Dutch, and students need to be able to read Dutch in order to use them. In Indonesia itself, where Dutch is no longer the official language of state and is no longer widely spoken, lawyers still need to know Dutch, because many of the legal documents that form the precedents are written in Dutch.

Dutch is still spoken in the Netherlands Antilles and in Surinam (the former Dutch Guiana). If the Dutch had not been forced out of New Amsterdam (now New York) by the British in the second Anglo-Dutch War (1665–1667), Dutch would undoubtedly still be widely spoken along the East Coast of North America. It was in use in churches in New York until 1763.

Even though Dutch immigrants are quick to take up the language of their adopted lands, in the United States, Canada, New Zealand, and Australia—countries that absorbed large numbers of Dutch immigrants—Dutch is still spoken in some homes. There are a number of Dutch-language newspapers serving this audience. *De Hollandse Krant* (The Dutch Newspaper), for example, is published in Langley, British

Columbia, and is distributed widely both in Canada and the United States. Universities in these countries often offer Dutch and Dutch studies. The University of Melbourne, for instance, has a large Dutch department.

In South Africa, Dutch has had a very widespread, long-lasting impact. In the seventeenth century, travel to the Dutch East Indies (Indonesia) was by a long sea voyage around the southern tip of Africa. (The Suez Canal did not open a shorter route to the Far East until 1869.) In 1652, a Dutch colony was established on the Cape of Good Hope to serve as a way station on the trip to the Dutch East Indies, where ships could take on fresh drinking water and provisions and the sick could be tended. Afrikaans, which is spoken by 6 million people in South Africa, is based on the seventeenth-century Dutch of those colonists. Even the arrival of large numbers of British, who eventually took total control of South Africa, did not entirely displace Afrikaans with English. Dutch and Afrikaans are so closely related that educated native speakers can read each other's newspapers with a little extra effort.

LAND SURFACE AREA

The total land surface area of Holland is 33,948 square kilometers, or 13,107 square miles. This excludes all inland and territorial waters wider than 6 meters, or 20 feet. If all the water surface area is included, Holland has an area of 41,526 square kilometers, or 16,033 square miles. Holland is smaller than Denmark but larger than Belgium. It is located in northwestern Europe, bordered on the east by Germany, on the south by Belgium, and on the west and north by the North Sea. Holland's North Sea coastline is longer (642 km) than its border with either Belgium (407 km) or Germany (556 km).

Holland is located between 50°45′ and 53°52′ north latitude and between 3°21′ and 7°13′ east longitude. That places it south of Ketchikan, Alaska (55°25′ N, 131°40′ W), but north of Quebec (46°50′ N, 71°15′ W). The capital of the northern province of Groningen (53°13′ N) is almost on the same parallel as Goose Bay, Labrador (53°15′ N). At this latitude, the shortest day of the year—December 21—is only 7 hours and 43 minutes long. The longest—June 21—is 16 hours and 46 minutes long.

Climate

Despite its northern latitude, Holland has a moderate climate, with cool summers and mild winters. The average temperature in January is

2°C, or 35°F. The average temperature in July is 17°C, or 63°F. The North Sea has an extensive influence on the weather near the coast, moderating temperatures there. The average number of days on which the temperature drops below the freezing point on the coast is forty. Farther inland in the province of Drenthe, the average is eighty days.

The year 1996 had the warmest July since 1706, when the first reliable recording of weather data was begun. This record-breaking warm summer is part of a new trend in the climate of Holland. The five warmest years of the century have all occurred since 1987. In the ninety-five-month period following August 1987, the yearly average temperature was 1°C higher than for the period 1901–1987. The average temperature for July 1995, for example, was 20.1°C, which is 3.1°C higher than the pre-1987 average for July.

Until very recently, Dutch homes, offices, and stores were only rarely air-conditioned. Now, however, sales of home, car, and commercial air conditioners are on the rise, as the Dutch seek relief from what for them is the unusually oppressive summer heat. The question of the greenhouse effect is a topical one in Holland these days.

The average yearly rainfall is between 700 and 800 millimeters. The closer you are to the coast, the more rainfall you get.

The Battle to Keep Their Heads above Water

Holland literally means "land in a hollow." About 27% of the country is below sea level, and that is where about 60% of the population lives. The average elevation is only 11 meters, or 37 feet, above sea level. Holland is so low because it lies in the deltas of three rivers—the Rhine (in Dutch: Rijn), the Meuse (in Dutch: Maas), and the Scheldt (in Dutch: Schelde)—where they flow into the North Sea. Much of the country's soil was deposited by these rivers on their way to the sea. In addition to its rivers, Holland has one of Europe's most extensive networks of canals. Because there is water everywhere you go, swimming is a required subject in grade school as a practical safety measure for children.

The elevation rises as you move from west to east. The highest point is in the southeast. Vaalserberg in the province of Limburg is 321 meters (1,053 feet) above sea level. This part of the country is characterized by low ridges and gently rolling hills. The region is rich in coal, which was mined there from the sixteenth century until 1974, when the natural gas fields near Slochteren in Groningen caused a shift away from coal to gas as a fuel and resulted in the closing of the mines, due to the low price of natural gas and the high price of labor for the mines.

The lowest point in the country is 6.7 meters (22 feet) below sea level in the Prince Alexander Polder—"polder" is the word the Dutch use for land reclaimed from under the sea—northeast of Rotterdam.

In the west, the flat Dutch landscape is crisscrossed with drainage ditches that help keep the lowlands dry. The windmills—first used in the thirteenth century—that used to stand at the ends of these checkerboards to pump the water out, have been replaced by smaller and less obvious electric pumps that often run on solar cells. The windmills that used to drive the pumps and grind grain are now tourist attractions and museums, but there are still working windmills in Holland. Huge windmill parks now convert the ever-present wind from the North Sea into electricity. In 1995, there were about 1,000 power-generating windmills with an average capacity of 250 megawatts. That is enough power to supply about 150,000 households.

The largest wind-driven electric power plant in Europe is in Eemsmond in the northern province of Groningen. The plant has 94 wind turbines, which produce 73 million kilowatt-hours per year—enough to power 24,000 households. The plant is a joint project between the Dutch firm EDON and the American firm Kenetech. Operation of the plant is remotely controlled from a Kenetech facility in California.

The fight to keep the lowlands above water has been long and hard. Dutch character reflects that struggle. The need to work together to keep their heads above water lies at the foundation of the renowned Dutch tolerance and government by consensus. To paraphrase Benjamin Franklin (1706–1790), they had to learn to swim together or, most assuredly, they would have all drowned separately.

The Dutch are hardworking, determined, and do not give up easily. Since 1200, there have been at least twenty major floods. The Frisians, who settled in the northern part of present-day Holland over 2,000 years ago, built huge earth mounds called *terpen* to protect them and their livestock from high tides and floods. Eventually, some of these mounds were connected by earthwork walls for additional protection. These were the first dikes.

In the course of their history, the Dutch have improved their techniques for fighting the sea. Earthwork mounds gave way to stone and concrete, and windmills gave way to electric pumps. Today, the Dutch are world-recognized masters of hydraulic engineering.

Diking in shallows to recover land from under the water has allowed the Dutch to expand the surface area of the country without having to take land from someone else, as other nations have at times done. The largest and best-known polders are in the former Zuiderzee (*zuider* =

south; *zee* = sea). The Zuiderzee was not always a sea. Until the thirteenth century, it was a low-lying marshland inhabited by the Frisians. In 1287, the North Sea broke through the dunes that had kept it out, flooding the marshes. It was over 600 years before the Dutch were able to win back the land that had once been theirs from the sea.

In 1916, large parts of the country to the north of Amsterdam were flooded during a heavy storm. This was the impetus to start the project to reclaim the land under the Zuiderzee that had first been published in 1886 by Cornelis Lely (1854–1929). Sixteen years later, in 1932, the Dutch closed the Afsluitdijk (the Barrier Dike). The dike had been built as two separate arms reaching out from the shores of the provinces of North Holland and Friesland across what once was 32 kilometers of open water. At the point where the two arms of the dike meet, there is a memorial plaque commemorating the closing of the dike. The Dutch see the dike as a monument to their success in the constant struggle to keep their land above water.

Closed off from the sea, the Zuiderzee eventually became a freshwater lake and was renamed the IJsselmeer (*IJssel* = name of a river feeding the lake; *meer* = lake). With the lake isolated from the restless sea, it became possible to drain parts of the lake and turn them into polders. The four polders reclaimed from under the IJsselmeer add 165,000 hectares, or 408,000 acres, to the land surface area of Holland.

In February 1953, the Afsluitdijk held, but dikes in the south failed, following severe winter storms. Flooding covered 1,500 square kilometers, or 579 square miles; 1,835 people died in the flood, and more than 70,000 lost their homes. The Dutch reaction was a major water control project called the Delta Works. The rivers between the Scheldt and the New Water Way canal were closed off from the sea. The Scheldt and the New Water Way could not be closed off, because they are used by seagoing vessels to reach ports farther inland. For them, the Dutch built dams with floodgates that can be opened and closed as necessary. The floodgates in the Scheldt were completed in 1986. Work on the floodgates for the New Water Way is still in progress.

Even though the Delta Works project is a great advancement, the Dutch have not won their battle with the water yet. The Afsluitdijk and the Delta Works focused on the danger of flooding from the sea, but in February 1995, rising rivers in the south of the country were the danger. A quarter of a million people had to be evacuated, but there were only two deaths associated with the flood. The government swiftly took action to improve flood control on this front as well. Flood control takes up a large portion of the nation's gross national product (GNP), but it is money well spent considering that 60% of the populace lives below sea level. It is expected that 2 billion guilders ($1 billion) will have to be spent on dike maintenance and improvements between 1994 and 2000.

Natural Resources

Holland has large natural gas fields in the north of the country, in the province of Groningen, and smaller deposits offshore in the North Sea. They were first discovered in 1959. The fields near the town of Slochteren were then estimated to hold nearly 2,800 million cubic meters. This is the largest gas field in Western Europe. The present Dutch natural gas reserves from all fields are estimated to total 1,765 billion cubic meters. Natural gas production in 1997 was about 84 billion cubic meters, around half of which is exported to Belgium, Germany, France, Italy, and Switzerland.

Holland also has small, primarily offshore oil fields, which produce around 3.6 million tons of crude oil, or about 15% of its total domestic requirements (1995). From 1970 to 1994, Holland managed to reduce oil's percentage of the country's energy requirements from 58% to 36%. Much of the change is the result of substituting natural gas for oil, but successful efforts at energy conservation also contributed to reducing consumption.

Holland's other natural resources are salt and clay. Salt is used in the chemical industry. In fact, the "Z" in the name of the Dutch chemical and pharmaceutical conglomerate AKZO-Nobel stands for the Dutch word for salt (*zout*). Clay is used in the production of pottery and ceramics for which the town of Delft is famous. The golden age of Delft was between 1650 and 1750, when the Dutch attempted to reproduce the Chinese and, later, Japanese imported porcelain, which—especially the blue-and-white variety—was in high demand in Europe. At its height, there were more than thirty factories producing faience (tin-glazed earthenware) in Delft. By 1854, there was only one left. The industry collapsed because of competition from the new products developed by the Germans and the English. The pottery industry was revived in Delft by Joost Thooft (1838–1884), who introduced a new glazing process (clear glaze on stoneware) in 1876. Today, Delft Blue stoneware is imitated in China to be sold to tourists in Holland.

Fauna/Flora

Holland is one of the least-forested countries in Europe. Woodlands, chiefly pine, cover only about 8% of the total land area. The country is a haven for all sorts of migrating water fowl, because of all the water to be found there.

Transportation

Holland's location on the rivers flowing into the North Sea is one of its major assets. The Dutch capitalized on this location in the seventeenth century to become a major world trading power. Today Holland is a major transshipment and logistics center for Europe. Transportation accounts for approximately 8% of the GNP. It also accounts for about 40% of Holland's oil consumption each year.

More than 400 million tons of freight are delivered to Holland each year by sea, by inland waterway, and by road. Most of those shipments are destined not for Holland, but for some other European country. Forty percent of all the goods imported to Europe from Japan, for example, are shipped via Holland. Of the fifty largest exporters in the United States, around twenty have their distribution facilities in Europe. About half of them are located in Holland. Transshipments and exports (including natural gas exports via pipeline) amount to 350 million tons a year. The Dutch like to advertise their central location and transportation facilities as "the front door to Europe." Exports account for 51% of the Dutch GNP.

The port of Rotterdam is the world's leading port in terms of total cargo handled. In 1997, it handled 307.3 million tons of cargo. Together with Amsterdam, it handles 37% of all European Union (EU) seaborne imports. The other major seaports in Holland are Velsen/IJmuiden, Eemshaven, Vlissingen, Terneuzen, Vlaardingen, and Delfzijl.

Schiphol Airport in Amsterdam is the fourth largest handler of airfreight in Western Europe. It handles over a million tons of freight per year. It is also the main air-passenger terminal in Holland. In 1997, 31.4 million passengers transited Schiphol. There are flights from Schiphol to 227 destinations in 97 countries. This makes Schiphol the third best-connected airport in the world after Heathrow (London) and Charles De Gaulle (Paris). All totaled in 1997, there were 349,500 takeoffs and landings from Schiphol. The airport's location is typically Dutch. It is located 13 feet below sea level in a polder that was drained in the nineteenth century. Its name literally means "ship's hollow." There are also international airports in Rotterdam (Zestienhoven) and in Maastricht (Beek).

The best-known and largest Dutch airline is KLM (Koninklijke Luchtvaart Maatschappij [Royal Air Travel Company]). It is the world's longest continuously operating airline, having been in regularly scheduled service since 1920. The other airlines operating in Holland are Martinair,

Transavia, and Air Holland. They are charter operators, though Martinair also provides airfreight services.

There are 4,832 kilometers or 3,002 miles of inland waterways. The Rhine delta, the North Sea Canal, and the Scheldt basin handle a total of 71.6 million tons of freight per year. The Dutch inland waterway shipping fleet numbers over 6,000 vessels. It is the largest of its kind in the world and carries two-thirds of the waterborne cargo moved in the EU.

There is a 9,000-kilometer/5,625-mile-long pipeline that transports oil from the port in Rotterdam and natural gas from the gas fields in Groningen to customers throughout Holland and into Belgium, France, and Germany. Of the approximately 87 million tons of oil imported to Holland each year, about 54 million tons are reexported as refined oil products.

There are 2,798 kilometers or 1,739 miles of rail lines in Holland, of which 70% are electrified. Dutch Rail is the most heavily traveled rail network in Europe. There are 366 passenger stations spread around the country. Around a million people a year take one or more of the 2,425 daily scheduled trains. Public subsidies for passenger travel are falling, even though the government is trying to win more people back to public transportation, away from private automobiles, to reduce the impact of auto emissions on the environment. Dutch Rail also has 6,401 freight cars and 71 freight stations. In 1991, the amount of cargo moved by train was 18.4 million tons. By 1996, it had risen to 20.8 million tons.

The Dutch Rail network used to be entirely government owned and operated. Then, rail travel was subsidized from general government revenues. The government's new policy is intended to make Dutch Rail completely independent economically. Politicians are now discovering, however, that an independent, profit-making Dutch Rail will make decisions that are counter to government transportation goals—ticket prices and the continued operation of unprofitable, but socially necessary, rail lines topping the list. Nevertheless, the use of passenger trains is growing. In 1985, people rode 9.2 billion passenger-kilometers on the train. By 1996, that number had increased to over 14 billion.

Bicycles are a major mode of transportation in Holland. Because the country is so flat and everything so close together, it is easy to get around on them. Bikes are not just for children in Holland. People use them regularly to get to work and to go shopping. Postal workers deliver the mail on bikes. Mothers take their children to school by bike. Each year, the Dutch travel billions of kilometers by bike. In 1996, they traveled 12.5 billion kilometers, a figure that is expected to reach 14 billion by the year 2000.

In 1996, there were about 16 million bicycles in Holland, or slightly more than one for every inhabitant. About 1.3 million new bicycles are sold every year. In 1996, bicycle sales totaled 950 million guilders ($475 million), and bicycle repairs totaled 349 million guilders ($174.5 million). There are 19,000 kilometers or 11,807 miles of bicycle paths and specially marked bike lanes on the streets. There are even traffic lights for cyclists.

You can rent a bike at almost eighty Dutch Rail stations, just like you can rent a car at an airport in the United States. There are also bike repair shops at train stations so that people who bike to the train station on their way to work can leave their bike to be repaired and pick it up when they come back that evening.

For those who insist on driving a car, there are 105,000 kilometers or 65,247 miles of surfaced roads, including 2,100 kilometers or 1,305 miles of divided highways. The number of cars in Holland has grown explosively since the seventies. It is growing faster than the populace. As of August 1, 1996, there were 5.6 million privately owned vehicles registered in Holland. That works out to an average of 365 cars per 1,000 inhabitants. In terms of the total surface area of Holland, it translates to 165 vehicles and 3 kilometers of paved road per square kilometer. An average of 2.3 million cars make the home-to-work commute each day. Traffic jams during rush hour are a way of life in Holland. It is estimated that 26 million hours are lost each year in traffic jams.

Almost 15% of Dutch households have two or more cars, while less than one family in ten does not have a car. As the number of cars increases, so does the number of auto fatalities. There were 1,334 fatalities in 1995. Still, Holland is the fourth safest country to drive in, with 8.6 fatalities per 100,000 inhabitants. Only the United Kingdom (6.4), Sweden (6.5), and Norway (7.0) have lower numbers of fatalities. In the United States, there are 15.9 fatalities per 100,000 inhabitants.

More than 75% of all the kilometers traveled in Holland are by car; 60% of all car trips are for a distance of less than 7.5 kilometers. The government is making a special effort to get more people to bike or take public transportation to work through the use of financial disincentives for driving, such as the high taxes on gasoline. Nevertheless, about one-third of trips of 7.5 kilometers or less are made by car. A case study in Dordrecht showed that up to 55 million guilders ($27.5 million) could be saved over seven years if all such short trips were made by bike instead of by car.

Convenience is one reason that people take the car instead of bike to work or to go shopping, but another consideration is the fear that their bike will be stolen. Twenty-seven percent of the Dutch no longer ride their bikes for this reason. One million are stolen every year. The average price a fence will pay for a stolen bike is between 10 and 25 guilders

($5.00–12.50). The average price of a new bike is 710 guilders ($355). Bikes can be insured against theft in Holland, just like cars are insured in America.

Public transportation is well developed. Buses and trams connect with trains to provide a convenient network that offers connections throughout the country. During the day in urban areas, there is a connection to or from downtown every 15 minutes. In the evening, the frequency drops to every 30 minutes. Downtown, buses or trams run every 5–7 minutes.

Despite governmental disincentives for driving and incentives for taking public transportation, only about 10% of all travel was by public transportation in 1996. There are around 20,000 taxis operating in Holland.

Communications

The state monopoly of the PTT (Post, Telephone, and Telegraph) ended in 1989, when it was privatized as KPN (Koninklijke Post Nederland [Royal Dutch Telecom]). Holland has a high-quality, modern communications infrastructure. As of 1995, all the telephone exchanges were digital. Mobile telephones are in wide use. There is a new initiative to bring fiber-optic cables into consumers' homes by pulling the fiber-optic cable through the existing natural gas distribution pipelines. This will provide consumers with high-bandwidth connections for voice data and video.

MAJOR CITIES

The Randstad Conurbation

The most heavily populated area in Holland is the Randstad (*rand* = edge; *stad* = city). This is a term that was coined by Dutch aviation pioneer Albert Plesman (1889–1953) in the 1930s. It describes the urban agglomeration in the west of the country that encompasses the cities of Dordrecht, Rotterdam, Delft, The Hague, Leiden, Haarlem, Amsterdam, and Utrecht. These heavily populated urban areas form a horseshoe-shaped area that opens to the southeast. The less heavily populated and less urbanized area in the center of the horseshoe is known as the "green heart."

The majority of political and economic activity takes place in the west of the country in the Randstad. The government, recognizing the pressure on the infrastructure of the area, is taking steps to encourage people and businesses to move out of the Randstad. One of these steps is locating government ministries in other areas of the country. The part of the Ministry of Education that deals with student grants, for example, was moved to Groningen. Another step is the expansion of the transportation infrastructure in other parts of the country. Despite the improved accessibility of the northern and southern provinces, many people still think of them as far away. The east of Gelderland is referred to as the Achterhoek (Outback).

The Dutch have a unique sense of distance, defined by the size of the country in which they live. In Holland, if children live a two-hour drive away, you would think that they lived on the other side of the world to hear the family talk about it. In America, you might well drive two hours to eat at a restaurant you like, and your parents might live two time zones away. The feeling of a Dutch family in The Hague, whose son moved to Groningen (three hours away by train) in the north of Holland, is the same as an American family's in Alabama, whose son has moved to California (five hours by plane and three time zones away).

Amsterdam

Amsterdam began as a settlement on the Amstel River in the thirteenth century. The first documentary evidence of its existence is in the year 1275. Its original name was Amstelledamme, meaning the dam on the river Amstel. Though Amsterdam is officially the capital of Holland, the Parliament, the government, the embassies, and the Crown are located in The Hague. Amsterdam's designation as the capital is to honor its prominence during the Golden Age.

Despite some competition from Rotterdam, Amsterdam is the cultural center of Holland. It is home to the Rijksmuseum (National Museum), which is famous for its collection of paintings by Dutch and Flemish masters. The most famous of these is Rembrandt van Rijn (1606–1669). *The Nightwatch* (1642) is his best-known work on display there. The Stedelijk Museum (City Museum) houses an outstanding collection of more modern artists, chief among whom is Vincent van Gogh (1853–1890). Its collection also encompasses a number of Dutch twentieth-century artists such as Piet Mondrian (1872–1944), Kees van Dongen (1877–1968), and Karel Appel (1921–   ).

Amsterdam is the home of the Concertgebouw Orchestra, one of the leading symphony orchestras in the world. There is also a large number of theaters spread throughout the city. Amsterdam is also the home to two of the eight universities in the Netherlands. In the sixties, it was the focal point of the antiestablishment protests for which that decade is famous. Today it is overrun with tourists.

In a series of posters published by Dutch Rail, advertising how inexpensive it is to travel from one city to another, Amsterdam is depicted by a picture of a red lightbulb. The association is immediately clear to the Dutch. Amsterdam's red-light district is (in)famous. Prostitution is legal, regulated, and taxed in Holland.

Rotterdam

Rotterdam emerged as a port when a dam was built across the river Rotte in the seventeenth century to create a deep, sheltered waterway. Up to the nineteenth century, it was overshadowed by, first, the port at Antwerp and, later, by the port at Amsterdam. Rapid industrialization upstream along the Rhine led to increased river traffic and a need for direct access to the North Sea. The result was the New Water Way, which was opened in 1872. This deepwater channel to the sea is the key to Rotterdam's success as a port.

While Rotterdam was extensively damaged by German bombing in May 1940 at the beginning of World War II, it recovered and went on to become the world's largest port in terms of total tonnage handled. When measured in the number of containers (twenty-feet equivalent units [TEU]) handled, however, Hong Kong and Singapore are ahead of Rotterdam, which handled only 5 million TEU in 1997. Despite heavy competition from other European ports, Rotterdam still has a 42% market share of all goods transported by ship. To remain competitive, however, Rotterdam will have to modernize its infrastructure to be able to move more containers, which is a more efficient way to handle goods. Rotterdam's advantage over the other European ports as a container harbor is that it can accommodate ships with deeper drafts. This is an important consideration as modern container ships are becoming larger and draw more water.

Only 36% of the population of Rotterdam has lived there for twenty-five years or more, and that number is declining. The trend is for better-educated and better-paid people to leave the city. In contrast to the rest of Holland, the average age of the population of Rotterdam is getting lower, not higher.

About 40% of the population can be considered aliens, that is, not ethnically Dutch. The Dutch are also quick to point out that more than 25% of the population is *allochtoon*, that is, not European in origin. Projections are that these non-Europeans will provide more than 80% of the population growth in Rotterdam in the near future. Younger Rotterdamers, who have grown up in a multiracial city, discriminate less than their parents, but they still respond negatively to questionnaires about the change in the racial makeup of the city and the effects that it has.

Public safety, especially after dark, is one of the biggest problems reported by residents in public opinion polls. Problems with junkies and drugs score highest among their public safety concerns.

The Hague

The Hague is the third largest city in Holland. In Dutch it is known as Den Haag. The name derives from the original name of the count's residence: 's-Gravenhage (the count's hedge), which William II (1234–1256) started building in about 1248. While the exact date is uncertain, this is the year that the city officially uses for its birthday. The buildings of the interior court of the count's residence—*het Binnenhof* in Dutch—are still in use today to house the Parliament. The outer court buildings—*het Buitenhof* in Dutch—were demolished to ease vehicular traffic in 1923.

While Dutch monarchs go to Amsterdam to be coronated, The Hague is the seat of government and home to the civil service. Every third Tuesday of September, the monarch rides to *het Binnenhof* in a golden coach to open Parliament. The royal family maintains three palaces in The Hague: Paleis Lange Voorhout, Paleis Noordeinde, and Huis ten Bosch, which is the royal residence. The Hague is also home to a number of the international bodies of the United Nations. The World Court, the International Criminal Tribunal for the Former Yugoslavia (ICTFY), and the headquarters of the Organization for the Prohibition of Chemical Weapons (OPCW) are located here. All the foreign embassies are located here as well.

The *Binnenhof* complex also houses the Mauritshuis Museum, which has a number of Vermeers and Rembrandts. The renowned Netherlands Dance Theater also calls The Hague its home. Every other year, the Holland Dance Festival is held there, while the world-famous North Sea Jazz Festival is held every year.

Utrecht

Utrecht is the fourth largest city in Holland. In 1996, 234,254 people called it home. It is the oldest of the four big cities. In A.D. 48, the Romans built a castellum on an island formed by an arm of the Rhine at what was known as Trecht (ford). This was part of the northern Roman frontier that defended the empire from the barbarians to the north. In 695, the site of the castellum became the seat of the evangelistic efforts of Bishop Willibrord (658–739), who brought Christianity to the Frisians. The present cathedral in Utrecht stands on the same spot as the castellum.

Utrecht was the first city in Europe to receive the right to hold a yearly fair. Godebald, who served as bishop from 1114 to 1127, extended that right in 1127. Today, Utrecht is host to over 100 trade fairs and exhibitions, which attract more than 2 million visitors each year.

The University of Utrecht was founded in 1636. This university has the only veterinary faculty in Holland, and its is the only foreign veterinary degree that is accredited by the United States and Canada. Graduates from this program are eligible to practice veterinary medicine in North America.

Utrecht is the headquarters of Dutch Rail and the home of the Dutch mint. The Holland Music Festival, which focuses on medieval and baroque music, is held there.

THE TWELVE PROVINCES

Drenthe

This is the least-populated province of Holland, with a density of 172 inhabitants per square kilometer. It is home to five of Holland's six national parks. The Dutch go to Drenthe on vacation to get away from it all. The capital of Drenthe is Assen.

After World War II, government policy encouraged industrialization in the north, and southeast Drenthe thus houses the largest industrial concentration in the north. The plastics, metal, optical, and precision-instrument industries are well represented there. While Drenthe retains its rural character, the importance of agriculture is much less now than it was right after World War II. It is, however, the fastest growing horticultural area in all of Holland.

Drenthe is famous for its hunebeds. These are megalithic graves, built by the people who lived in this area about 5,000 years ago. Of the fifty-four surviving hunebeds in Holland, fifty-two are in Drenthe. It is also famous as the site of the discovery of the Pesse canoe (ca. 6,000 B.C.), the oldest known boat.

Flevoland

The four IJsselmeer/Zuiderzee polders form Holland's newest province of Flevoland, which officially became the twelfth province in 1986. Flevoland takes its name from the Roman names for the area: Flevo (as appears

North
Sea

Groningen

Friesland

Drenthe

Noord-
Holland

Flevo-
land

Overijssel

Zuid-
Holland

Utrecht

Gelderland

Germany

Noord-Brabant

Zeeland

Limburg

Belgium

The Twelve Provinces of Holland

in the work of the writer Pomponius) and Flevum (as appears in Plinius). In Roman times, there was no Zuiderzee. Pomponius described Flevo as an area on the right arm of the Rhine that widened into a lake and then narrowed again before continuing its journey to the sea. It was only in the thirteenth century that the area became completely flooded and not until the fourteenth that the name "Zuiderzee" was first used for it.

The capital of the province is Lelystad. It is named in honor of the man whose vision made the IJsselmeer polders possible, Cornelis Lely. It was his land reclamation plan, published in 1886, that was the basis for the Zuiderzee Works project. The two oldest polders, the Wieringermeer Polder and the Northeast Polder, are used for agriculture. The East Flevoland Polder combines agricultural and commercial uses of the land with residential areas. The newest polder, South Flevoland, has been zoned for residential, commercial, and recreational use, with a goal of alleviating some of the congestion in the Randstad. Almere, in South Flevoland, is the fastest growing municipality in Holland. It is a bedroom community for Amsterdam.

Friesland

Friesland is the second least-populated province, with a population density of 182 inhabitants per square kilometer—only Drenthe has fewer. The capital of Friesland is Leeuwarden. In a Dutch Rail poster, Leeuwarden is depicted by a black-and-white Frisian cow about to deposit a cow pie. The corresponding picture on the poster for destination in the south of the country is a fruit pie, for which Limburg is famous. All the Dutch who see the poster get the connection, because Friesland is famous for its production of milk and butter. It has excellent grazing lands and a long growing season. The Frisians have been cattlemen since Roman times. Their taxes to the Romans were paid in cowhides and horns.

Friesland is also home—weather permitting—to the Eleven-City Tour. This long-distance race on ice skates has been held only fifteen times this century. It attracts thousands of participants, who cover a grueling 200-kilometer course across frozen lakes and canals that takes them through eleven cities.

Gelderland

Gelderland is the largest province in Holland. It has an area of 5,131 square kilometers. It is home to Holland's sixth national park, Hoge

Veluwe, which is famous for its free-roaming deer. The capital of the province is Arnhem.

Gelderland is mainly an agricultural province, and it hosts the Agricultural College in Wageningen. The province has twice as many cows and chickens per hectare as the national average. The number of pigs is one and a half times the national average. The Betuwe region is famous as the fruit basket of Holland.

The Betuwe area is also the homeland of the Germanic tribe the Batavians, of whom the Romans wrote and for whom the Batavian Republic (1795–1806) was named during the period of French domination. The capital of the Dutch East Indies (now Indonesia), Batavia (now Jakarta), was also named for this tribe. In ancient German, the name *Betuwe* means "the good lands." The name *Veluwe,* where the national park is located, means "the bad lands."

Each year, the city of Nijmegen, originally a Roman frontier town and border garrison, hosts the grueling sporting event called the Vierdaagse (Four-Day) March. Male participants cover a different 50-kilometer course each day. (The course is 40 km for women.) Aptly, the picture on the Dutch Rail poster for travel to Nijmegen is a bare foot covered with Band Aids. The Vierdaagse is popularly known as the "Blister Fest."

Groningen

The capital of the province of Groningen is the city of Groningen, which was one of the cities of the Hanseatic League, an ancient association of German towns promoting and protecting commerce. Here, as in Drenthe, there is abundant evidence of the prehistoric inhabitants of the area. There are about 400 Frisian *terpen* and two hunebeds in the province. It is a thinly populated province (238 inhabitants per square kilometer), and agriculture is still a major part of its economy. It used to be considered very poor, but today it is the home of one of the world's largest natural gas fields, which was discovered near the town of Slochteren in 1959.

In an attempt to stimulate industrial growth in the region, the government designated Delfzijl and Eemshaven as regional growth centers. Companies that relocated there would enjoy reduced energy costs and direct government subsidies. The policy was not successful, however, because too many Dutch businesspeople view Groningen as too far away from the Randstad: three hours by train.

Limburg

The capital of Limburg is Maastricht. This province, which borders predominantly Catholic Belgium, was 90% Catholic through the mid-to-late 1960s, when the pillars—self-imposed segregation—started to break down. Carnival—the traditional Roman Catholic festival still observed in many European countries—is celebrated here and in neighboring North Brabant in a big way. The name Maastricht is commonly used to refer to the treaty on European monetary and political union, which was concluded in Maastricht in 1991.

This is the only province where anything that looks like hills can be found. Limburg used to be the center of the coal industry, at one time producing over 65% of Holland's need for coal. The discovery of the gas fields near Slochteren in Groningen, however, caused a shift away from coal to gas as a fuel and resulted in the closing of the mines in the seventies. To soften the blow of the mine closings on the economy, the government moved the Central Statistical Bureau to Limburg. The Dutch State Mines, the company that had run the mines, turned its attention to chemicals and is now a major producer.

Overijssel

Overijssel is located on the eastern border with Germany. The province takes its name from the river IJssel, which flows into the IJsselmeer. The capital is Zwolle, famous as the home of the Dutch statesman Johan Rudolf Thorbecke (1798–1872), who is considered the spiritual father of the democratic constitutional reform of 1848.

Twente in Overijssel used to be famous for its textile industry, employing 30% of the working population of Overijssel in 1950. But in the seventies, the textile industry collapsed. The industrial base then shifted to metals, chemicals, rubber, and meatpacking. The area around Hengelo and Enschede is one of the country's more important industrial centers. Enschede is the site of the Twente Technical University, one of the youngest of the Dutch universities, founded in 1961. It is primarily a technical school, but it requires that 10% of a student's course load be in the humanities.

Noord-Brabant (North Brabant)

The capital of Noord-Brabant is 's-Hertogenbosch. This province was originally part of Catholic Belgium, and, like Limburg, through the mid-to-late 1960s it was still 90% Catholic. The Carnival celebrations here and in neighboring Limburg are a highlight of the year. The province is called North Brabant, because it was split off from the original province of Brabant, which continues to exist today in Belgium. The capital of Vlaams (Flemish) Brabant is Brussels.

Eindhoven used to be home to the headquarters of the multinational electronics giant Philips, but it moved to Amsterdam—in the Randstad, of course. A single lightbulb is the picture that Dutch Rail uses to advertise travel to Eindhoven. Its companion destination, Amsterdam, is depicted with a red lightbulb. Everyone who sees the poster gets the picture, even though Philips no longer produces lightbulbs in Holland. Production was moved to Poland, where labor costs are lower.

Kaatsheuvel is home to the Efteling, a Dutch version of Disneyland. The Efteling started as a fairy tale park, based on the artistry of Anton Pieck (1895–1987) and has grown into a major amusement park. In Europe, only Disneyland Paris is bigger.

Noord/Zuid-Holland (North/South Holland)

The capital of Noord-Holland is Haarlem, for which the district of Harlem in New York is named. It is the second most populous province, with 928 inhabitants per square kilometer. The Hague is the capital of Zuid-Holland, the most heavily populated province, with a population density of 1,166 inhabitants per square kilometer. Together, these two provinces encompass the bulk of the Randstad, the nation's capital and the seat of government, and most of the cities that tourists visit. Amsterdam, the cheese market in Alkmaar, and the international airport at Schiphol are in North Holland. The miniature city of Madurodam, Gouda (home of the cheese that no one outside of Holland can pronounce properly), and Rotterdam are in South Holland.

Until the period of French domination (1795–1813), these two provinces were one. As a single political unit, the province of Holland was the driving force behind the Dutch expansion. William the Silent (1533–1584), who led the fight for independence from the Spanish, had his power base here. This was the center of power, art, culture, and learning during the Golden Age. It was because of the province of Holland's leading role in the affairs of the Republic of the Seven United Provinces that the names Holland and the Netherlands are used interchangeably. It is a case of the name of the most important part being used for the whole.

Hilversum, home to the radio and television broadcasting center, is located in the province. All programming for the state-owned, noncommercial broadcast networks originates here. The shortwave voice of Holland, Radio Netherlands International, also originates from here. (The current transmission schedule is available on the Internet at: <http://www.rnw.nl>.) Commercial Dutch-language television programming originates in Luxembourg.

Utrecht

The province of Utrecht is located in the center of the country. Its capital is the city of Utrecht. Together with North and South Holland, Utrecht is a part of the Randstad conurbation. It is the third most densely populated province, with 789 inhabitants per square kilometer. The fourth most densely populated province, Limburg, is comparatively much less crowded, with only 523 inhabitants per square kilometer.

Zeeland

The capital of Zeeland is Middelburg. This is the fourth least-populated province, with a population density of 205 inhabitants per square kilometer. It is located in the southwest corner of Holland on the border with Belgium. It is famous as the most sunny part of Holland and as a recreation area. It is also a major agricultural area, well known for its potatoes, onions, and sugar beets. In schools, Dutch children are taught to associate Zeeland with the Delta Works flood control project.

New Zealand in the Pacific Ocean was discovered by Dutch explorers from here, who named it after their home province. Australia used to be called New Holland for the same reason.

The Scheldt—a major international waterway—runs through the middle of the province from west to east. Ships sail to the harbors in Antwerp, Ghent, Terneuzen, and Vlissingen via the Scheldt. All the land south of the Scheldt up to the Belgian border is called Zeeuws-Vlaanderen (the part of Flanders that belongs to Zeeland). The province on the other side of the border in Belgium is called simply Vlaanderen (Flanders).

Poor rail and road connections with Holland north of the Scheldt mean that it is often faster to cross Belgium to get to Zeeuws-Vlaanderen than to wait for the ferry. A tunnel under the Scheldt is planned for construction early in the twenty-first century.

2

The Economy

THE EXCHANGE RATE

The monetary unit in Holland is the guilder. The current official exchange rate is approximately 2 Dutch guilders to 1 U.S. dollar—f2:\$1. The Dutch equivalent of the dollar sign (\$) is f. This stylized letter "F" stands for the word *florijn* (florin). Dutch paper money has raised symbols on it that can be "read" by the blind so that they will know how much each bill is worth. For the sighted, each denomination is a different color. In 2002, the guilder will be replaced by the common European currency, the Euro. The symbol for the Euro is €. On December 31, 1998, the European Commission fixed the exchange rate between the Euro and the guilder at €1:f2.20371.

THE BIG MAC EXCHANGE RATE

In theory, the exchange rate is based on what it would cost to buy identical goods and services in each of the currencies to be exchanged. In fact, it is not. The best proof of that is the Big Mac exchange rate. Wherever in the world you go, nothing is more identical than the food at McDonald's. If the theory is correct, the price of a Big Mac meal would be the same in both countries. The price of a Big Mac meal in Indiana is $3.19 plus 16 cents tax, or ƒ6.70 at the current exchange rate of ƒ2:$1. In Holland, the same Big Mac meal costs ƒ9.95. Tax is included in this price, but ketchup for your french fries is not—it costs 50 Dutch cents extra. That makes the Dutch price ƒ10.45 or $5.23 at the current exchange rate. For a Big Mac meal to cost exactly the same in both countries, the exchange rate would have to be closer to ƒ3:$1.

MINIMUM WAGE

The minimum wage in Holland is not a single amount but a variable amount based on age. It starts at age fifteen, the lowest age at which you can legally work, and increases yearly to age twenty-three, after which it is the same for everybody. The minimum wage was last raised in 1996. The minimum wage for a fifteen-year-old, for example, is ƒ152.60 ($76.30) per week. For the Dutch thirty-eight-hour work week, this comes to ƒ4.02 ($2.01) per hour. For a twenty-three-year-old, the minimum wage is ƒ508.00 ($254.00) per week before taxes and withholdings. For a thirty-eight-hour work week, this comes to ƒ13.37 ($6.69) per hour. After taxes and withholdings, however, the average take-home pay will be about ƒ384.00 ($192.00) per week, or ƒ10.11 ($5.06) per hour. Taxes and with-holdings for the fifteen-year-old would be minimal, only about ƒ1.60 ($0.80) per week.

The real comparison of the minimum wage in Holland and in Amer-ica is not simply what the official exchange rate says that ƒ13.37 is worth in dollars. The real comparison is what you can buy with it. The twenty-three-year-old Dutch minimum-wage worker (ƒ13.37 per hour) has to work 46.9 minutes before taxes and withholdings to buy a Big Mac meal (ƒ10.45). In America, the minimum-wage worker ($5.15 per hour) has to work only 39.03 minutes for the same Big Mac meal ($3.35). If you apply the Big Mac exchange rate to the Dutch minimum wage of ƒ13.37 per hour, it shows that the Dutch minimum wage is really less than the American minimum wage. At ƒ3:$1, the Dutch minimum wage is $4.46 per hour, not the $6.68 per hour that it appears to be using the official ex-change rate of ƒ2:$1.

PLASTIC MONEY

Holland ranks number one in Europe in the use of plastic money (debit or credit cards), with 91% of the Dutch having one form or another of plas-tic money. In second-place Germany, only 57% have plastic money (1996).

GROSS DOMESTIC PRODUCT

In the 1990s, the Dutch economy has been growing at about 2.5% annually, slightly faster than the average for the European Community. The gross domestic product (GDP` for 1997 was ƒ706 billion. This equates to about ƒ45,572 per inhabitant. The 1997 GDP was up ƒ163.43 billion from the 1991 GDP of ƒ542.57 billion and up ƒ38.4 billion from the 1996 GDP of ƒ667.6 billion.

The average disposable income is also climbing. In 1990, it was ƒ40,500. By 1994, it had climbed more than 10% to ƒ44,200. In 1996, the modal disposable income for a family of four with two incomes was ƒ65,000. The modal disposable income for the country as a whole was ƒ34,870 (ƒ52,000 before taxes).

PERSONAL WEALTH

At the start of 1995, the amassed wealth of all Dutch households was ƒ1,230 billion, less their combined debts (mostly mortgages) of ƒ350 billion, for a total of ƒ880 billion. This included the value of all the homes that are privately owned, which made up 57% of the total. The average price of a house is ƒ271,000 (1997). The total value of privately owned housing is ƒ700 billion. The number of households with an amassed wealth of over 1 million guilders was 116,000. The average stock holding was ƒ230,000 (1995).

THE STOCK EXCHANGE

The Amsterdam Stock Exchange (AEX) is the oldest in the world. It was founded in the early seventeenth century. It is the ninth largest exchange, with all the listed stocks worth over 1 trillion guilders. The best year in its history was 1997, with the AEX index, which measures the price movement of the twenty-five most widely traded stocks listed on the exchange, closing at ƒ913.67, a climb of 41% for the year. This was more than double the average market gain for the last fourteen years (19%). Also good years for the AEX were 1995 and 1996, with increases of 17% and 30%, respectively.

INFLATION

Using 1980 as the base year, the 1997 price index is 149.5. That means that something bought in 1997 is 149.5% more expensive than the same thing bought in 1980. During the 1990s, inflation rates have remained in the range of 2.0% to 3.2%. In 1997, the consumer price index rose 2.25%.

THE PUBLIC DEBT

In 1997, the public debt (budget deficit) was only 2.4% of GDP. This was below the treaty limit of 3% of GDP, required for participation in the single European currency. The level of fiscal discipline that this implies is reflected in the attitude and philosophy of the chairman of the European Central Bank, Willem Duisenberg, who comes from Holland. The fiscal policies that the bank sets will affect each of the member states of the EMU.

TAXES

The collective burden of tax and Social Security premiums amounted to about 53% of the national income of ƒ522 billion in 1994. The income tax is graduated. The more income, the higher the tax. In 1986, the minimum rate was set at 16% and the maximum rate was 72%. In 1985, income tax provided 37% of all central governmental revenue. In 1998, the minimum rate was set at 36.5% and the maximum at 60%. At these rates, the income tax provides only slightly less than 25% of government revenue.

Holland also has a wealth tax of 0.7%, which is levied on the personal net worth of individuals. Florida has a similar tax, but the tax rate there is 0.1% up to $200,000 and 0.2% above that.

The BTW (Belasting op de Toegevoegde Waarde, or value-added tax) was introduced in 1969 under pressure from the European Community. It is a tax paid by the end consumer, and it is levied on the value added to goods and services at each stage of production. The basic rate is 17.5%. Certain essential goods and services such as food, nonalcoholic drinks, medicine, newspapers, shoe repair, and passenger transport are taxed at only 5%. Goods for export, medical, cultural, and educational services are exempt. The BTW accounts for more than a quarter of the government's revenue.

HOUSING

During World War II, more than 25% of Holland's housing stock of 2 million units was damaged. The housing shortage remained acute until the 1950s, when an accelerated program of housing construction was initiated. From 1948 to 1985, nearly 4 million housing units were added,

bringing the total housing stock up to 5,384,100 units. By 1996, almost another million units had been added, bringing the total housing stock up
to 6,282,500. That is 405 units per 1,000 inhabitants. Of these, 49%
(3,066,600) were privately owned. Of the rental units, 75% (2,387,350)
were state owned, and only 25% (816,725) were privately owned.

In 1985, the average price of a privately owned home was ƒ112,510. By
1997, it had more than doubled to ƒ271,000. At 7.1%, a mortgage for this
amount in Holland would be ƒ1,821 per month. In contrast, the average
rent in 1996 was ƒ625.

Housing construction in Holland is government directed. The government determines how much housing is to be built each year, based on its
projections. On the basis of national estimates, each municipality is allocated an amount of housing that it can construct. The municipality is responsible for actual construction. Central government approval is
needed for all construction over a specific cost.

The most expensive housing park in Holland is in Bloemendaal in
North Holland, where the average house price is ƒ457,000. The next most
expensive city for housing is Laren (the Hollywood of Holland), where
the average house price is ƒ402,000. The least expensive housing is in Rei-
derland in Groningen, where the average house price is ƒ86,000. Leeuwarden, in Friesland, is close on its heels, with an average house price of
ƒ87,000 (1997). The total estimated value of all housing in Holland is ƒ1.6
trillion.

INDUSTRY

Holland has limited natural resources. Its economy is based to a large
extent on import and export services. It is, in essence, trading on its location near the sea in the delta of three major navigable European rivers, as
it has done from the earliest of times. This is what made Holland a major
world power during the Golden Age in the seventeenth century.

Because it is dependent on international trade, the Dutch economy is
affected by events abroad over which Holland has no control, such as
currency fluctuations and the economic developments of its trading partners. That is one of the reasons why Holland is such a strong supporter
of the European Economic Union.

Service industries are a major force in the economy. Banks, trading
companies, ship brokers, oil refining, logistics, warehousing, and call
centers all play a large part in the economy. The multilingual, highly
skilled workforce makes Holland an attractive location for international
firms to obtain these services.

During and after the American Revolution, loans from Dutch banks helped to keep the new Republic afloat. More recently, the Dutch ING Bank bought out the humbled British merchant bank Barings, after Barings failed following a stock-trading scandal. The ING Bank also owns Poland's retail and commercial banking group, Slaski, SA. In the United States, it recently bought the Furman Selz investment bank in New York and the life insurance provider Equitable of Iowa. It has offices in more than fifty countries and holds seats on more than sixty stock, futures, and commodities exchanges.

Royal Dutch Shell/Shell Group is the world's largest publicly held company. It owns and operates one of the world's largest oil refineries on Curaçao, off the coast of Venezuela. Its refinery in the Rotterdam suburb of Pernis is the largest oil refinery in Europe. In addition to oil, the company has interest in petrochemicals, coal, and metals. Its 1997 revenues were $128.155 billion.

Chemicals are produced near the petroleum refineries at the ports of Rotterdam and Amsterdam, as well as in south Limburg and in Zeeland. The chemical industry accounts for an average of 25% of Holland's oil consumption.

AKZO-Nobel, headquartered in Twente, is a multinational company that produces health-care products, coatings, chemicals, and fibers. It employs approximately 69,000 people in more than sixty countries. In 1997, it had revenues of $12.05 billion.

Hoogovens in IJmuiden is one of the most important iron and steel producers in the world. It produces approximately 6 million tons of steel and 350,000 tons of aluminum annually, employing 23,000 workers worldwide. In 1996, it had revenues of $3.9 billion.

Dutch consumer products conglomerates are also prominent on the world market. Philips is one of the world's largest electronics companies. Its product line ranges from compact disc players to lightbulbs, from medical systems to semiconductors. Philips employs 267,200 people in over sixty countries. In 1997, revenues totaled $39.2 billion.

Unilever is a joint Dutch-British consumer products conglomerate that sells food and home and personal-care products in over 160 countries. It owns over a thousand brand names, including such well-known ones as Chicken Tonight, Lawry's, Lipton, Ragu, Birds Eye, Magnum, Klondike, I Can't Believe It's Not Butter, Lux, and Dove. In 1997, it had revenues of $48.721 billion.

The Albert Heijn supermarket chain owns over 3,000 supermarkets worldwide in Holland, Portugal, the Czech Republic, Poland, Southeast Asia, Brazil, and America. Albert Heijn U.S.A. is the leading supermarket company on the East Coast, with approximately 900 stores in 14 states. In America, its supermarkets do not operate under the Albert Heijn name but as BI-LO, Giant, Stop & Shop, and Tops Markets.

TOURISM

Tourists spend about ƒ42 billion annually (1997) in Holland, making tourism a significant part of the Dutch economy. Close to 300,000 people work in the tourist industry. Amsterdam is fourth in the list of European cities most visited by foreign tourists. In 1997, for example, Amsterdam had 6.3 million overnight stays, compared to 47.5 million for London, 18 million for Paris, and 9.3 million for Rome.

AGRICULTURE

Agriculture is important to the Dutch economy, because agricultural products represent 20% of all exports from Holland. Dutch agriculture is one of the most efficient in the world, but the extensive use of fertilizer is a pollution problem, as is phosphate pollution from all the manure produced by domestic livestock. This problem is only just being recognized in the United States, while the Dutch have been wrestling with it since the 1980s. The Dutch have not found a solution yet. It is a politically sensitive issue that is being dealt with in typical Dutch fashion: a seemingly endless series of regulations requiring permits and paperwork.

Much of Holland is so low and the ground so wet that the ground is only suitable for use as grassland. This is why dairy farming is so prominent. The names of the Dutch towns Gouda and Edam are famous around the world for the cheeses that are produced there.

Scientific and technological advances have allowed Dutch agricultural productivity to increase, while the number of people employed in agriculture is decreasing. Yields per hectare have risen dramatically. In 1970, the winter wheat harvest was only 4,500 kilograms per hectare. In 1992, it had almost doubled to 8,100 kilograms per hectare.

In the 1870s, Dutch farmers were faced with competition from "cheap" imported foods, primarily from the New World. They began to move away from traditional cash crops into "high-value" crops that they could export at a profit.

Thousands of greenhouses in the west of the country form a virtual sea of glass between The Hague and Rotterdam in the north, and the Hook of Holland in the south. It is there that Dutch farmers grow both vegetables and flowers out of season for export and for domestic consumption.

Tulips are an important part of the Dutch economy. Holland is the world's leading exporter of tulips, irises, daffodils, and hyacinths. The Dutch grow about 65% of the world's flower bulbs. The center of the flower industry is near the towns of Lisse, where the seemingly endless fields of blooming tulips attract thousands of tourists every spring, and Aalsmeer, where the wholesale tulip auctions are held.

Though tulips are the national symbol, they originated in Turkey. The name "tulip" is really the Turkish word for turban, which refers to the shape of the blossom. Tulips first came to Europe in the sixteenth century. The Austrian ambassador saw the flower in Turkey and brought some bulbs with him when he returned to Vienna. A Dutch horticulturist at the Austrian court introduced tulips to Holland.

CHIEF EXPORTS

In 1995, Holland exported ƒ370 million worth of cut flowers to Great Britain and ƒ117 million to the United States. It exports about 7 billion flower bulbs annually. Of these, about 1 billion go to the United States.

Holland is the world's largest exporter of cheese, butter, and powdered milk. Over half of all the milk produced in Holland is turned into cheese. The total production of cheese for 1997 was 690,000 tons. Of this, 520,000 tons were exported.

Holland is also the largest beer exporting country in the world. The largest Dutch brewery is Heineken. It is the second largest brewery in the world. Only Anheuser-Busch is larger. Heineken beer is exported to 170 countries, and it has its own breweries in 50 countries. In 1996, Heineken had total revenues of $6.75 million, employing 32,000 workers worldwide.

Holland is the third largest investor in the United States, investing some $67 billion and employing 323,000 Americans. Examples of large Dutch investors in the United States are: Royal Dutch Shell, AKZO-Nobel, Unilever, Philips Electronics, Polygram, Albert Heijn, OCE, ASM Lithography, Reed Elsevier, Heidemij, AEGON, ABN/AMRO, Rabobank, and ING Bank.

Between 1992 and 1996, Dutch investment in Canada increased 63% to 7.35 billion Canadian dollars (about ƒ10 billion). This makes Holland the third largest investor in Canada, after the United States and the United Kingdom. The Dutch are attracted to Canada because of its low taxes and labor and real estate costs, as well as its European feel. The North American Free Trade Agreement also gives the Dutch free access to the American market from Canada. Examples of large Dutch investors are:

Unilever, Shell Canada (the seventh largest company in Canada), ING Bank, and Gist-Brocades (Bio-Intermediair).

LABOR FORCE

The thirty-eight-hour week was introduced in 1985. For statistical purposes, the Dutch consider employment for as few as thirty hours per week a full-time job. Flexible working arrangements are on the increase in Holland. The number of part-time and less-than-full-time jobs is increasing. In 1996, workers with temporary contracts accounted for 12% of those employed. Workers with part-time jobs accounted for 38%. Workers with permanent, full-time, staff positions still made up the majority of those employed: 58%. By law the minimum number of paid vacation days is fifteen, but twenty-three days are generally given.

UNEMPLOYMENT

The total working population is approximately 6.7 million. The seventies and eighties were a period of economic decline, not only in Holland, but all over the industrialized world. The oil crises of 1973 and 1979 were clearly a factor. Between 1963 and 1972 the average GDP growth in the industrialized nations was 4.7%, while in the ten years that followed it shrank to 2.5%. Inflation climbing from 4.2% to 7.5% accompanied GDP decline. Production growth in the G-7 (the seven largest industrialized countries) reached new lows in 1974–1975 and 1979–1982, while unemployment increased.

The 1980s was the decade of the Dutch unemployment explosion. In 1970, 1.2% of the workforce was unemployed. By 1980, it had climbed to 6.5%. The explosion reached its peak in the middle of the decade, at about 13% of the workforce in 1986. After that, it began to drop at a rate of about 3,000 per month, until it reached 312,000 in early 1992. That year, unemployment began to climb again at a rate of about 10,000 per month, until it peaked in early 1994 at 9.9%, just below the European Community average for that year of 10.7%. Following that, it began to drop again at a rate of about 2,000 per month. In 1997, unemployment fell even faster: about 8,000 per month. By the end of the year, it had reached 375,000 (5.6% of the workforce), 65,000 less than in 1996.

These figures, however, do not paint an entirely realistic picture of unemployment in Holland. The decreasing unemployment figures for Holland are due in part to a decrease in the number of new claims for unemployment insurance and not to an increase in the number of people obtaining a job. Too often in Holland being laid off means unemployment for good. When broadly defined to include programs like WAO (Disability Benefits Act) and VUT (early retirements), unemployment levels have remained stuck at the levels of the mid-1980s. The most problematic populations in terms of the unemployment of the eighties—women and young people—are no longer the focus of attention at the Central Labor Bureau. Their place has been taken by the worker over forty. Age discrimination is rampant in Holland, and people over forty who lose their job have trouble finding another one.

TRADE UNIONS

About 25% of waged employees are members of a trade union. There are three main trade unions: the Federatie van Nederlandse Vakverenigingen (Federation of Dutch Trade Unions), the Christelijk Nationaal Vakverbond (Christian National Federation of Trade Unions), and the Vakcentrale voor Middelbaar en Hoger Personeel (Trade Central for Middle and Upper Management). Dutch society strives for consensus; therefore, Dutch labor leaders try to avoid confronting management with a strike. Holland has one of the lowest percentages of days lost to strikes of the European Community.

3

The Political System

The Kingdom of the Netherlands is a constitutional monarchy. The royal family is the House of Orange-Nassau, which traces its lineage to Prince William of Orange (1533–1584), who later became William I—the first stadholder in the Netherlands—known as William the Silent. Succession to the throne is hereditary, passing to the firstborn child—either male or female—of the reigning sovereign. The present monarch is Queen Beatrix (1938–   ). Her son, Crown Prince William Alexander (1967–   ), is the heir apparent to the throne.

Executive power is exercised by the Crown and the cabinet of ministers. The party or coalition of parties that has a majority of the seats in the lower house of Parliament appoints the ministers to the cabinet. Ministers, however, may not be both members of the Parliament and members of the cabinet. Anyone given a portfolio in the government who has also been elected to Parliament must give up his or her seat there.

The sovereign is advised by the Council of State, which was instituted in 1532. The Council is appointed by the sovereign, who serves as its president. The vice president, however, is responsible for the day-to-day operation of the Council. There are a maximum of twenty-eight councilors, who are appointed for life and retire at age seventy. One of these will be the crown prince or princess, once he or she reaches age eighteen.

The Council is normally an advisory body, which considers all legislation before it goes to the Parliament, but it wields executive powers when it implements orders of the sovereign and judicial powers when it acts in disputes concerning the government.

The Parliament is known as the Staten-Generaal (States-General). It consists of two chambers. The Eerste Kamer (First Chamber) has seventy-five members, elected for six years by the Provinciale Staten (Provincial Councils). The Tweede Kamer (Second Chamber) has 150 members, elected on the basis of proportional representation by popular vote for four-year terms. The minimal age for election to the Second Chamber is twenty-one, and for the First Chamber it is twenty-five. The minimum voting age, however, is eighteen.

The Dutch do not restrict voting rights to citizens only. Legal resident aliens, who are not citizens, can vote in local elections. In 1981, 1982, and 1986, more than 80% of the electorate voted. Recently, however, voter participation has fallen so low that politicians are considering restoring mandatory voting, which was abolished in Holland in 1970 but is still the law in neighboring Belgium. The turnout in the 1998 parliamentary elections was 73.2%. This decline in voter turnout is partially explained by the present good state of the economy, which is traceable to the policies of the coalition government that was returned to power in the 1997 elections. The voters were comfortable and saw no real electoral challenge to the incumbents.

Only the sovereign, together with the government (cabinet of ministers), and the Second Chamber have the right to introduce legislation. The First Chamber cannot amend legislation or initiate it. It can only ratify or reject laws passed by the Second Chamber. The Second Chamber also prepares the budget and has the right to question ministers.

The monarch signs all bills approved by the States-General, but, to become law, bills must also be signed by the responsible minister. Should the sovereign for some reason not sign a bill that has been passed by the States-General, the government falls and a new government has to be formed. The government can also fall if it loses its majority in the States-General. Since World War II, only five governing cabinets have served the full four years.

Every year on the third Tuesday in September, the monarch opens the new session of the States-General with a speech from the throne. This speech outlines the government's program for the coming legislative year.

The Dutch electoral system insures that each political party gets the number of seats that is proportional to the number of votes that the party's candidates obtained in the election. The total number of votes cast is divided by the number of seats to be filled (150 for the Second Chamber). The result is the number of votes that are required for a seat. The total number of votes received by each party is divided by the number of votes required for a seat, and that is the number of seats that the party gets. If a party does not get at least that many votes, it does not get a seat.

Who actually gets a seat is determined by the party. The party makes up a list of candidates, arranged in the order of the candidate's importance to the party. The seats that the party wins in the election are assigned to candidates, based on the candidate's position on the list. Voting is, therefore, more a question of which party to vote for than a question of which candidate.

Following elections to the Second Chamber, or when the government falls, the monarch appoints a *formateur* to form a new government. If the *formateur* cannot create a new government, another *formateur* is appointed and, if necessary, another and another until a successful governing cabinet is formed. For example, the Labor Party (Partij van de Arbeid [PvdA]) won a plurality of seats in the elections of 1977, and a PvdA party *formateur* was named, but the PvdA was unable to form a government. This failure allowed a coalition of Christian Democratic and other parties to form a government instead.

POLITICAL PARTIES

Holland has a large number of political parties. Twelve parties won seats in the 1994 parliamentary elections to the Second Chamber. Twenty-two parties contested seats in the 1998 parliamentary elections, but only nine got enough votes to win seats. The parliamentary elections of 1933, though, had the largest number of parties contesting seats: fifty-four.

Verzuiling (pillarization) along religious lines was responsible for creating a number of these parties, but the general trend now is political polarization along conservative/liberal lines. As no single party holds a majority in the Second Chamber of the States-General, the governing cabinet is a coalition of various parties, whose combined number of seats in the Second Chamber of the States-General does give them a majority. The governing coalition cabinet that emerged from the 1998 parliamentary elections holds a parliamentary majority of forty-five seats for the Labor Party, thirty-nine seats for the People's Party for Freedom and Democracy (Volkspartij voor Vrijheid en Democratie [VVD]), and fourteen seats for D'66 (Democraten '66 [Democrats 1966]). Together, the three parties hold 98 of the 150 seats (65%) in the Second Chamber, which is enough to insure the passage of the legislation that furthers the coalition's policies.

The VVD is a liberal party in the European, rather than in the American, sense of the word. It advocates free enterprise, separation of church and state, and individual liberties. The liberal tendencies of the VVD trace their roots to the constitutional reform of 1848, which laid the groundwork for parliamentary democracy in Holland. It is, generally speaking, the most conservative of the political parties.

The Christen-Democratisch Appel (CDA; Christian Democratic Appeal Coalition), which favors democratic government and a middle-of-the-road social policy, was originally three separate religious parties: one Catholic and two Protestant. The three parties trace their origins to the political battle over the funding of schools that held center stage in Dutch politics in the nineteenth century and the first part of the twentieth century. Equal state funding for public (secular) and private (religious, denominational) schools eventually became the law of the land in the constitutional amendment of 1917.

Through the 1970s, the religious party with the largest membership was the Katholieke Volkspartij (KVP; Catholic People's Party). In 1977, it joined with the Christelijk-Historische Unie (Christian Historical Union) and the Anti-Revolutionaire Partij (Anti-Revolutionay Party) to form the CDA in order to challenge the lead that the PvdA had won in the 1972 elections. The PvdA won more seats than the CDA in 1977, but when it was unable to form a government, the CDA formed a governing cabinet instead.

This governing Christian Democratic coalition remained in power until 1994, when it was replaced by a coalition of social democrats and liberals (PvdA, D'66, and VVD). Together, the coalition held 92 of the 150 seats (61%) in Parliament. This new governing cabinet was called the *paars* (purple) cabinet because purple is a combination of the color for the PvdA (red) and the color for the VVD (blue). In this election, the Green Left Alliance (discussed further below) played the pivotal role. It blocked a VVD-CDA coalition, and the VVD was forced to join with the PvdA to form a government.

The CDA supports free enterprise and holds to the principle that government activity should not replace, but should supplement, private-sector action. Politically, the CDA stands between the individualism of the VVD and the governmentalism of the PvdA.

The PvdA is a European social democratic party (left of center). It was established in 1946, when its policy concerns were the postwar reconstruction of Dutch society and, in particular, the establishment of the welfare state. It now follows mainly national interests instead of strictly socialist ones.

The fourth major party is D'66. It grew out of an increasing wave of discontent with the other major political parties and the erosion of party discipline in the mid-1960s. Its political fortunes have varied widely since it was founded in 1966. The 1994 election brought it twenty-four seats in the Second Chamber, twice the party's average over the last twenty years. In the 1998 elections, the number of seats that the party won in the Second Chamber again dropped to fourteen. Politically, D'66 is a center-left party, somewhere between the CDA and the PvdA. The party has a pro-European platform, which supports ethnic and religious tolerance. Its strongest support is from young urban professionals.

The largest left-wing coalition is the Green Left Alliance (Groen Links). It is a combination of the Communistische Partij Nederland (Communist Party of the Netherlands), the Evangelische Volkspartij (Evangelical People's Party), the Politieke Partij Radikalen (PPR; Radical Party), and the Pacifistisch Socialistische Partij (Pacifist Socialist Party).

The Algemeen Ouderen Verbond (AOV; General Federation of Seniors) is a reflection of the shifting demographics in Holland. The baby boomers of the turbulent sixties are becoming the militant elderly of the nineties. In 1996, 22.8% of the populace was fifty-five or older. Political militancy among the fifty-five-plus segment of the population is a reaction to the age discrimination that is prevalent in Holland (see the discussion in Chapter 12 for more detail). In the 1994 parliamentary elections, the AOV won even more seats (six) than Green Left (five). In 1997, the AOV merged with the other seniors' party, Unie 55+ (Union 55+), which had only one seat in the Second Chamber. In the 1998 elections, however, the AOV did not win any seats at all in the Second Chamber.

PROVINCIAL GOVERNMENT

Holland is divided into twelve provinces. Each province is governed by a Provincial Council (Provinciale Staten), an Executive Council, and the Queen's Commissioner. The Provincial Councils are directly elected by the voters for four-year terms. The number of members is based on the number of residents in the province. The Provincial Councils, in turn, elect the deputies who will represent the province in the First Chamber.

The Queen's Commissioner is appointed by the queen. He or she serves as the president of both the Provincial Council and the Executive

Council. The Executive Council is responsible for the day-to-day running of the government of the province. It consists of six to eight members, appointed from among the elected members of the Provincial Council. Just as in the United States, the central government is in the process of devolving more power to the provincial and municipal authorities, because local authorities are supposed to understand local problems better. The process, however, is simultaneously being reversed as problems arise with policy implementation at the local level. At present, the reversal is only ad hoc, but it is a harbinger of a change in the direction of the policy pendulum.

MUNICIPAL GOVERNMENT

The twelve provinces are further divided into 647 *gemeenten* (municipalities). They are administered by local Councils, which are elected by popular vote for four-year terms. In contrast to the national elections, aliens, who have lived in Holland for five years, but who are not Dutch citizens, can vote in these municipal elections.

Just as in the provinces, the day-to-day running of the municipal government is the job of an Executive Board, consisting of two to six members, appointed from the elected local Council. Both the Council and the Board are headed by the *Burgemeester* (mayor), who is appointed by the monarch.

Due to the very high population density, city planning is a dire necessity in Holland. It is the municipalities that plan everything and approve every building proposal. That gives them a considerable amount of power in the community.

THE JUDICIARY

The judicial system is largely a combination of Roman and Napoleonic law. There is no trial by jury. Independent judges, who cannot be removed except for malfeasance or incapacity, hear all the cases. The judges must, however, retire at age seventy.

There are sixty-two cantonal courts. Most of these courts are just a single magistrate. They deal with cases of petty crime and civil cases up to ƒ500. Above them are the nineteen district courts. These are the courts that first hear criminal cases and civil cases not handled by the cantonal courts. There are five Courts of Appeal to hear appeals of cases ruled on by the lower courts.

The Hoge Raad (Supreme Court) of the Netherlands ensures that the law is applied consistently and reviews the judgments of the lower courts. It cannot, however, declare laws unconstitutional, as the Supreme Court of the United States can.

Holland is not as litigious as the United States. Instead of suing one another for real or imagined damages, as Americans do, the Dutch all carry personal liability insurance policies that pay for them. The insurance companies, not the courts, decide who gets how much. If the insurance companies cannot work it out, there is an ombudsman's office and, in addition to the courts, a system of binding arbitration that is supported by trade and consumer groups. They handle cases regarding breach of contract that would be tried as civil cases in the courts in America. The death penalty was abolished in 1870.

MEMBERSHIP IN INTERNATIONAL ORGANIZATIONS

Holland is a founding member of the United Nations. It participates in the North Atlantic Treaty Organization (NATO), the European Union, the World Trade Organization (the successor to the General Agreement on Tariffs and Trade), the Law of the Sea Treaty, the Organization for Economic Cooperation and Development (OECD), the European Bank for Reconstruction and Development, and the International Monetary Fund (IMF). It is the seat of the International Court of Justice, the Iran Claims Tribunal, the International Criminal Tribunal on Rwanda and the former Yugoslavia, and the Organization for the Prohibition of Chemical Weapons (OPCW).

FOREIGN AID

In 1975, Holland was the second country (Sweden was first) to achieve the goal of allocating at least 0.7% of GNP to official development aid. Now, Holland is the fourth largest foreign aid donor. It gives about 1% of its gross national product in foreign aid. Large amounts of aid are channeled through multilateral organizations like the UN Development Program, the International Development Association, and the EU, rather than given directly to recipient states. Private, not state, organizations control a lot of the foreign aid that the Dutch provide. These are "co-financing" projects, and the private donor organizations have almost total autonomy in their choice of project.

Dutch development assistance—as defined by the OECD—totaled about $4 billion in 1995. Dutch priorities for that year were the environment, women in development, the alleviation of urban poverty, and research.

4

Society

THE POPULATION

In 1829, the Dutch began conducting a census every ten years. The last official census, however, was in 1971. It was conducted amid considerable protest about the issue of privacy. Population numbers after the census of 1971 are based on estimates made using municipal records. Even though Holland requires citizens to register with the municipal government, Dutch statisticians view their population data as flawed and would like to return to a true census, if the privacy issues could be resolved. The population figures below show the rapid growth of the population in the twentieth century, which has tripled in the number of people living in the country since 1900.

1900	5,104,000	1960	11,417,000
1910	5,858,000	1970	12,958,000
1920	6,831,000	1980	14,209,000
1930	7,832,000	1990	14,893,000
1940	8,834,000	1996	15,494,000
1950	10,027,000	2000	16,000,000 (projection)

Holland has the highest average population density in the world, with a 1996 density of 373 inhabitants per square kilometer. If the water surface area is excluded, the population density rises to 456 inhabitants per square kilometer. (Japan's average population density is only 334 inhabitants per square kilometer.) Of the 15,494,000 Dutch, 7,662,000 or 49.5% are men and 7,832,000 or 50.5% are women. The average life expectancy for men is 74.8 years. For women, it is 80.7 years (1997).

Age Differentials

The demographic processes in Holland are much like those in the United States. The older segment of the population is growing faster than the younger segment, as more women become better educated, enter the workforce, postpone starting a family, and have fewer children. The sixty-five-plus segment of the population makes up about 13% of the total, while the birth-to-nineteen age group makes up about 25%. It is projected, however, that by the year 2050, the sixty-five-plus segment will make up over 21%, while the birth-to-nineteen age group will represent just over 22% of the population. This trend, however, is not as noticeable in the *allochtoon* segment of the population, where nonworking mothers and large families are still the norm.

Ethnic/Racial Makeup

The Dutch are ethnically homogeneous. They are descended from the Germanic tribes that once inhabited the region. The collapse of the Dutch Empire and the economic boom of the sixties, however, caused a shift in the ethnic makeup of the country.

When Indonesia gained its independence in 1949, about 300,000 people repatriated or emigrated to Holland. After Surinam gained its independence in 1975, another 130,000 people joined them. The economic boom and the need for unskilled laborers in the sixties and seventies also increased the number of non-Dutch inhabitants. Turks and Moroccans came to fill the void in the labor market, and many of them stayed.

Most recently, waves of asylum seekers have been drawn to Holland by the liberal social benefits that Holland offers residents. The result has been a changing racial climate that is testing the fabled tolerance of the Dutch. In the mid-1990s, the Dutch introduced new, stricter regulations for granting asylum and obtaining residence permits. This led to reductions in the number of asylum seekers in 1995 and 1996. In 1996, the number of asylum seekers had dropped to 23,000. Of the 725,400 aliens residing in Holland in 1996:

- 282,300 were from Surinam
- 154,300 were Turkish nationals
- 149,800 were Moroccan nationals
- 33,500 were from the former Yugoslavia

There are two words in Dutch for "alien": *buitenlander* and *allochtoon*. The dictionary treats them both equally, but in practice, *allochtoon* is most often used for aliens of color and *buitenlander* for aliens who are white. The *allochtoon* population consists of Moroccans, Turks, and those from the northern Mediterranean countries (Greece, Italy, Portugal, Spain, and the former Yugoslavia), from Surinam, and from the Cape Verde Islands and the Netherlands Antilles. Even though those of Indonesian descent would seem to qualify to be called *allochtoon* because of their skin color, they are not. They are better accepted than the other ethnic minorities and are not generally referred to as *allochtoon*, but as Indonesians. The birthrate for the *allochtoon* segment of the population is much higher than for the ethnic Dutch. This will cause a further shift in race differentials in the next century.

Immigration

In 1996, 109,000 people immigrated to Holland. This was 13% more than in 1995, when only 96,000 people immigrated. The increase is due to a reduction in unemployment, which made it easier for immigrants to obtain a residence permit. Emigration from Holland is hardly significant. There was a big wave of Dutch emigrants in the period right after World War II, when the country was in ruins, jobs were scarce, and the government encouraged people to leave to seek their fortunes elsewhere. More than half a million Dutch moved to America, Canada, Australia, New Zealand, and South Africa at that time.

Socioeconomic Classes

Of the thirty poorest districts in Holland (1997), eight are in The Hague, seven in Rotterdam, and four in Amsterdam. For example, in the Schildersbuurt district of The Hague—a predominantly *allochtoon* district near the Hollands Spoor train station—disposable income is 33% below the national average. The disposable income in The Hague as a whole, however, is only 4% below that in Rotterdam and Amsterdam (1997).

Unemployment is also above the nationwide average in these cities. In The Hague, it is only 8.7%, but in Rotterdam, it is 14.2% and in Amsterdam, 14.0% (1997). All of these cities have large *allochtoon* populations.

CULTURAL LIFE

Tolerance

The Dutch have long tolerated different political ideas and views. Tolerance, however, is not the indiscriminate acceptance of diversity; it is the recognition of someone else's right to be different, as long as that difference is not intrusive. Dutch tolerance led to society breaking down into a sort of voluntary segregation, known in Dutch as *verzuiling* (pillarization). This separation of one social group from another kept frictions over their differences to a minimum. The Protestant and Catholic *zuilen* date back to the sixteenth and seventeenth centuries, the time of the revolt against Spain. When the Protestants displaced the Catholics as the ruling power in society, the Catholics formed a closed "pillar" within society to preserve their own Catholic identity. The Dutch sense of tolerance, which allowed them to do so, was an unusual concept in this time of religious wars.

The nineteenth century was a time of sweeping social change in Europe. Liberalism became increasingly popular in Holland. The liberals believed that freedom, self-responsibility, tolerance, and social justice were the requisites for an ideal society. The Protestants and Catholics closed ranks in their individual pillars, maintaining their own religious identities, as economic and political power shifted to the liberal, secular elements of society. At the end of the nineteenth century, liberalism was joined by socialism as a new force in society. The socialists represented the interests of the workers and farmhands. They became the fourth pillar in Dutch society. Each of them was tolerant of, but isolated from, the others. Each maintained its own values and let the others maintain theirs.

At the height of *verzuiling*, almost all social activities were voluntarily segregated on the basis of religious or philosophical views. For instance, there were separate Catholic, Protestant, liberal, and Socialist sports clubs, newspapers, schools, insurance companies, labor unions, agricultural associations, and political parties. The *zuilen* did not start to break down until the 1960s, under the influence of television, which erased the boundaries between the pillars by exposing people to each other's differences. (See Chapter 12 for a more complete explanation.)

Religion

Complete religious freedom is guaranteed by the constitution, and such freedom conforms to the Dutch tradition of tolerance. In the seventeenth century, the Dutch created a haven for personal and religious freedom, unmatched anywhere in Europe. They hosted the Pilgrims between 1608 and 1620, while the Pilgrims searched for religious freedom from the Anglican Church. The ascendant Protestants tolerated the Catholics.

Beginning in the 1950s, the influence of the Christian Church began to decline. In 1984, 36% of the populace aged eighteen and over were estimated to be Roman Catholic. By 1996, that number had dropped to 20%. The effects of the changing racial makeup of the country brought on by the loss of empire, by the need for guest workers, and by the influx of refugees seeking asylum can be seen in the number of Muslims and Hindus now residing in Holland. In 1986, there were 338,000 Muslims and 72,000 Hindus. It is projected that by the year 2020, Islam will be the second largest religion in Holland. By that time, 7% of the populace should be Muslim, while only 10% is expected to be Catholic.

The largest growth has been in the number of people professing no religious affiliation. This populace has grown from 2.2% in 1900, to 23.6% in 1971, and to almost 35% in 1984. By the year 2020, it is expected that 73% of the population will be nonreligious.

Education

Illiteracy is virtually nonexistent in Holland. School attendance is compulsory for children between the ages of five and sixteen. Most children attend nursery school before starting elementary school. Politicians are presently debating lowering the age for compulsory attendance to four.

Dutch schools are centrally guided but locally controlled. The Ministry of Education makes policy, but it cannot specify how that policy will be implemented. It is the individual school, in cooperation with the local municipal authority, that decides the specifics of how to achieve the policy goals set by the ministry.

This framework of guidance, not control, allows the state to fund all schools, both public (30%) and private (70%), both secular and religious, without impinging on each school's special focus. The Education Ministry can say that every student should learn to read Dutch, but it cannot say which textbook should be used to teach it. This allows secular schools to offer a secular curriculum and religious schools to offer a religious curriculum, both of which meet the national guidelines as well as the school's special focus.

The Dutch do not see state funding of all schools as a violation of the separation of church and state but, rather, as a guarantee of the parents' freedom of choice. Parents' choice can be guided by the religious or secular focus of the school, by its academic focus, or by both. In Amsterdam, for example, freedom of choice means de facto segregation. In the *oost* (east) district of the city, eight of the nine elementary schools are considered "black," because more than 75% of the pupils are *allochtoon*. Ethnic Dutch (*autochtoon*) parents tend to send their children to the one "white" Montessori school in the district or to take them to schools outside the district. *Allochtoon* parents, on the other hand, tend to send their children to schools where children of their ethnic minority dominate. The elementary school De Kaap is the Moroccan school, in which Moroccan children make up 70% of its 188 pupils. De Kraanvogel is the school for those from Surinam. Het Palet is the school for the Turks.

To help schools provide extra resources for these students, funding is allocated on the basis of a sliding scale that determines the statistical value of one enrollment. One teacher's position is funded for each thirty-two statistical students. A student from a home where Dutch is not the first language, for example, counts as 1.9 students. A student from a home where the parents have minimal education, or are poorly paid, or are unemployed counts as 1.25 students.

Schools in Holland are in session throughout the year. This, however, brings with it a side effect that needs to be considered in the American debate over year-round schools. Because there is only one six-week school break in the summer, families with children all wish to go on vacation during that time, which risks the country grinding to a halt, as offices, shops, and factories empty and roads, hotels, and vacation destinations fill to overflowing. To counteract this problem, Holland has been divided into three school regions, and the timing of the long school break is rotated among the three regions so that each year, one of the regions will have its break early in the summer, the second late in the summer, and the third in the middle. Each year the timing of the break alternates per region, so that all have an opportunity to vary their vacations.

There is no school lunch program in Holland. Children go home for lunch each day unless special arrangements are made for them to stay. Staying for lunch in a Dutch school is much like after-school care in U.S. schools. It is a pay-as-you-go service provided by the Parent-Teacher Organization. There is no food provided. Children who stay have to bring their own lunch from home. A by-product of this feature of the Dutch school system is that mothers of elementary schoolchildren find it hard to have full-time jobs, for they have to make four trips a day to school to drop off and pick up their children.

Nor is there a school-specific transportation system in Holland. Children who ride the bus are expected to use the same buses that their parents take to work. This affects both the school budget (it does not have to include money for busing) and the children's experience of going to and from school (the atmosphere on a yellow American school bus is much different than that on a regularly scheduled Dutch bus during rush hour). Most Dutch children walk or bike to school.

Schools in Holland have considerable Turkish and Moroccan student minorities. The state tries to ensure that these students will not be disadvantaged in school by making them equal to 1.9 statistical students. Extra lessons in their own language and culture are available to them if their parents choose for the children to attend. The school staff feels, however, that their minority students could better use the time spent on parental language and culture to learn Dutch language and culture instead. Their reasoning is that most, if not all, of the children will never return to live in their parents' home country, so a good command of Dutch language and culture will make them better equipped to succeed in their new homeland.

In predominantly ethnic minority schools, such as the ones in Amsterdam, a significant problem is the parents' lack of desire to be integrated into Dutch society. They continue to live in their own culture and to speak their native language at home, to the exclusion of things Dutch. When, for example, a teacher at one of these schools gave her second- and third-grade classes a homework assignment to watch a television program about the environment for discussion in class the next day, over half the class could not watch the program, because their parents program their sets to omit all the Dutch television channels. They have only Moroccan channels to watch.

For children from families like these, school is the only place that they can learn Dutch. When there is a single predominant ethnic group in a school, it is easy for the children to speak their native language among themselves, which weakens their need to speak Dutch. Studies have shown that a deficiency in Dutch language skills leads to poorer performance in other school subjects. Poor Dutch and academic skills mean that these children will not be able to get ahead in Dutch society and will remain confined to the ethnic ghettos in which they now live.

Until 1970, French was offered in elementary school as an elective. In 1970, the law was changed to make English the foreign language of choice in elementary school. English is taught beginning in the fifth grade, and it continues through high school. In addition to English, college-bound high school students also have to take German and French. Those who take the classical *Gymnasium* track learn Latin and Greek. Those who take the *Atheneum* track do not. Students who will take a terminal high school degree or go on to a technical or vocational college continue with English and must choose one of the following for a second foreign language: German, French, Spanish, Russian, Arabic, Turkish, Frisian, or Italian.

Universities

Entry to a college requires either an *Atheneum* or a *Gymnasium* track high school diploma. Holland has eight universities. Leiden is the oldest, established in 1575 by William of Orange to commemorate the city's resistance to the Spanish in the War of Independence. The story goes that the citizens of Leiden could choose between a university and an exemption from taxes. They chose the university, because they thought that the tax exemption could one day be rescinded. The other universities are in Groningen (established in 1614), Utrecht (1636), Nijmegen (1923), Maastricht (1976), and Rotterdam (1973), with the final two in Amsterdam.

The University of Amsterdam began in 1632 as the Athenaeum Illustre. It retained that title until 1877, when it was designated a university. The Vrije (Free) University of Amsterdam was founded in 1878 as part of the "Battle of the Schools" fought in the Dutch political arena of the nineteenth century. It was a private initiative by orthodox Protestants, under the leadership of Abraham Kuyper (1837–1920), who wanted a university free from church and state, one that would be bound only by God's word.

In addition to these, there is one agricultural and three technical/engineering colleges, plus two business schools. The three technical colleges are in Delft (established in 1905), Eindhoven (1957), and Twente (1961). Wageningen (1876) is the home of the Agricultural College. The business schools are in Tilburg (1927) and Nijenrode (1946).

The Dutch government gives each university and vocational school student between the ages of eighteen and twenty-seven a basic scholarship. The original intention of this payment was to cover the student's living costs. Government economy moves, however, reduced the basic scholarship for a single student living away from home to ƒ425 per month in 1997 from ƒ570 in 1992.

After paying tuition, the single student living away from home will have less than ƒ200 per month to live on. In the Randstad, the rent for a small room is easily twice that much. In 1996, the Ministry of Education's model budget for a single student living away from home was ƒ1200 per month. The difference between the model budget amount and the basic scholarship is supposed to be made up by supplementary scholarships for students with demonstrable needs and by student loans. The goal of the Stoeb Law, which regulates government student scholarships, is "to place the heaviest burden on the strongest shoulders." It is colloquially known as the "Students Stand on Their Own Legs Law."

There were 159,500 students enrolled in Dutch universities and colleges in 1997. The total number of students enrolled that year fell 3% from 1996 because of new regulations that make it impossible for someone to remain a student indefinitely at government expense. Degrees now have to be completed in six years. The number of freshmen, however, rose 4% to 29,100.

Beginning in 1996, economic changes limited scholarship payments to students to four years. Before 1991, the payments could, in theory and sometimes in practice, be drawn almost forever. The new regulations created what is called the "achievement scholarship." Students have to achieve certain goals for the money they receive to be considered a grant. If they do not meet these requirements, the money they receive is a loan, which has to be paid back with interest. During their first year of study, they have to accumulate a certain number of credit hours, and they have to complete their degrees within six years. Government payments to students also now stop at age twenty-seven, whether the student has completed his or her degree or not. Those who wish to continue studying after that have to take out a student loan.

In addition to a student grant/loan, Dutch students also get a pass for public transportation and for the Dutch Rail network. This benefit was introduced when the government first began reducing benefits under the student grant/loan program. The government thought that it would be cheaper to give the students the pass than to give them the money to pay for their transportation to school and back. The students quickly saw a way to make money with their passes to compensate for their reduced scholarships. They began offering courier services throughout the country. Since students traveled free on Dutch Rail, they could take a package from The Hague to Groningen, study on the train, and pocket the whole fee. The government quickly caught on, however, and now Dutch Rail passes for students living away from home are valid only on weekends.

THE ARTS

Visual Arts

Holland has over 800 museums, making it the country with the highest museum density per square kilometer in the world. The outstanding museums in Amsterdam are the Rijksmuseum, the Stedelijk Museum, the Van Gogh Museum, and the Tropical Museum. In Rotterdam, the Boymans-van Beuningen Museum is of interest. In The Hague, it is the Mauritshuis Museum with its collection of Vermeers that is worth seeing. The Frans Hals Museum in Haarlem has a world-renowned collection of old masters. Other collections of major interest are at the Centraal Museum in Utrecht, the Museum of Natural History in Leiden, Teyler's Museum in Haarlem, and the Folklore Museum in Arnhem, and the Krüller-Möller Museum in Otterlo.

In the late Middle Ages, artists from Flanders and Brabant introduced new styles and techniques. Hubert (ca. 1370–1426) and Jan (ca. 1395–1441) van Eyck discovered the use of oil paint. Hieronymus Bosch (ca. 1450–1516), who came from Aachen but who worked all his life in Den Bosch, is considered by some to be the first surrealist painter. He developed a vivid fantasy world of his own.

Later, Vincent van Gogh (1853–1890) was the forerunner of expressionism, while Piet Mondrian (1872–1944) was one of the leading cubists. His works became progressively more and more abstract until objects finally disappeared from his canvases altogether. They became surfaces with horizontal lines in a particular pattern or compositions of square colored blocks, sometimes combined with black lines. Mondrian's theories were specifically two-dimensional. They dealt with the tension, equilibrium, and movement of geometric planes based on their color and shape.

Willem de Kooning (1904–1997), another prominent artist, was born in Rotterdam. He emigrated to America in 1926. At first he had to work as a sign painter and commercial artist to support himself, but now he is recognized as a master of abstract expressionism. While his works adorn many an American museum, there is not one to be seen in his hometown of Rotterdam.

The well-known graphic artist M. C. Escher (1898–1972) is also from Holland. His prints are almost mathematical in quality, presenting repeating images and offering the viewer strange perspectives.

The Cobra movement (1948–1951) included Dutch artists Karel Appel (1921–   ), Eugène Brands (1913–   ), Corneille (a.k.a. Cornelis van Beverloo; 1922–   ), Constant (Nieuwenhuys; 1920–   ), Jan Nieuwenhuys (1922–1986), Anton Rooskens (1906–1976), and Theo Wolverkamp

(1925–   ). Its name was a conflation of the initial letters of the names of the capital cities of the countries of origin of the first members of the group: Copenhagen, Brussels, and Amsterdam.

The conceptual artists Ger van Elk (1941–   ) and Jan Dibbets (1941–   ) work with photographs and paint. They are considered among the most innovative Dutch artists being shown in the United States.

Music

Modern-day Holland has a great music tradition with orchestras that tour the world. These include the Amsterdam Concertgebouw Orchestra, The Hague Residentie Orchestra, the Rotterdam Philharmonic, the Netherlands Chamber Orchestra, the Netherlands Chamber Choir, the Netherlands Woodwind Ensemble, and the Eighteenth Century Orchestra. The Concertgebouw Orchestra in Amsterdam is perhaps the most famous. It made its first tour of America in 1954.

Pop music is equally well represented. Golden Earring, Normaal, BZN, the Nits, the Scene, 2 Unlimited, Trockener Kecks, and Lois Lane play to full houses all over the country. Pop festivals are organized throughout the year. Pinkpop is the most famous of them.

Dance

The contemporary success of Dutch ballet dates to the mid-1950s, when Sonia Gaskell (1904–1974), a Russian émigré, took charge of the New Dutch Ballet in 1954. In 1961, the Amsterdam Ballet was amalgamated with the New Dutch Ballet to form the Dutch National Ballet, and Gaskell remained at its head. She left the company in 1968 and returned to Paris, after which Rudi van Dantzig (1933–   ) took over the leadership of the company. The National Ballet's repertoire consists mainly of classical ballets, with the exception of the works of twentieth-century choreographers like the Russian-born, American dancer George Balanchine (1904–1983).

In 1959, while still under Madame Gaskell's direction, the National Ballet split in two. A splinter group left to form the Netherlands Dance Theater (NDT) in The Hague. In 1978, Czech choreographer Jiri Kylian (1947–   ) took over the company. Kylian's unique and personal style of choreography defies academic categorization. In 1981, the Netherlands Dance Theater became the first Dutch dance troop to perform at the Met in New York.

The NDT consists of three parts. The "main group" (NDT1) is complemented by a young, experimental company of dancers aged seventeen to twenty-two (NDT2) and by a group of mature (over age forty) dancers and artists (NDT3). Each of them has its own repertoire reflecting the specific qualities that dancers have at each of those stages of life.

Theater

Holland has a large number of professional theater companies, which perform in Dutch. Internationally renowned productions, such as *Cats, The Phantom of the Opera,* and *Les Miserables* are translated into Dutch and presented with great success. The Dutch musical *Cyrano* reversed the process and was well received on Broadway in 1993.

The weekly magazine *Vrij Nederland* lists all the plays being staged throughout the country. During the month of January 1998, it showed that forty-five different plays were being presented to the public in any one week. Opera and musicals were being produced in much lower numbers. There were three operas running simultaneously and six musicals. Cabaret shows were the most widely presented form of live theater entertainment, with fifty-four shows running at one time.

The impresario Joop van den Ende, who sent touring companies all over the country, is, however, cutting back on the number of theaters with which he deals. Beginning with the 1998–1999 season, his touring companies will only play in ten large, centrally located theaters, rather than the thirty-five theaters spread all over the country that they had played before. The change was prompted by the cost of tearing down the performance space and setting it back up again, as well as by the fact that the smaller theaters could not draw large enough crowds to pay for the cost of production. In the new season, the shows will remain open longer at each theater in the hope that the public will travel to the show instead of requiring that the show travel to them.

Festivals

There are a number of theater, dance, and music festivals held annually in Holland. The most prominent of these is the Holland Festival. It has been held in June each year since its inception in 1947. It is a showcase of international developments in the performing arts. The best foreign avant-garde, experimental theater groups, opera companies, mimes, performers, and musicians are given the spotlight for the month. In addition to the talents of their guests, the Dutch also show off what they themselves can do. The Amsterdam Concertgebouw Orchestra, the Amsterdam Philharmonic Orchestra, the Dutch National Ballet, the Netherlands Dance Theater, The Hague Residentie Orchestra, and the Rotterdam Philharmonic are all regular participants.

The Holland Music Festival is held in Utrecht. It focuses on baroque and medieval music. The North Sea Jazz Festival is held annually in The Hague. The Theater Festival, held in The Hague and Antwerp (Belgium), showcases the most important Dutch and Flemish theater productions of the year. The Holland Dance Festival, held every other year, hosts leading Dutch and foreign companies. The annual Utrecht Film Festival in September screens all the Dutch films produced the previous year. The Poetry International Festival is held annually in June in Rotterdam. Poets from all over the world attend to read their works.

Motion Pictures

The Dutch film industry is very small. There are only ten to fifteen films produced in Holland each year, and most of those are documentaries. The Ministry of Welfare, Health, and Cultural Affairs provides financing for Dutch film production through the Netherlands Film fund. The fund offers producers interest-free loans for up to 60% of production costs to a maximum of ƒ800,000.

In 1997, there were 19 million paid admissions to Dutch theaters, a 13% increase over 1996. The average number of paid admissions has remained constant for the last ten years at around 15 million. The movies that attracted the most viewers in 1997 were: *Bean, The Lost World: Jurassic Park, Men in Black, The English Patient,* and *101 Dalmatians.* The most popular Dutch-produced movies were: *All Stars*, a soccer comedy, directed by Jean van de Velde; *Karakter* (Character), the 1997 Oscar winner for best foreign film, directed by Mike van Diem (1959–   ); and *De Gordel van Smaragd* (Belt of Emerald), a story of Holland's Indonesian past, directed by Orlow Seunke (1952–   ).

The Academy of Motion Picture Arts and Sciences award for best foreign-language film, which was first created in 1956, has gone to Dutch films three times: in 1986 for *De Aanslag* (The Assault), directed by Fons Rademakers (1920–   ); in 1995 for *Antonia* (Antonia's Line), directed by Marleen Gorris (1948–   ); and in 1997 for van Diem's *Karakter,* his directorial debut for a feature film. In addition to the winners, Dutch films have garnered two nominations: 1959: *Dorp aan de rivier* (Village on the River), directed by Fons Rademakers; and 1973: *Turks fruit* (Turkish Delight), directed by Paul Verhoeven (1938–   ). Other Dutch films of note by Dutch directors are:

- *Keetje Tippel* (Katie's Passion; 1975), *Soldaat van Oranje* (Soldier of Orange; 1979), and *De Vierde man* (The Fourth Man; 1983) by Paul Verhoeven.

- *Als twee druppels water* (The Spitting Image; 1963), *Max Havelaar* (1976), and *Mijn vriend* (The Judge's Friend; 1979) by Fons Rademakers.

- *De Stilte rond Christine M.* (Question of Silence; 1982), *Gebroken spiegels* (Broken Mirrors; 1984), and *Mrs. Dalloway* (1997) by Marleen Gorris.

- *De Smaak van water* (The Taste of Water; 1982), *Pervola: Sporen in de sneeuw* (Pervola: Tracks in the Snow; 1985), and *Siberia* (1995) by Orlow Seunke.

- *Vliegende Hollander* (The Flying Dutchman; 1995) by Jos Stelling (1945–).

Successful Dutch filmmakers and actors often go abroad to work. *Robocop* (1987), *Total Recall* (1990), and *Starship Troopers* (1997) were produced by Verhoeven. Jeroen Krabbé (1944–), who worked for Verhoeven in *Soldier of Orange* and *The Fourth Man,* has played in such films as *The Disappearance of Garcia Lorca* (1997), *The Fugitive* (1993), and *The Living Daylights* (1987). Rutger Hauer (1944–), who worked with both Verhoeven and Krabbé in *Soldier of Orange,* has starred in *Hostile Waters* (1997), *Amelia Earhart: The Final Flight* (1994), and *Blind Fury* (1990). Sylvia Kristel (1952–), who became internationally famous as the star of the erotic French film *Emmanuelle* (1974) and its sequels, has played in *The Nude Bomb* (1980), *Mata Hari* (1985), *Dracula's Widow* (1987), and *Hot Blood* (1990).

Dutch motion picture theater screens, however, are dominated by American films. The January 1998 edition of *Vrij Nederland* listed the movies showing on 135 screens in Amsterdam, Rotterdam, and The Hague: The number of screens showing Dutch-made films ranged from a low of 4 to a high of 8, while the number of screens showing American-made movies ranged from 62 to 73.

Studio, the Dutch equivalent of *TV Guide,* gives a summary of all the movies that will be shown on television each week. During the week of August 9–15, 1997, of the twenty-six movies to be aired, eighteen (69%) were American. Only one was a Dutch production. The rest came from Australia, Brazil, France, Greece, Italy, and the United Kingdom. All of them were shown in the original language with Dutch subtitles.

Books

The Dutch book trade comes off better than the Dutch motion picture industry. Of the 191 books reviewed in the *Nieuwe Rotterdamse Courant* (*NRC*), translated as the New Rotterdam Courier (the Dutch equivalent of the *New York Times*) during the month of January 1998, eighty-five (45% of the total) were original Dutch titles. Still, Holland imports more English-language books than any other non-English-speaking country. Untranslated original English-language works from the United Kingdom, the United States, Canada, and Australia accounted for fifty (26%) of the books reviewed in the *NRC*. Translations (forty-two, or 22% of the total) and works in a language other than English (fourteen, or 7%) made up the rest of the reviews. The large number of non-Dutch books, films, and television shows that are read and seen by the Dutch public gives the Dutch a very broad international outlook.

An icon in everyone's literary perception of Holland is the story of Hans Brinker, who put his finger in the dike to save a town from flooding. As sure as you are that every Dutch(wo)man you meet in Holland knows the story of Hans Brinker, the Dutch are all just as sure that Americans know the stories of Arendsoog (Eagle Eye) and Witte Veder (White Feather). *Hans Brinker* was written in 1865 by American writer Mary Mapes Dodge (1831–1905), who had never been to Holland and made up the story of the little boy with his finger in the dike. Arendsoog and Witte Veder are the heroes of a series of Western novels for children written by Jan Nowee (1901–1958) and his son Paul (1936–1993), who never set foot in America. The Eagle Eye series has sold over 5 million copies in Holland.

Postwar Dutch literature has been dominated by three novelists: Willem Frederik Hermans (1921–1995), Harry Mulisch (1927–), and Gerard Reve (1923–). Hella Haasse (1918–), Jan Wolkers (1925–), Cees Nooteboom (1933–), Tessa de Loo (1946–) and Maarten 't Hart (1944–) are other major postwar writers. While twentieth-century Dutch authors are very interesting, only a few have been translated into English. A short list of English translations of works by Dutch authors can be found in the Bibliography of Translations of Works. Reading some of them can give you a feeling for what life is like in Holland.

The Foundation for the Production and Translation of Dutch Literature publishes the magazine *Books from Holland and Flanders* with book reviews and translations of short stories and excerpts of new books.

The Oscar winner for the best foreign film in 1986, *De Aanslag*, was based on the 1982 novel of the same name by Mulisch. The film *Karakter*, which won an Oscar for the best foreign film in 1997, was also based on the 1938 novel of the same name by Ferdinand Bordewijk (1884–1965), as was the Oscar nominee for 1973 *Turks fruit,* based on the 1969 novel by Jan Wolkers. Wolkers is an interesting personality as well as a writer. He refused to accept the prestigious Constantijn Huygens literary prize in 1982 and the P. C. Hooft literary prize in 1989.

Leon de Winter (1954–   ) is not only a writer, but also a film director. He directed *Hoffman's honger* (Hoffman's Hunger; 1993), a four-part television series based on his novel (1990) of the same name, and *Junkieverdriet* (Junkie's Sorrow), a film about the poet Jotie 't Hooft (1956–1977), who died of an overdose at age twenty-one. The film was named for a volume of poetry of the same name (1976) by 't Hooft.

Simon Vestdijk (1898–1971), originally trained as a psychiatrist, was an extremely subtle and gifted novelist, poet, and essayist, who was well familiar with the works of major American authors. He published a study of Emily Dickinson (1830–1886) and translated some of her finest poems into Dutch. Herman Melville's (1819–1891) *Moby-Dick* inspired one of Vestdijk's essays. He was also an authority on William Faulkner (1897–1962) at a time when interest in the future Nobel Prize winner had faded in America.

The extremely popular children's writer Annie M. G. Schmidt (1911–1995), with over sixty books to her credit, got an F in Dutch in middle school. She has been widely translated into English as well as Czech, Danish, Frisian, French, German, Greek, Hebrew, Italian, Japanese, Lithuanian, Norwegian, Slovenian, Spanish, Swedish, and Russian. Her most famous series of stories is about a little boy and girl named Jip and Janneke.

Dick Bruna (1927–   ) and Rien Poortvliet (1932–1995) are both well known in America from their illustrated books. Bruna's children's books rely on the illustrations to convey the story and hardly require any translation. They tell the story of Miffy the rabbit (Nijntje, in Dutch). The Miffy series contains such titles as: *Miffy Goes to School, Miffy at the Seaside, Miffy in the Snow,* and *Miffy at the Museum.* Rien Poortvliet's book *Gnomes* was a great success in the United States and even turned into a Saturday morning cartoon series. It was followed by the sequel *Secrets of the Gnomes,* and by his books of animal illustrations: *The Living Forest: A World of Animals* and *Rien Poortvliet's Horses.*

Television

For many people in Holland, television is the medium that keeps them in touch with events going on in the world outside their door. The average Dutch viewer watched 2 hours and 35 minutes of television per day in 1997. The most-watched programs were sports events, with the coverage of the grueling Eleven-City Tour over a course of frozen canals and rivers drawing a 94% share. The most popular program is the news on the noncommercial public network, with a 69% share. The most popular channel is the commercial RTL4 with a 20.2% share. The three noncommercial public channels together have a 38.8% share.

A look at the Dutch *Studio* for one week in August in 1997 shows how pervasive American programming is. On Monday, Dutch viewers could have seen: *As the World Turns, Bad Girls* (movie), *Baywatch, Beach Patrol, Birdland* (miniseries), *The Bold and the Beautiful, Cheers, Days of Our Lives, Disney Cartoon Express, Dynasty, Evening Shade, Golden Girls, Growing Pains, Hercules, Highway Patrol, Hollywood Love and Sex* (documentary miniseries), *Hollywood Remembers, Jerry Springer, L.A. Heat, The Late Show with David Letterman, Magnum, P.I., Marker, Married with Children, MASH, On the Edge, The Oprah Winfrey Show, The Outer Limits, The Real World, Rescue 911, Sanford and Son, Santa Barbara, Scruples* (movie), *Shadow of Obsession* (movie), *Sideshow* (documentary), *Taxi, Tropical Heat, Walker, Texas Ranger,* and *The Waltons.*

Not only is American programming pervasive, it is being watched. An editorial in the *NRC* described the pomp, circumstance, and drama of Queen Beatrix's sixtieth birthday celebration as *"Dynasty* squared," and the description was just as understandable to the Dutch reader as it would have been to an American reader when *Dynasty* was a prime-time weekly phenomenon in America and few dared miss it. The average family pays ƒ400 per year in membership fees for the public networks and in cable subscriptions.

The Press

Freedom of the press is guaranteed by Holland's constitution. Indeed, Holland has long been a place where things that could not be published elsewhere were published. The Dutch were the first to issue regular newspapers. One of the oldest newspapers, the *Weecklijke Courante van Europa,* was founded in 1656. It continued to be published until World War II as the *Oprechte Haarlemsche Courant.*

In the mid-nineteenth century, however, periodicals became less and less independent and more and more a medium for a particular party or group. The editor in chief was often the party leader. The Dutch even have a word for this kind of publication to distinguish it from independent periodicals: *opinieblad* (opinion paper). Opinion papers were the cornerstones of pillarization. In the 1960s, the new medium of television, with the power to captivate audiences of all religious and political persuasions, began to break down the pillars.

At the same time that the newspapers were losing support among their constituent pillars, they also began to lose advertising revenue to television, once advertising was finally permitted on television in 1967. Since two-thirds of the operating costs of newspapers are covered by advertising, the print media had to take action. In typical Dutch fashion, part of the revenue stream from television advertising was temporarily redirected to the print media to help them cope with the change in the situation.

The shift of advertising revenue away from the print media to television resulted in mergers in the print media and changes in editorial policy. The liberal *NRC*, founded in 1844, and the *Handelsblad*, founded in 1828, merged into the *NRC-Handelsblad*. The Catholic daily *De Tijd* chose to become a weekly in 1974 rather than accept government subsidies. The Catholic *De Volkskrant* took on a progressive, liberal tone. The Protestant *Trouw*, which had begun as an organ of the Dutch resistance during World War II, took a turn to ecumenicalism and now represents all Christian faiths. Other papers gave up trying to reach the national market and managed to find a niche, regional market that allowed them to survive. *Het Vrije Volk*, once the party organ for the PvdA, found it could survive as a regional paper in Rotterdam, which has always been seen as the center of the Dutch workers' movement. Consolidation in the print media has considerably reduced the number of media companies. There are now five media companies, which control 96% of the countries daily papers.

Just as with television, the need to attract larger audiences to keep up with growing costs forced the papers to take a middle-of-the-road line at the expense not only of their religious and social views, but also of the quality of their reporting. Sensationalism, gossip, and sports sell more papers than lucid, insightful reporting on the events of the day. That can be seen in the circulation figures for the major newspapers. The largest national newspapers (arranged by daily circulation) are:

	1986	1997
De Telegraaf (Amsterdam) (right-wing, conservative, sensationalist)	706,000	763,400
Algemeen Dagblad (Rotterdam) (liberal, conservative, Protestant)	398,000	403,310

De Volkskrant (Amsterdam)	285,400	372,100
(left-of-center, Catholic, quality newspaper)		
NRC-Handelsblad (Rotterdam)	191,800	275,830
(liberal, quality business newspaper)		
Trouw (Amsterdam)	122,600	121,600
(left-of-center, ecumenical)		

The total number of daily papers printed by all publishers in 1997, both regional and national, was 4,752,791. That translates to 74 daily papers per 100 households. Dutch newspapers are sold primarily on a subscription basis: 90% of the figures above represent subscriptions. There are no Sunday editions of the national dailies. *De Krant op zondag* (The Paper on Sunday) is more advertising than news.

The Internet

About 60% of all the households in Holland have access to a personal computer (PC). Word processing is the reason most often (80%) given for having a PC. In Europe, Sweden and Denmark lead the way in projected sales of PCs with 90 sales per 1,000 inhabitants. Holland is the next largest European market for PCs with 75 PC sales per 1,000. Germany and the United Kingdom trail with 65 and 62 per 1,000, respectively; both will experience growth in projected PC sales to 76 and 68 per 1,000. But Holland will remain a European leader in the adoption of this new technology, with expected sales climbing to 80 per 1,000 in 1998, while sales in Sweden and Denmark level off at 92 per 1,000. In 1997, 14% of the Dutch had an Internet connection, and almost all of them used their connection at least once a week. This number was expected to double by 1998.

Sports

Soccer is very popular in Holland. The Dutch national team won the European championship in 1988, but it has never won the World Cup. It was, however, the runner-up in 1974 and 1978.

Soccer hooliganism is, unfortunately, a major concern in Holland. A prearranged fight between supporters of the Ajax soccer team (Amsterdam) and the Feyenoord team (Rotterdam) in March 1997 ended in the death of an Ajax fan. The government quickly responded to the public outcry for a crackdown on soccer violence. The police announced that they would increase their infiltration of hooligan groups, provide a larger police presence at matches, and improve the collection and exchange of information on known offenders. In addition, it was announced that so-called high-risk matches could be attended only by supporters from one of the sides, but not the other. The April 1998 win by Ajax over Feyenoord, playing in Rotterdam to a booing crowd of Feyenoord supporters without one single Ajax supporter present, brought into question the common wisdom of home field advantage.

The Dutch are particularly good in speed skating. When it gets cold enough, thousands of people take part in the grueling Eleven-City Tour, which follows canals and lakes for over 200 kilometers. In 1997, the winning time for men was 6 hours and 49 minutes; the winning woman's time was 7 hours 49 minutes. Since it is run entirely out-of-doors, it can be held only when weather permits, thus there have been only 15 Eleven-City Tours this century. The 1963 tour was the worst. Due to extremely poor weather conditions, only 1% of the participants reached the finish line.

The crown prince, William Alexander, is a member of the International Olympic Committee. He personally attended the Olympic Summer Games in Atlanta (1996) and the Winter Games in Nagano (1998). During the 1996 Summer Olympics, the Dutch won nineteen medals, four of which were gold. The Dutch gold medals were in men's volleyball, men's field hockey, men's rowing eights, and men's mountain biking. Holland finished fourteenth in the overall medal standings. In 1998, the men's field hockey team repeated its success by winning the World Cup tournament. The Dutch women's team finished second. During the 1998 Winter Olympics, the Dutch won eleven medals, five of which were gold. This is an amazing feat for a country with no mountains or snowfall of which to speak. All the medals were won in speed skating events. Many competitors in the speed skating races wore the new Dutch-developed clap skate, an articulated skate that has a blade hinged at the toe and loose at the heel, like a cross-country ski.

Tennis is also very popular in Holland. Richard Krajicek (1971–), who was born in The Hague of Czech parents, won the 1996 Wimbledon men's title. In 1998, Paul Haarhuis (1966–) and Jacco Eltingh (1970–) won the men's double title. Betty Stöve (1945–) is a multiple Wimbledon and U.S. Open champion.

During the summer, the Dutch hold the (in)famous Four-Day March at Nijmegen. Participants cover four different 50-kilometer routes (for women the routes are 40 kilometers). In 1998, 37,849 entrants from 51 countries took part in the eighty-second annual Four-Day March. Of these, 5,340 dropped out before reaching the finish. In 1997, seven of the participants covered the distance for the fiftieth time.

For less-avid walkers, the Dutch hold four-day evening walks during the summer. These walks offer a choice of 5-, 10-, or 15-kilometer routes and are very popular. Whole schools sign up and walk the route carrying the school flag. On the fourth day, the participants make a triumphal march to the finish led by a brass band. Family members who did not take part in the walk line the streets and hand flowers to the participants.

Part II

The History of the Nation

5

From the Ice Age to the Middle Ages

It is estimated that in the course of the last 700,000 years, the northern polar ice cap has advanced to the south about ten times. The ice advanced as far as present-day Holland only one time. That was during the next-to-the-last Ice Age, the Saale Ice Advance. This ice advance took place between 200,000 and 180,000 years ago. During this time, the present area of Holland was covered with ice as far south as Haarlem-Apeldoorn-Nijmegen. As the ice advanced, it pushed rocks and soil in front of it like a bulldozer. The massive rocks that were used to build the hunebeds—megalithic graves—in the province of Drenthe were brought to Holland in this way.

The rivers that cross Holland from east to west today used to flow farther to the north before reaching the sea. The changes in the landscape produced by the bulldozer-like advancing ice, are what made them flow to the west. The ice advanced, freezing all the water in its path, the sea level dropped 150 meters, or 490 feet. Humanoids lived in the area of present-day Holland before the Saale Ice Advance. Remains of humanoid inhabitants have been found near Maastricht, on the edges of the Veluwe in Gelderland, and in Drenthe. They were found together with the remains of rhinoceros, crocodiles, hippopotamuses, and forest elephants, indicating a very different climate than is found in Holland today.

The Saale Ice Advance was followed by a period of about 60,000 years when the area was warm again. Then, about 120,000 years ago, the ice began to advance once more. This ice advance is known as the Weichsel Ice Advance. The ice sheet did not extend into what is now Holland, but the temperatures there dropped to a level that changed the ground into frozen tundra, where no trees can grow. Only lichens, mosses, and stunted shrubs can survive in this type of climate. The rivers again dried up, but the sea level fell only about 135 meters (443 feet) this time. The prevailing westerly wind—that to this day still comes off the North Sea—picked up the silt from the bottom of the dry seabed and blew it inland. This created a belt of fertile soil that stretches across south Limburg and much of present-day Europe. This type of soil is know as "loess."

The Weichsel Ice Advance ended about 10,000 B.C. The tundra gradually receded to be replaced by forests. The reindeer that had been important to the peoples living on the tundra left and were replaced by forest deer, elk, wild cows, and pigs. Stone Age campsites have been found in Twente and in Brabant from around this time.

As the ice melted, the landscape of the low-lying areas of present-day Holland took shape. These areas became nothing more than swamps and everglades as the North Sea began to fill up again. Around 7,000 B.C., the land bridge between Normandy and England broke down, and England became an island.

Around 6,500 B.C., humanoids in Drenthe were making dugout canoes. This is the age of the Pesse canoe, named for the village of Pesse in Drenthe, near which it was found. It is the oldest boat ever found. A wooden paddle has been found in Star Carr in Yorkshire that is 1,000 years older, but Holland has the honor of the oldest boat. The canoe was dug out of a pine tree trunk. It is 3 meters (10 feet) long and 44 centimeters (18 inches) wide. In 1998, another prehistoric dugout, presumed to be of the same age, was found near Hardinxveldt, in the province of South Holland. This dugout was 5.5 meters (18 feet) long and 45 centimeters (18 inches) wide.

At the time that Egyptian civilization reached its peak, about 5,000 years ago, the inhabitants of what is now Limburg were just beginning to make the transition from nomadic hunters and fishermen to settled farmers, raising domestic animals. This was also the time that the Funnel Beaker people—named for the type of pottery they made—built the so-called giants' graves, or hunebeds. The name comes from the old word for "giant," *huyn*.

There are fifty-four known giants' graves, mostly in the province of Drenthe. The largest hunebed is near the town of Borger. It is 22 meters (72 feet) long, and its largest stone weighs 23,000 kilograms (50,600 pounds). Many of the hunebeds in Holland were plundered either for their grave goods or for the stones themselves, which were used to make roads and to reinforce dikes. Traces of thirty-four other hunebeds have been found, including two in Groningen, two in Overijssel, and one in Friesland. There is speculation that at one time there were well over 100 altogether.

In the late Stone Age (about 4,000–3,000 years ago), flint was mined in south Limburg. Flint was used for arrow points, axes, knives, scrapers, and drill bits. It was a very important natural resource and was in great demand. Flint from these mines has been found as far north as Münster and as far south as Frankfurt am Main in Germany, pointing to the existence of an extensive trading network. When the Bronze Age began, about 3,000 years ago, the importance of flint declined and the mines closed.

When the sea stopped rising, about 3,000 B.C., the sand carried downstream by the Rhine and the Meuse began to combine with the sand carried up the coast by the current that flows through the channel between France and England. The sand was deposited on the coast of Holland and became the sand barriers that protect the land from the sea. As the areas behind these sand barriers dried out, they became peat bogs.

About 1,000 B.C., the sea began to rise again, flooding large areas of what would become Holland. The remains of a 4,000-year-old hunting camp north of Rotterdam was found 8 meters (26 feet) below current sea level. It was during this period that the inhabitants began to build large mounds to keep their houses above water when the tide came in. In Friesland, this type of mound was called a *terp*; in Groningen, it was called a *wierd*, and in North Holland, a *werf* (compare the word "wharf"). In Gelderland, it was called a *woerd*. The highest remaining *terp* is in Hoogebeintum in Friesland. It rises 9 meters (30 feet) above the surrounding countryside.

The Roman historian Plinius described the north of present-day Holland as a country of strong tides that caused one to question whether the ground belonged to the land or to the sea:

> There a poor folk inhabits high hills or mounds that they have raised with their own hands to a level that they know from experience to be above the highest flood. That is where they have built their huts. When the water covers the surrounding area, they resemble sailors and when the water recedes, shipwreck victims.[1]

The arrival of the Romans in the wilds of northwest Europe just before the birth of Christ marked the beginning of history for present-day Holland. Everything that went before that is prehistoric. That means that it is based on archeological and geological data, not on written records. History came to the area with the Romans, who knew how to write and preserve their written records.

THE ROMAN NETHERLANDS

The oldest recorded history of the peoples of present-day Holland is Roman. When the Romans came to the wilds of northwest Europe, the Rhine River formed the boundary between the Celtic tribes to the south and the Germanic tribes to the north. The Romans brought "civilization" to the area. They introduced the written word. Roman engineers built roads and bridges. They taught new farming techniques and stimulated trade.

The Belgian tribes south of the Rhine were separated from the rest of Celtic Gaul, still farther to the south, by the woods of the Ardennes. To the north of the Rhine, the Germanic tribe known as the Batavians lived on an island in the delta of the Rhine, in the present-day province of Gelderland. Farther north along the coast, another Germanic tribe, the Frisians, lived in the Bourtange marshes from the area of the present-day Zuiderzee/IJsselmeer—which did not become a lake until the severe floods of the thirteenth century—to the river Eems.

Belgium was named for one of the tribes of mixed Celtic and Germanic origin that inhabited the area between the rivers Marne and Seine in the south and the Rhine in the north. The territory of the Belgae extended eastward from the North Sea to the Moselle River. They spoke the same language as the Celts of greater Gaul to the south but were much less civilized than the other Celts. On the other hand, they were much stronger and had more endurance than the other Celts, and Julius Caesar (100–44 B.C.) praised them as the bravest of the Celts.

Caesar's conquest of the Belgian tribes began in 57 B.C., but the Belgians were not finally subjugated until 52 B.C. The Romans ruthlessly suppressed all opposition to their control of the territory. The tribe called the Nevrii swore to die rather than surrender to the Romans, and die they did. Caesar, at the head of eight legions, annihilated them and moved on. The account of the Nevrii's honor and valor in the Roman chronicles so impressed the English poet John Blackie (1809–1895) that he immortalized their struggle in his poem "A Song of Heroes" (1890).

Under Augustus in 15 B.C., the territory of the Belgian tribes was designated the Roman province of Gallica Belgica. This was the outer edge of the empire, where the fortified Roman border followed the Rhine. Once it was established, the frontier held until the third century A.D.

As a result of internal weakness within the empire and pressure from the peoples without, the frontier began to give way in the third century, and large areas of territory were lost. The northern frontier was pulled back to the Roman road from Cologne to Boulogne. Below this line, Gallo-Roman civilization survived for another two centuries. Above it, the Germanic tribes replaced the Gauls. This Roman road became the language border that now splits Belgium. To the north of it, they speak Dutch (or Flemish, as it is called in Belgium), and to the south of it, they speak French.

The Batavians had originally been a part of the Chatti, who lived in the area of present-day Hessen in Germany. About 100 B.C., the Batavians were exiled from Hessen, following an internal disagreement among the Chatti. They subsequently settled on the island in the Rhine delta on which the Romans found them. When Batavians arrived at the island, it was uninhabited. The previous—probably Celtic—inhabitants of the island had deserted it after a major flood that had swept away not only their houses, but the trees and vegetation as well.

In 13 B.C., during the governorship of Drusus, the Romans formed an alliance with the Batavians. The Batavians were not incorporated into the empire as the Belgians were, but they were considered *Socii* (allies). Their alliance with the Romans freed them from Roman taxes but required them to provide troops to the Roman legions. Those sent to fight in the legions remained there until death or for twenty-five years, whichever came first.

According to the Roman historian Tacitus, the Batavians were the bravest of the Germans, and the Romans respected them for this trait. The Batavian cavalry was famous throughout the empire. Batavian valor turned the tide at the battle of Pharsalus (48 B.C.), when Caesar defeated Gnaeus Pompeius (106–48 B.C.) in a struggle for control of Rome. A Batavian legion was the imperial bodyguard from the death of Julius Caesar to the time of Vespasian (A.D. 9–79). Their loyalty to Rome was complete. They even fought with Rome against the neighboring Germanic tribes.

When, however, Roman power wavered, the Batavians sought to regain their freedom. In the confusion surrounding the struggle for the Roman throne after Nero's murder, the Batavians rose up against Roman rule under the leadership of Gaius Julius Civilis, in the year of the three caesars (Galba, Otho, and Vitellius: A.D. 68–69). Civilis was a Batavian noble, whose German name was not recorded in the Roman annals of the revolt. He was Roman educated and had served in the legions for twenty-five years.

Civilis formed a confederation of the tribes of the Lowlands, both Celtic and German. For a short while, the Batavian commonwealth was free of Rome. When Vespasian won the fight for the Roman Crown, he turned his attention to the Lowlands. As the might of Rome's legions focused on them, the Celtic tribes sued for a separate peace. Civilis, finally recognizing the inevitable, also began negotiations with the Romans. The Roman chronicle breaks off at this point in 70 B.C., so the fate of Civilis is not known. The Batavians, however, continued their alliance with Rome until the Silian Franks overran this part of the empire at the end of the third century. One of the last appearances of the Batavian cavalry in history is at the battle of Strasbourg in 357, against the Alemanni. After that, the Batavians disappear from the stage of history.

Even though the Batavians had vanished from the territory and history of Holland, they continued to live in the Dutch imagination as the forefathers of the Dutch people. In the eighteenth century, "Batavia" came to be used as a poetic name for Holland. Dutch settlers in America named cities Batavia in New York, Ohio, Illinois, Iowa, and Wisconsin. Dutch colonial officials in the Dutch East Indies named the capital Batavia, and *Batavia* was the proud name of a sailing ship belonging to the Dutch East India Company. Furthermore, the republic declared at the beginning of the period of French domination was called the "Batavian Republic"; and in this century, Batavus is even the name of a popular brand of bicycle manufactured in Holland.

It is the Frisians, however, who have been on the territory of what is now Holland longer than anyone else. The Frisians, together with the Angles and the Saxons, were a part of the Ingaevones, one of the three groups of Germans identified by Tacitus. The other two were the Istaevones and the Hermiones, whose name survives in the present-day word for Germany. The Frisians moved into the Lowlands, probably from the area of present-day Schleswig-Holstein, displacing the Celts, who had lived there earlier. They were the first German tribe to develop commerce. Frisian traders could be found as far afield as Basel and Saint-Denis. They were the main form of contact between the Germans and the Celts.

The Frisians did not come under Roman dominion until 12 B.C., when Drusus, with the aid of the Roman fleet, brought the German coast, including the Frisians, under Roman control. Unlike the Batavians, who were exempt from Roman taxes, the Frisians were required to pay a tribute in cowhides and horns. In A.D. 28, they revolted against the Romans and managed to remain free until A.D. 47, when they were again brought back under Roman control by Domitius Corbulo. In A.D. 69, following the death of Nero, the Frisians, like the Batavians, broke free of Rome. Unlike the Batavians, however, the Frisians—whose name is based on the word "free"—remained independent until the eighth century, when Karel (Charles) Martel (688–741) finally defeated them and forced them to convert to Christianity. Even under Charles the Great (a.k.a. Charlemagne, 742–814), they remained the free Frisians, keeping their own laws and rejecting the feudal system, which Charles introduced.

Being "free" used to have a much more literal meaning than it does today and those who had won the right to be called free were proud of it. Liberia (compare: "liberty") was established as a homeland for freed African slaves from America. In Russia, the Cossacks, whose name in Turkish means "free man," have a similar history to that of the Frisians. Unfortunately, history has no record of from what the Frisians had been freed.

When the Roman Empire fell in Western Europe around A.D. 400, Europe entered the Dark Ages.

FROM THE DARK TO THE MIDDLE AGES

With the fall of the Roman Empire, "culture," "civilization," and "history" disappeared for centuries. That was the time of great population shifts known as the migration of the peoples, which were caused by the advance of the Huns from the east, led by Attila. Not much is known about this period, because there were not very many written records to begin with and very few of them survived. For this reason, it is known as the Dark Ages.

The migration of the peoples changed the makeup of the population of what is now Holland. The Batavians and the other smaller tribes that the Romans had enumerated in their histories of the area disappeared. The area was now occupied by the Frisians along the coast, the Saxons in the east, and the Franks in the south. It was the Franks, who became the dominant power in Europe.

In the beginning, the Franks were far from being a cohesive whole. They were a loose alliance of German tribes—the Salians, the Ripuarians, and the Chatti—related to one another by long association and custom. There was no central power as there had been under the Romans. It was the Salian king Chlodowech I, also known as Clovis (466–511), of the

Merovingian line of kings, who began the reconsolidation of power in Europe. In 481, he succeeded his father, Childeric I, as king of a small kingdom in southwest Belgium in the area of Doornik. In 486, he defeated the Roman Syagrius, who ruled in the area around Paris, and the last Roman possession in Gaul passed into Frankish control. By 493, he had subjugated all the Salian tribes. In 506, he defeated the German tribe the Alemanni, the name of which is the origin of the French word for "German": *allemand*.

On Christmas Day of that year, Clovis accepted Christianity, not out of deep conviction, but because of a promise he had made on the battlefield. If God let him win the battle against the Alemanni, he had promised he would let himself be baptized. This made his dealings with the romanized inhabitants of Gaul and his wife—who was already a Christian—much easier. It also gained him the support of the Church of Rome. His later successes against the Burgundians and the Visigoths laid the foundation for the modern French state.

When Clovis died in 511, in accordance with the German customs on inheritance, his kingdom was divided among his sons. This scenario was to be repeated time and time again throughout European history. The constant divisions of kingdoms and empires, which had been united through power of will and of arms, weakened the forces of peace and stability, as brother fought brother for power, and held back the advance of civilization. Viking inheritance law, on the other hand, gave preference to the firstborn son. This strengthened the power of the king and pushed his brothers out to seek their fortune elsewhere. This is one of the factors that led to the Viking invasions of Europe in the ninth century.

Clovis's empire was not again reunited until the seventh century, when Chlotar II and his son Dagobert pulled it together from 602 to 639, but after them, it was divided again. The kings who followed them were weak rulers, who depended on their stewards to do the dirty work of leadership for them.

The empire was again reunited in 687 by Pépin the Younger (a.k.a. Pépin II, ?–714), the steward of the Merovingian king. In 689, Pépin defeated Radbod, the king of the Frisians, at Dorestad. The victory gave Pépin mastery of south Friesland. Radbod was forced to give his daughter, Theodeswinde, to Pépin's son, Grimoald, in marriage and to allow Christianity to be preached in Friesland. This victory made it possible for Bishop Willibrord to establish the seat of his bishopric in Utrecht in 695 and begin the conversion of the Frisians to Christianity—a conversion that was accomplished more by the sword than by the Good Book.

When Pépin died, Radbod took back the south of Friesland and expanded his territory as far as Cologne, marking the greatest expanse of Frisian power. In 717, Pépin's illegitimate son, Karel Martel, defeated Radbod again, and Radbod had to permit Christianity to be preached once more.

Neither Radbod nor his son, Poppo, who succeeded him, ever accepted Christianity themselves. When Bishop Wolframnus was about to baptize Radbod, Radbod asked where his departed ancestors were. The bishop's imprudent answer was that Radbod's ancestors were in hell, as was the fate of all unbelievers. Radbod refused to be baptized, even under threat. He said that he would rather feast with his ancestors in hell than enjoy the meager salvation of Christianity with strangers in heaven. Poppo continued his father's resistance to Christianity through 734, when he, along with a large number of Frisians, was killed in the battle of Boorn as they fought against Karel Martel.

Karel Martel (the Hammer) was the first Karel (Charles) in the Carolingian line of kings, which was shortly to replace the weak Merovingian line on the throne. The Carolingian line lasted until 987 in France and 911 in Germany. Karel Martel's greatest victory for the advancement of Christianity was not his defeat of the Frisians, but his defeat of the Muslims in 732 near Poitiers. This victory is credited with stemming the westward advance of the Muslims and keeping Western Europe Christian.

Karel Martel was followed by his son Pépin III—the Short (714–768). In 751, Pépin III locked the last of the Merovingian kings, Childeric III, away in a cloister and took the Crown of the Frankish Empire in fact as well as in deed. Because the Pope wanted the help of the Franks against the Longobards, he gave his blessing to Pépin's somewhat dubious ascension to the throne.

For a while around 800, it looked as if Pépin's son, Charles the Great (Charlemagne), who ruled from 768 to 814, would restore order to Western Europe. His reign was a period of political stability and the rebirth of learning. In 800, the Pope crowned him the first Holy Roman Emperor. This return to Roman-style civilization was known as the "Carolingian Renaissance." It did not last long, however. Following Charles's death, his empire—which covered France, Belgium, Holland, Germany, Switzerland, Austria, northern Italy, northern Spain, parts of the present-day Czech Republic, and parts of the former Yugoslavia—was divided by inheritance, and another two centuries of disorder and insecurity followed.

The Viking invasions began in about A.D. 850, and lasted until 1007, when they inexplicably stopped. At first they were just plundering expeditions, with the Vikings sailing up the rivers that crisscrossed the Lowlands. Eventually, the Vikings established camps and built their own settlements.

In 841, Rurik, a member of the family of the Danish king, together with his brother Harald, was given a fiefdom by Emperor Lothair I (795–855), Charlemagne's grandson, who had inherited the third of the empire that included present-day Holland. After Harald died, Rurik clashed with Lothair, and Lothair had him imprisoned. Rurik escaped and, in 850, forced Lothair to grant him dominion over the Frisian lands, from the river Meuse to the river Vlie in the north of the country. In exchange, Rurik promised to defend his fiefdom against marauding Vikings—his own kinsmen. After Rurik died (between 876 and 882), his lands were passed to Godfried, the Norman, who was most likely his nephew.

Emperor Charles III—the Fat (839–888)—who was Charlemagne's grandson and Holy Roman Emperor from 881 to 887, gave Godfried Friesland to buy him off. (Charles much preferred buying the Vikings off to fighting them off.) Godfried took the Christian faith in 882 and was given Gisela, the daughter of Lothair II (ca. 835–869) in marriage. When Charles suspected Godfried of plotting with one of Lothair II's sons to take over more territory, Charles had him murdered around 885. Godfried's death marked the end of Norman rule in Friesland.

In the eleventh century, the feudal principalities that Charlemagne had introduced to make his empire function, became the basis of the provinces that were to play a major role in Dutch history. As the ties between the emperor and his vassals grew weaker, the dukes, counts, and bishops, who had originally been officials of the emperor, transformed their fiefs into independent lordships. The most important of these were the duchies (the domain of a duke) of Brabant and Gelre, the counties (the domain of a count) of Flanders and Holland, and the bishopric (the domain of a bishop) of Utrecht.

After A.D. 1000, the Flemish cloth trade began to flourish along the Scheldt. The towns of Ghent, Doornik, Ieperen, Valenciennes, Rijssel, and Torhout became important textile centers producing cloth for the northern European market. Later, they were joined by towns in Brabant, like Brussels, Louvain, and Mechelen. Bruges, at the crossing of the trade routes, became a trade center. These towns developed into the large trading and industrial cities of the twelfth and thirteenth centuries.

The period of the thirteenth and fourteenth centuries was one of relative peace and prosperity. The cities gained enough power to wrest concessions from the counts and the dukes, giving them a degree of independence. The advantages of being located on the sea and on three navigable rivers with access to the rest of Europe became clear. The Low Countries became a natural center of trade. This was the period that saw the development of towns like Amsterdam (founded in 1275) and Rotterdam (first mentioned in the chronicles in 1283).

THE HOUSE OF BURGUNDY

In the fifteenth century, Philip the Good of Burgundy (a.k.a. Philip III, 1396–1467)—considered the founder of the modern Dutch and Belgian states—began to unite the provinces of the Netherlands under control of the House of Burgundy by means of treaties and marriage. When his father, John the Fearless, was killed in 1419, Philip had control of Flanders, Artois, and Mechelen, which his father had acquired in 1385 as a result of his marriage to Margaret, the only daughter of the count of Flanders. In 1429, Philip acquired Namur. In 1430, Brabant and Limburg. In 1433, he wrested Holland, Zeeland, and Henegouwen from his aunt Jacoba of Bavaria (1401–1436). In 1451, he added Luxembourg. He further expanded his control by making his nephew, Lodewijk of Bourbon, the bishop of Luik (1455) and his illegitimate son, David, the bishop of Utrecht (1456).

Philip wanted to unify all the provinces. To make this possible, he saw that laws, weights, and measures would have to be the same in all of them. (This is the same course that the European Parliament is following today to bring about European unity.) To this end, in 1464, he created the first States-General, consisting of representatives from the Provincial Councils. The States-General did not have any executive powers and was called to session only to approve taxes.

The balance of power rested with the southern provinces, with Brabant in particular, where the dukes of Burgundy held their court, in Brussels. They ruled Brabant personally. The other provinces were ruled through appointees, known as "stadholders." The provinces were not yet truly unified, however. They each viewed the other as separate countries and would not let officials from one enter the other.

Philip the Good was succeeded by his son, Charles the Bold (1433–1477), who brought the provinces of Gelre and Zutphen under Burgundian control. Like his father before him, Charles wanted to be crowned king of his dominions. He was negotiating with Emperor Frederick III (1415–1493) of the House of Hapsburg to be crowned king and had even pledged his daughter, Mary of Burgundy (1457–1482), to Frederick's son, Maximilian (1459–1519), to seal the bargain. The emperor had agreed to crown him, but in the face of staunch political opposition to the coronation, he disappeared on the eve of it (1473), and the ceremony did not go through. The wedding eventually did, however, in 1477, shortly after Charles's death. His lands passed to Mary, and with her marriage to Maximilian, the Netherlands came under Hapsburg rule.

After the unexpected death of Charles in 1477, the States-General took advantage of the helpless position of Mary to increase its rights. Mary was forced to buy the help of the States-General against France with the "Great Privileges" charter. This charter granted the States-General the right of consent to declarations of war, the right of the sovereign to marry, and the right to levy taxes. In addition, the States-General could convene as often as it wished without waiting for the sovereign to call it to session. Only natives of the province could be appointed to high office, and all documents had to be in the local language. Unfortunately, Philip the Handsome—Mary and Maximilian's son—would put an end to this when he took power in 1494.

PRELUDE TO REVOLUTION

After Mary's death in 1482 (she fell from a horse while hunting), there was opposition to Maximilian acting as regent for their three-year-old son Philip (1478–1506). Maximilian suppressed the opposition, despite being taken captive by the people of the town of Bruges for a while in 1488. When Maximilian's father died in 1493, Maximilian became emperor and in 1494, at the age of fourteen, Philip the Handsome took charge of the Netherlands. Under his rule, the province of Gelre, which had never been very obedient, broke away in 1499.

Through Philip's marriage to Joan, daughter of Ferdinand II and Isabella, he was in line for the Spanish Crown. But Philip died unexpectedly in Spain in 1506, and Joan went mad. Their six-year-old son, Charles V (1500–1558), became ruler of the Netherlands. His aunt Margaretha (Margaret of Austria [1480–1530])—Philip's sister—became regent. Under Charles V, the province of Gelre once again joined the Netherlands in 1543. It had been preceded by Friesland in 1524 and Groningen in 1538. That brought the total number of provinces to seventeen.

When his grandfather Ferdinand II died in 1516, Charles became the king of Spain. In 1519, when his other grandfather, Maximilian, died, he inherited his crown as well. Charles V had been born in Ghent and considered himself a Netherlander. Within his worldwide empire, the Netherlanders had unrestricted rights to conduct trade and had a majority share of the world's trade volume. The center of trading activity was in Antwerp. In addition to trade and industry, agriculture, cattle herding, fishing, science, and the arts also flourished under Charles's reign. The same cannot be said about his son, Philip II.

At the age of fifty-five, Charles abdicated in favor of his son Philip II, who, until age twenty-two, had lived in Spain. Philip had never even been to the Netherlands, nor could he speak Dutch. Charles died three years later in a cloister in Spain. The stage was now set for the Dutch revolution against Spain: the Eighty Years' War.

NOTE

1. Quoted in Jan Romein and Annie Romein, *De lage landen bij de zee: een geschiedenis van het Nederlandse volk* (The Low Countries by the Sea: A History of the Dutch People) (Utrecht: W. de Haan, 1949), pp. 26–27.

6

Reformation, Rebellion, and the Republic

When King Charles V of Spain abdicated in 1555, control of the Low Countries went to his son, Philip II (1527–1598). Philip's absolutism brought the trouble that had been developing for years in the Netherlands to the surface. The Dutch nobles were opposed to rule by a foreign sovereign, and Philip was an "absentee monarch." He never visited the Low Countries again after he returned to Spain in 1559, following his father's death. The cities, which had been almost completely self-governing, resented the increasing restrictions on their independence. The merchants were convinced that they could be much more successful traders if they were independent of Spain. One of the more important factors in the increasing discontent, however, was religion.

The first half of the sixteenth century was the period of the Protestant Reformation, which had begun in Germany with Martin Luther (1483–1546). It was the teachings of French-born John Calvin (1509–1564), however, that had a profound effect on the course of Dutch history. Calvin gave more thought to social and economic factors than other reformers. While Luther sought a return to primitive simplicity, Calvin promoted economic development by preaching the virtues of thrift, industry, sobriety, and responsibility. Unlike Luther, who believed in the political subordination of the church to the state, Calvin saw the state as subordinate to the church. For him, the state was an institution created by God to defend the church and uphold the law. In the event that a ruler proved to be a tyrant, it was Calvin's view that the lower levels of government, rather than the common citizens, should be the ones to resist the tyrant. The results of both these precepts are clearly visible in the course of Dutch history.

Philip demanded absolute loyalty to the Spanish Crown; and for Philip, that also meant absolute loyalty to the Roman Catholic Church. Because the Dutch did not revolt until Philip took power, though, does not mean that Charles V had been tolerant of Protestant reforms. He was not. In May 1521, he signed the Edict of Worms, which outlawed Luther and all his followers. In 1550, he signed another edict under which Protestant heretics were burned at the stake. His parting words to the Netherlands that he had united were: "Remain united, uphold the law and suppress heresy." Many people in the Netherlands, however, were Protestants. In Charles's eyes, that was heresy.

When Philip left the Netherlands for Spain in 1559, after the Peace of Cateau-Cambrésis, which put an end to the war between France and Spain over the control of Italy, he named his illegitimate half sister, Margaret of Parma (1522–1586), vicereine of the Netherlands. She was familiar with the customs of the Netherlands and acquainted with Spanish politics. A courageous woman with a firm character, a sharp mind, and a feeling for the use of power, she tried to control the situation with tact.

Philip appointed Cardinal (as of 1561) Antoine Perrenot de Granvelle (1517–1586) as her adviser, but Granvelle assumed an overly influential role in the government of the Netherlands and became, essentially, the prime minister. In 1563, William of Orange (stadholder of Holland, Zeeland, and Utrecht), the fourth Count of Egmond (stadholder of Flanders and Artois) and the Count of Hoorne (stadholder of Gelre and Zutphen) wrote a letter, offering their resignation from the Council of State should Granvelle not be recalled. Margaret demanded that Philip recall Granvelle, and after his departure in 1564, she tried to work with the Dutch nobility to preserve the peace.

In 1566, the lesser Dutch nobles concluded a pact called the "Compromis." They joined together in the Compromis to oppose the Inquisition and edicts limiting freedom of religion. The Compromis is recorded as having begun in Brussels at the wedding of Margaret's son, which had brought a large number of nobles together for the celebration. The Compromis passed secretly from hand to hand and soon had collected the signatures of over 500 nobles, both Catholic and Protestant. William of Orange (William the Silent), however, was reluctant to sign the pact and advised against recruiting troops, as some of the leaders of the Compromis were demanding.

William the Silent was the son of the Count of Nassau. He had been baptized as a Catholic, but he was raised as a Protestant until he was eleven. In 1534, he inherited the title of the Prince of Orange. For William to be able to accept his inheritance, however, Charles V insisted that William be raised as a Catholic at the royal court. William's parents, knowing that the vicereine of the Netherlands, Mary of Hungary (1505–1558)—Charles's sister—was not entirely hostile to Protestant ideas, agreed, and William went to the court to be raised as a Catholic under her tutelage.

When Charles V abdicated in 1555, William was very much in his good graces. William was appointed to the Council of State and made a member of the Order of the Golden Fleece. When Philip II left for Spain in 1559, William was appointed stadholder of Holland, Zeeland, and Utrecht. In the Council of State, he was the voice of the resistance to Philip's absolutism and defender of the freedoms and rights of the cities and provinces.

William arranged meetings between the upper and lesser nobles in Breda and in Hoogstraten, but the only results of these meetings were a warning to the vicereine from the fourth Count of Egmond of the danger posed by the Compromis and a petition prepared on William's advice for presentation to Margaret. The petition was delivered on April 5, 1566, with the signatures of over 200 nobles.

Initially, the results of the nobles' action were positive. Persecution came almost to a halt, and the Protestants were able to practice their religious beliefs more openly. That, however, worked to their disadvantage. The more openly the Protestants manifested themselves, the more concerned the government in Brussels became. The vicereine began recruiting troops.

When their protests to the vicereine were unsuccessful, the leaders of the Compromis also began making preparations for armed action with foreign support. At the same time, they prepared a second petition, which they presented to Margaret on July 28, 1566.

The "Iconoclastic fury,"[1] which began on August 10, panicked Margaret and the leaders of the Compromis into an accord. Margaret promised an amnesty and the maintenance of the status quo in religious affairs but prohibited a further expansion of Protestantism. The leaders of the Compromis—the lower nobility—promised to take action to stop the fury. Most members of the upper nobility rejected even the few concessions that Margaret had made in the accord and continued the repression of the

Protestants. William was the only exception. He proclaimed religious freedom in his provinces.

In the wake of the accord, the Compromis fell apart. Some of its
members were afraid of the Iconoclastic fury turning into a popular
uprising, which would have swept away not only the Catholic Inquisition and the king, but them as well. This inclined them to accept Margaret's concessions. Other members of the Compromis rejected
Margaret's prohibition on the expansion of Protestantism. Realizing
that Philip would never approve of the accord, others began to collect
money among the Calvinist middle class to raise an army for the defense of the Reformation. Their assessment of the situation was correct.
Philip did not approve.

In 1567, Philip sent the Duke of Alva, Fernando Alvarez de Toledo
(1507–1582), at the head of an army of Spanish and Italian troops to the
Netherlands. Alva was a trusted military officer and a veteran of campaigns in France, Italy, Africa, Hungary, and Germany under Charles V.
When Margaret saw that the powers Philip had given Alva made her
presence in the Netherlands meaningless, she abdicated her regency and
left for Italy to join her husband.

Also in 1567, Alva replaced William as stadholder of Holland, Zeeland,
and Utrecht with the Count of Bossu (1542–1578). The first free assembly
of the States-General—held in Dordrecht in July 1572—tried to give the
revolution a legal basis. It recognized William of Orange as the legal stadholder instead of Bossu. This was strictly a political move to put the right
spin on the revolution. The goal was to make the revolution appear to be
against Alva and not against Philip.

It was the eloquence and diplomacy of Philip de Marnix (1540–1598),
Lord of Saint Aldegonde—alleged to be the author of the Compromis—
who swayed the delegates of the session to elect William stadholder.
Marnix is also reputed to be the author of the Dutch national anthem,
"Wilhelmus," which is dedicated to William. Its lyrics are an acrostic, in
which the first letters in each line form his name "Willem van Nassov,"
when read in sequence from top to bottom.

Alva's powers allowed him—in the rigorous defense of the Catholic
faith and the Spanish Crown—to seize even the most prominent and
honored citizens of the country, execute them, and confiscate their property. Alva's reign of terror lasted for six years, from 1567 to 1573. The tribunal he convened to defend the faith and Spanish rule was popularly
known as the "Council of Blood." Within its first three months, it had ex-
ecuted 18,000 people. Among the first to be called to appear before the
Council of Blood were Egmond, Hoorne, and William of Orange. William

and his brother Lodewijk wisely refused to appear. Hoorne and Egmond were beheaded.

The slightest suspicion, even libelous accusations by one's enemies, was sufficient for conviction, and the council knew only one sentence: death and confiscation of property. The terror increased. Executions numbered in the thousands. Confiscated property was valued at 30 million talers (the currency at the time). Trade and industry ground to a halt. Hundreds of thousands of refugees fled the country. During the Spanish offensive of 1572–1573, the populaces of the towns of Mechelen, Zutphen, Naarden, and Haarlem were massacred.

The members of the Compromis, who had taken up armed struggle against the Spanish, called themselves the *Geuzen* (Beggars). The name reputedly stems from the presentation of the first petition to Margaret of Parma in 1566. Berlaymont (1510–1578)—one of Margaret's councilors— allegedly whispered to the vicereine in French: *"ce ne sont que des gueux"* (they are only beggars). The militant members of the Compromis took up this name as a badge of honor.

The name *Geuzen* is a linguistic artifact of the time. It can be used only in this context. It shows that the language of the court of the Spanish Netherlands was neither Spanish nor Dutch. It was French. The Dutch spelling of the name is only a representation of the sounds of the French word *beggar* with a Dutch plural ending. It bears no resemblance to the Dutch word *bedelaar* (beggar).

Alva gained the upper hand on the ground battle, but the *Geuzen* took to the sea, attacking the Spanish fleet and Spanish coastal positions. Their first success was the capture of the town of Den Briel in April 1572. After that, they freed the rest of the northern Dutch coast little by little.

During the campaign of 1572, as the Spanish moved toward Amsterdam, which was still pro-Spanish at that time, they encountered a fleet of *Watergeuzen* (Water Beggars) frozen in the ice. To the amazement of the Spanish, the Dutch were able to move forward across the ice to engage them without falling down. The Spanish report of the incident shows that the Spanish were not familiar with ice skates. There was no single Spanish word for them. The report conveys the idea of what the Dutch had on their feet with a long description. The Spanish were so impressed with the ability to walk and fight on ice without falling down that Alva ordered 7,000 skates for his troops.

Until the late 1570s, problems with the Turks rivaled those with the Dutch, and Philip had to keep moving his limited forces back and forth between the Mediterranean and the Netherlands, unable to achieve a decisive victory in either theater. This allowed the Dutch to keep up their struggle with what was then the world's leading superpower. Even though Alva had been victorious on the battlefield up to the end, he lost hope of achieving his goals and asked to be relieved.

Alva left the Netherlands in December of 1573 to be replaced by Luis de Requeséns y Zúñiga (1528–1576). Requeséns was more moderate than Alva. He announced a general pardon, but it excluded the heretics. He abolished the Council of Blood and the extra taxes that had been levied by Alva. Nevertheless, he was unable to overcome the religious differences between Catholics and Protestants to achieve a peace settlement.

In 1574, Requeséns defeated Dutch forces led by Lodewijk (1538–1574) and Hendrik of Orange (1550–1574)—William's brothers—at the battle of Mokerheide. Both of them were killed in the battle. In May 1574, the Spanish lay siege to Leiden, but William broke the siege in October by breaking the dikes and flooding the surrounding countryside. The lifting of the siege is still celebrated in Leiden today. Requeséns's military operations against the Dutch were hampered by a continuing lack of money to pay for them. After Requeséns's unexpected death in March 1576, Spanish forces were in a state of confusion.

Because they had not been paid, mutinous Spanish troops moved from the rebellious north of the Netherlands to the rich south and began plundering Flanders and Brabant. That pushed these two provinces, which had not been involved in the uprising until then, to call on William of Orange to restore order. Negotiations began on October 19 in Ghent. Between November 4 and 7, Spanish troops plundered the city of Antwerp, and more than 7,000 people were killed. This incident—known as the "Spanish fury"—helped speed the conclusion of the negotiations. The settlement that was signed on November 8 is known as the "Pacification of Ghent," because it resolved the conflict between William, the provinces of Holland and Zeeland, and their allies on the one side and the southern provinces, except Luxembourg, plus Utrecht on the other. The agreement achieved the following:

- It restored William—pending the confirmation of the States-General—to the position of stadholder of Holland, Zeeland, and Utrecht that he had held before Alva's arrival.
- It suspended the application of the edicts against heresy until the States-General could take legislative action.
- It provided for the release of prisoners and the return of confiscated property.

- It prohibited taking any action against the Roman Catholic Church, except in the provinces of Holland and Zeeland, where Catholicism was already prohibited.

The result was the loss of all Spanish control over the Netherlands and the recognition of the Calvinists' monopoly position in Holland and Zeeland.

Pushed by a fear of Calvinist supremacy, some of the predominantly Catholic Walloon provinces of the southern Netherlands began extending feelers about a reconciliation with Philip II as early as February 1578. Margaret's son—Alessandre Farnese, Duke of Parma (1545–1592), who became governor of the Spanish Netherlands in 1578—deftly took advantage of the unrest in the Walloon provinces that was caused by fiery Calvinist demagogues and unruly Scottish mercenaries in the service of the Calvinists to reassert Spanish control in the south. If the cities and provinces would support the Roman Catholic faith and reaffirm their loyalty to the king, Parma promised to: let bygones be bygones; to withdraw foreign troops; to lift the taxes that had been levied due to the rebellion; and to return rights that the provinces and cities had had.

On January 6, 1579, the Provincial Council of Artois with delegates from Henegouwen and Dowaai, meeting in the capital of Artois, Atrecht, issued a manifest in which they guaranteed to uphold the provisions of the articles of the Pacification of Ghent, to preserve the Roman Catholic faith, and to be loyal to the king. The Union of Atrecht, as it came to be known, marked the beginning of the division of the Netherlands into present-day Belgium and Holland.

To counter the Union of Atrecht, on January 23, the northern provinces formed the "closer union" within the Pacification of Ghent and vowed to continue to fight for complete independence from Spain. The Union of Utrecht declared the solidarity of the signatories in their fight against the king and bound them not to conclude a separate peace with him or to enter into separate treaties with other powers. The signatories—with the exception of Holland and Zeeland—were free to decide the question of religious freedom as they wished, as long as no one was persecuted for their religious beliefs. In Holland and Zeeland, however, only the Reformed Church was to be permitted.

The Union of Utrecht defined the political framework for the government of the Seven United Provinces. It was, in essence, only a military union, and that was its shortcoming. Real power remained in the hands of the Provincial Councils, which were comprised of the nobility and the patricians from the cities. Their deputies at the States-General in The

Hague were bound by the instructions of their electors in the Provincial Councils, which hampered efforts to reach consensus on national issues when national interests conflicted with regional ones. Complex issues often required unanimous approval. Executive power rested in the hands of the stadholders, who were elected by the States-General and were not free to act independently of their political overlords.

The provinces were all jealous of their sovereign powers. The regents—members of the urban aristocracy—opposed moves to strengthen the central power in the United Provinces, because they wanted to preserve their position of power. Holland and Zeeland, in particular, wanted to preserve their leading role in the Union. Thanks to their wealth—they paid over 80% of the costs of the war with Spain—and large populations, they were the most powerful of the seven. The province of Holland, together with Amsterdam, had the most financial and political power, which is why the name "Holland" came to be associated with the whole of the country, rather than just the then-single province.

In 1581, the States-General published the Act of Abjuration, which two centuries later would serve as the model for the American Declaration of Independence. The justification of the act was the premise that the Provincial Councils were sovereign and that the lord of the land ruled only by virtue of the power delegated to him by the states. He could, therefore, be removed for acts of tyranny and actions counter to the rights and freedoms of the provinces. The act abjured the oath of loyalty that had been sworn to Philip and replaced it with an oath of loyalty to the United Netherlands.

William the Silent's military campaigns were successful. He allowed whole areas to be flooded to break the Spanish sieges of towns in the northern provinces. Philip put a price of 25,000 gold coins on William's head and promised to elevate the assassin to the nobility. There were two attempts on William's life. The second was successful. He was shot in Delft in 1584 by Balthazar Gérard (1562–1584). The Dutch had no prohibition on using cruel and unusual punishment on Gérard. They began by placing his hand into a red-hot waffle iron. The reward for taking William's life was paid to Gérard's next of kin. There was even an attempt to have Gérard declared a saint, but the pope wisely chose not to do so.

The separate peace with the southern provinces, gave Philip new hope, and he sent fresh armies to the Low Countries. Between 1579 and 1585, Philip was able to concentrate all his attention on the United Provinces. For a time after William's death, the Spanish were close to reestablishing their authority, but the renewed fighting with England and France forced Philip to divide his attention again.

By 1585, the Duke of Parma had managed to conquer all the southern provinces that had joined the rebellion and was threatening the northern provinces. In 1588, Philip sent the Spanish Armada to conquer England and take revenge for the death of the Catholic Mary Stuart (1542–1587). The Armada consisted of 130 ships of the line and 30 support ships. There were 2,000 volunteers from the upper nobility and 19,295 soldiers embarked. The ships were manned by 8,460 sailors and 2,088 slaves. The Armada had bad luck from the outset. Just after it had sailed from Lisbon, it encountered a storm that dispersed the ships. One sank and three were taken to French ports by mutinous slaves. The Armada's mission was to free the ports of Nieuwpoort and Dunkirk on the Flemish coast, embark Parma with an army of 31,000 and 4,000 horses, and take them to England. The mission was never fulfilled. The Armada encountered the English fleet. Rather than try to risk the return passage of the narrow English Channel, the fleet tried to return to Spain via the North Sea, where it encountered a major storm. By the time the Armada returned to Spain at the end of September, it had lost 75 ships of the line and 10,185 men.

In 1590, Philip ordered Parma and his troops across the border to try to halt the ascension of Henry IV (1553–1610) to the throne of France. Philip's goal was to place his daughter Isabella on the throne instead. This campaign, like that of the Great Armada, was also a failure.

With Spain's attention divided among France, England, and the Netherlands, Maurits of Nassau (1567–1625)—William the Silent's son—continued the fight after his father's death. He was able to capture Zeeland and Flanders, as well as all of the territory north of the rivers. It was not only Philip's lack of money and his acceptance of political imperatives over military ones that helped Maurits to succeed on the battlefield; it was also Maurits's reorganization of the Dutch army. He introduced training, discipline, and uniform armament for the troops. The battle of Turnhout in 1597 was the first time that sabers and carbines replaced the lances of the Dutch cavalry in actual combat with the Spanish. These new armaments were so much more powerful than the old that the Spanish suffered 2,350 casualties and lost 300 prisoners, while the Dutch suffered only 7 casualties.

Philip died in 1598, but the war dragged on until 1609, when Spain agreed to a cease-fire to last for twelve years. In 1607, Admiral Jacob van Heemskerck (1567–1607) led the Dutch fleet that attacked the Spanish in their home harbors at Gibraltar and defeated them. The ability of the Dutch to take the fight to the Spanish homeland was one of the factors that led the Spanish to the conclusion of the Twelve Years' Truce in 1609.

By the time that the truce was concluded, the frontiers of the United Provinces were secure.

Maurits's brother—Frederick Henry (1584–1647)—succeeded him, and when the war resumed in 1621, Frederick Henry extended Dutch control to north Brabant and north Limburg, as far south as Maastricht. That brought the territory then held by the Dutch more or less to the present-day frontiers of Holland. The army that had been created by Maurits was a showpiece. In 1625, no less than 26 counts of the House of Nassau, together with over 2,000 foreign officers and observers, were serving in the Dutch army to learn its tactics. The war continued for another twenty-three years. Thus the revolt against Spanish rule that had begun in 1568—the year after Alva's arrival—became the Eighty Years' War (1568–1609 and 1621–1648), initially led by William the Silent. By the time the final peace was concluded—with the Treaty of Westphalia of 1648, which also ended the Thirty Years' War[2]—the Dutch were led by William II (1626–1650), William the Silent's grandson. Thereafter, the Republic of the Seven United Provinces was recognized as an independent state.

WILLIAM AND MARY

Reflections of the great hate and mistrust between Protestants and Catholics that fanned the flames of the Eighty Years' War can still be seen today in Ireland. Though the Irish troubles are far from Holland, there is a Dutch connection. The Loyal Orange Institution, which was established in 1795 in Ulster to maintain Protestant ascendancy in Ireland in the face of growing agitation for Catholic emancipation, is named for William III (1650–1702), Prince of Orange, who was king of Great Britain and Ireland from 1689 to 1702, and under whose reign the position of the Protestant minority in Ireland was consolidated.

William, a Protestant, came to the English throne via his marriage in 1677 to his cousin Mary (1662–1694), the daughter of James, then Duke of York, later to become the king of England (1695). When James—a Catholic convert—had a son in 1688, fear of a Catholic heir to the throne led the Tories and the Whigs to put aside their differences. They invited William of Orange to come to England and depose his father-in-law. William landed in Devon in 1688 with an army of 15,000. He made his way to London with almost no opposition, and James fled to France. This short, successful, and bloodless campaign is known as the "Glorious Revolution."

In 1689, the English Parliament invited William and Mary to rule jointly, but on the condition that they accept the Declaration of Rights and the Bill of Rights, which greatly restricted the powers of the monarch and marked the shift of power from the Crown to Parliament. Under these rights, Catholics were barred from succession to the throne, the royal power to suspend and dispense with law was abolished, and the Crown was forbidden to levy taxes and to raise an army in peacetime without Parliament's consent.

James returned to England in an attempt to overthrow William in 1690, but William defeated him at the battle of the Boyne on July 12, a victory that is celebrated to this day by the Orangemen of Ulster, by marching through Catholic areas of the town. After William's victory at the Boyne and the Treaty of Limerick (1691), penal laws against Catholics in Ireland were increased in severity. The religious struggle that took the Dutch eighty years to resolve is still going on in Ireland now, over three centuries later.

NOTES

1. The Iconoclastic fury was a wave of destruction in the wake of increasing popularity of the Protestant reforms. It was directed against the icons and art of the Catholic Church. It was comparatively late in coming to the Netherlands. There had already been similar outbreaks in Wittenberg in 1522, in Zürich in 1523, in Copenhagen in 1530, in Münster in 1534, in Geneva in 1535, in Augsburg in 1537, in Scotland in 1559, and in France in 1566. In three weeks' time, by the end of August, more than 400 churches in the Netherlands had been irreparably damaged.

2. The Thirty Years' War was fought between the Catholics (the Hapsburgs of Austria and Spain and the Catholic German princes) and the Protestants (the Protestant German princes, France, Sweden, and Denmark, supported by England, Holland, and Russia).

7

The Union and the Golden Age

THE RISE OF THE DUTCH STATE

Long before the conclusion of the Eighty Years' War, the Dutch economy had been flourishing. The Twelve Years' Truce (1609–1621) permitted the United Provinces to blockade the Scheldt estuary, which prevented ships from reaching the port of Antwerp. This was a great blow to the economy of the southern Netherlands (now Belgium), which remained under Spanish control. The city of Amsterdam, in Holland, took over the lead in economic activity. It was, at that time, the busiest harbor in the world. Because of this, many of the merchants of Antwerp relocated their operations to the United Provinces. Many writers, artists, and master craftsmen followed them north. Holland became the new focus of trade and prosperity.

William Usselincx (1567–1647), who proposed founding a trading company for the Americas, was a refugee merchant from Antwerp. The renowned painter Frans Hals (ca. 1585–1666) was the son of an Antwerp linen merchant, who settled in Haarlem. Simon Stevin (1548–1620), who established daily use of decimal fractions, discovered the hydrostatic paradox, and wrote on optics, geography, and astronomy, was a native of Bruges.

During their struggle for freedom, the United Provinces became the richest nation in Europe. Dutch traders were everywhere. Their military might was considerable. Dutch arts and sciences were at the leading edge of development. The Dutch had rich colonies. In 1643, the Dutch merchant fleet consisted of 3,400 vessels with a capacity of 4 million tons. In 1648, a bank in Amsterdam had deposits of 300 million guilders in coin. There was so much money available that interest rates were only in the range of 2–3% and the high costs of the military could easily be covered by high taxes and duties. Philip II, on the other hand, bankrupted Spain three times in his fight against the Reformation. It was Holland's economic success that led to the seventeenth century being known as Holland's "Golden Age."

The Dutch became the importers, exporters, and transporters of the goods for half of Europe in the sixteenth and seventeenth centuries. In doing so, they built a reputation for being tightfisted and shrewd. In 1826, the British statesman George Canning (1770–1827) encapsulated their reputation in verse:

> *In matters of commerce, the fault of the Dutch*
> *is offering too little and asking too much.*

It was out of the fierce struggle for economic supremacy between England and Holland in the seventeenth century that the large number of pejorative phrases that begin with the word "Dutch" took root in the English language. A poem written by the English poet Edmund Waller (1606–1687), for instance, celebrating the victory of the British fleet over the Dutch on June 3, 1665, was one of the first written uses of "Dutch courage":

> *The Dutch their wine and brandy lose,*
> *Disarmed of that from which their courage grows.*

This war propaganda outlived the war and took on a life of its own, engendering terms like:

Dutch courage is the kind that comes out of a bottle.

Dutch treat is an invitation to a dinner that you have to pay for.

Dutch reckoning is guesswork.

A *Dutch nightingale* is a frog.

A *Dutch auction* is an auction where the asking price begins high and goes down.

This is just a sample of the inventiveness of English propagandists. There were many more besides, most of which have finally fallen into disuse.

PROSPERITY

Prosperity means that you have more money than you need and that some of it can be used to satisfy your mental appetites: your curiosity, your desire for elegance and for beauty. The Dutch of the Golden Age were prosperous indeed. The arts and sciences were well supported during this time.

In the seventeenth century, while Dutch explorers expanded the frontiers of the known world and took the Dutch Empire to the four corners of the globe, Dutch scientists, philosophers, and artists at home expanded the frontiers of knowledge and of art.

Abel Janszoon Tasman (ca. 1603–1659) discovered Tasmania and New Zealand and was the first to circumnavigate Australia, proving it to be an island. Willem Barents (1550?–1597) was the first navigator to sail north of Russia in search of the Northeast Passage and left his name on the Barents Sea. Henry Hudson (1565–1611), who was sailing for the Dutch in search of the Northwest Passage, gave his name to the Hudson River in New York State.

Christiaan Huygens (1629–1695) was the first effective observer of the Orion Nebula (a part of which is named for him) and designed the first pendulum clock, which was more accurate than the clocks that had preceded it. Antoni van Leeuwenhoek (1632–1723) is considered the father of research with a microscope. He discovered red blood cells. Hermann Boerhaave (1668–1738) introduced the clinical method of instruction for medicine.

In 1625, Hugo de Groot (1583–1645) published his treatise *De Jure Belli ac Pacis* (On the Law of War and Peace), which earned him the name "Father of International Law." The influential pantheistic philosopher Baruch (Benedict) Spinoza (1632–1677) was born in Amsterdam of Portuguese-Jewish parents. Spinoza's philosophical writings expressed the belief that God exists in everything in nature. It was his idea that man could approach God through an understanding of the natural world.

Just as Geoffrey Chaucer (ca. 1342–1400) and William Shakespeare (1564–1616) are considered the cornerstones of English literature, Joost van den Vondel (1587–1679), poet and playwright, and Pieter Cornelis-zoon Hooft (1581–1647), poet, playwright, and historian, are considered the quintessential writers of Dutch classical literature. The Dutch annual state prize for literature, in fact, is named for Hooft.

The greatest artist of the Golden Age was Rembrandt Harmenszoon van Rijn (1606–1669). Rembrandt worked with a wide range of themes, from portraits to landscapes, from interiors to historical scenes. Other artists of the time tended to specialize in one theme. Jan Havickszoon Steen (ca. 1626–1679) is best known for his paintings of interior scenes. His images are immortalized in the Dutch proverbial description of a messy room: Housekeeping by Jan Steen. Isaac van Ostade (1621–1649) specialized in landscapes and scenes of rural life. Michiel Janszoon van Mierevelt (1567–1641) specialized in portraits. As the court painter for the House of Orange, his somber, stereotypical portraits were all the rage. Jan Vermeer's (1632–1675) paintings, many of which can be seen in the Mauritshuis Museum in The Hague, reflect the icons of the time. The maps and globes, as well as the oriental rugs and tapestries, in his paintings remind the viewer of far-flung Dutch seaborne trade.

This was also the period in which the fabled Dutch tolerance came to the fore. Holland was open to people who had to leave their homes for political or religious reasons. French and Walloon Huguenots, German Lutherans, Portuguese Jews, Armenian Christians, and the Pilgrims all found their way to Holland. Press censorship was hardly existent, which was something quite unusual for seventeenth-century Europe. Many books that could not be published in other countries were published in Amsterdam and smuggled back into the countries that banned them.

The English historian George M. Trevelyan (1876–1962) offers a view of the impact that the Dutch had on England during Holland's Golden Age:

> Holland affected every department of English life, more perhaps than any other nation has ever done by the mere force of example. This little republic, which from 1600 to 1650 maintained its territory as a safe and prosperous oasis in the midst of the wilderness of fire and destruction around, was during most of those years the leader of mankind in most of the sciences and arts . . . the example to our merchants and politicians of a community which had attained prosperity, enlightenment and power by rebellion against a legitimate Prince.[1]

THE TRADING COMPANIES

During the seventeenth century, Dutch seafarers, searching for new trade routes, gave the small republic an empire sixty times its own size. By the time that the Dutch voyages of discovery began in the second half of the sixteenth century, the Spanish and Portuguese were already well-established world traders.

It was not until 1602 that the Verenigde Oostindische Compagnie (VOC; United East India Company) was established by charter and financed by public subscription. It had a monopoly on all trade east of the Cape of Good Hope and west of the Strait of Magellan. For a long time, the VOC was the largest commercial enterprise in the world.

In 1621—the year that the Twelve Years' Truce in the middle of the Eighty Years' War came to an end—the Westindische Compagnie (WIC; West India Company) was formed. William Usselincx had proposed founding a trading company for the Americas earlier, but his ideas were rejected by Johan van Oldenbarnevelt (1547–1619) and his supporters, who were trying to arrange the Twelve Years' Truce.

The WIC was given the monopoly on trade in the Western Hemisphere on the Atlantic Ocean. Unlike the VOC, the WIC could raid Spanish shipping on the high seas. A good deal of the WIC's finances came from the cargos that it captured from the Spanish. Raiding Spanish ships on the high seas was just a part of the Dutch war effort to win the Eighty Years' War. WIC raids reduced Spain's ability to pay for the war and increased Holland's. This tactic was nothing new in Dutch dealings with the Spanish. The *Watergeuzen* had financed their struggle with the Spanish before the Twelve Years' Truce in the same way. The activities—and profits—of these two companies were in large part responsible for the prosperity that made the Golden Age of Holland possible.

THE DECLINE OF THE DUTCH STATE

Dutch power began to decline in 1648 after the end of the Eighty Years' War. The war had been the glue that had held the country together politically. Disagreements between the stadholder and the powerful regents of the province of Holland eventually cost the United Provinces their place as a world superpower. Their place was taken up by their more populous neighbors: France and England, which, after about 1700, were the countries that determined the political, economic, and cultural trends of life in Western Europe.

Prince William II succeeded his father, Frederick Heny, as stadholder of all the provinces (except Friesland) and as captain-admiral-general of the Union. The States-General of Holland was afraid of the army because it was part of the base for the stadholder's central power. William refused the States-General's demands to reduce the size of the army and lower taxes and had six key opponents—members of the Aristocratic Party from the province of Holland—arrested.

When William II died unexpectedly of smallpox in 1650, the United Provinces entered the first Stadholderless Period (1650–1672). The Aristocratic and Loevestein (named for the castle where William II had held his opponents) Parties took advantage of the power vacuum caused by the fact that his son, William III (1650–1702), was not yet born and passed a resolution in 1651 that ensured that all the provinces would never be placed under a single stadholder.

In 1654, under the leadership of Johan de Witt (1625–1672), the Aristocratic Party went even further and passed a secret act that declared that the House of Orange should be removed from all government positions. This was followed by the Eternal Edict of the Provincial Council of the Province of Holland (1667) and the Harmonization Act of the States-General (1670). They were intended to forever separate the position of stadholder from that of commander in chief of the armed forces.

The regents of the Stadholderless Period soon ran into problems of their own. The British Parliament passed a series of laws called the "Navigation Acts" in 1650, 1651, and 1660. These acts were directly aimed at the Dutch, whose ships carried most of the seaborne trade at the time. They required that goods, entering or leaving England or its colonies, be carried in English ships. This was a great blow to the Dutch trade and led to the first (1652–1654) and second (1665–1667) Anglo-Dutch Wars.

With the conclusion of the Treaty of Breda at the end of the second Anglo-Dutch War, the provisions of the Navigation Acts were moderated—due, in part, to Michiel Adriaanszoon de Ruyter's (1607–1676) successful raid on the British naval base at Chatham—to allow goods that had come up the Rhine or Scheldt to be carried to England in Dutch ships. The Dutch lost New Netherland (now New York), but got Surinam, which had been captured in February 1667 by Abraham Crijnssen in exchange for it. The Navigation Acts remained in force until 1849.

The Dutch government, reluctant to spend the money and oversure of itself from its victory over the Spanish fleet, had neglected the navy and allowed it to degenerate into a mere collection of armed merchantmen. At the end of the second Anglo-Dutch War, the United Provinces concentrated all their attention on naval power, but their neglect of ground forces since the Treaty of Westphalia in 1648 soon caught up to them.

When Louis XIV (1638–1715), the French "Sun King," occupied the Spanish Netherlands (Belgium) in 1667, the government of the United Provinces concluded an alliance with England and Sweden (1668), which forced Louis to renounce most of his conquests. The alliance soon fell apart, however; and Louis, seeking revenge for defeat, declared war on the Netherlands in 1672, capturing four provinces and eighty-three

Dutch fortresses in short order. By the end of the third Anglo-Dutch War (1672–1674), the British had taken over the position of the world's leading sea power.

The Dutch people turned against the regents. Johan de Witt and his brother Cornelis were killed by an angry mob in The Hague on August 20, 1672. The young William III, who had led Dutch troops to victory over the French, was chosen the hereditary stadholder of five provinces in 1674. When peace was concluded by the Treaty of Nijmegen (1673), not only did Holland regain its lost territory, but it obtained Maastricht and favorable trade concessions from France as well.

In 1689, when William III became King William of England through his marriage to Mary Stuart, after fifty years of bitter commercial rivalry, relations between the two countries improved. England and Holland could now turn their attention to the real enemy: France. For the next twenty-five years—with one brief but uneasy interval—they were at war with France. First there was the Nine Years' War (1689–1697)[2] and then the War of Spanish Succession (1701–1714).[3]

When William III died accidentally in a fall from a horse, he left no male heir. Holland entered the second Stadholderless Period (1702–1747), and power once again fell into the hands of the Aristocratic Party. The wars had been very costly for the Dutch. Their national debt increased by nearly five times between 1688 and 1713. Holland had been at war or on the brink of war for almost the whole of the seventeenth century.

After the Peace of Utrecht (1713), which concluded the War of Spanish Succession, the Aristocratic Party followed a pacifist line. Ground and naval forces were neglected and went into decline. The militant entrepreneurs of the Golden Age had become the complacent rulers of the country, whose goal was preserving the status quo. Industry was paralyzed, and the standard of living fell. The ruling classes, however, continued to live in luxury, holding on to power.

The War of Austrian Succession (1740–1745)[4] brought the Netherlands out of its stupor. The war was conducted so poorly that the Dutch lost all their fortresses, which were at that time the key to any national defense. When the French invaded the Netherlands in 1747, the provinces of Zeeland and Holland felt that they had had enough of the Aristocrats and proclaimed a new stadholder.

William of Orange-Nassau-Dietz (1711–1751) was the hereditary stadholder of Friesland. In 1718, he became the stadholder of Groningen and in 1722, the stadholder of Drenthe and of Gelderland as well. In 1747, the other provinces followed their example, and he became William IV, the first hereditary stadholder and captain-admiral-general of all seven provinces. He was also given reign over the lands belonging to the States-General and the directorship of the VOC and the WIC. Despite his almost absolute power, William IV did not do anything to improve the political state of the country in the four short years of his reign.

When William IV died in 1751, his son, William V (1748–1806), was only three years old. His mother, the English Princess Anna of Hanover (1709–1759), served as regent until her death. Count Lodewijk Ernst (1718–1788) of Brunswick-Wolfenbüttel served as commander of the armed forces. Upon Anna's death, the states took the rights of the stadholder for themselves, and Lodewijk became William's guardian. This government maintained a policy of strict neutrality, except in the Indies, where the conquest of Ceylon was completed.

In 1766, at eighteen—the age of majority—William became stadholder. Lodewijk continued to influence him. Ten years later, when England declared war on the breakaway American states, they requested that the Netherlands supply troops to help them fight the "mutineers" in accordance with existing treaties. The Dutch refused to render that assistance. The result was the fourth Anglo-Dutch War (1780–1784). Even though the Netherlands was not ready for war—it would mean great losses for commerce and trade—the war was very popular with the populace. Even though the British ended the American Revolutionary War with the Treaty of Versailles in 1783, the Anglo-Dutch War continued until the Treaty of Paris in 1784.

NOTES

1. George M. Trevelyan, *England under the Stuarts* (New York: Putnam's, 1904), p. 50.

2. The Nine Years' War is known in historiography as the War of the League of Augsburg. This war was fought between France on the one side and the German Empire, Holland, Spain, England, and Brandenburg on the other to maintain the balance of power in Europe.

3. The War of Spanish Succession was fought by England and the Hapsburgs to keep the grandson of Louis XIV from becoming the king of Spain. As such, he could have united Spain, France, and the southern Netherlands (Belgium).

4. The War of Austrian Succession was fought by Prussia and France to keep Maria Theresia from ascending the throne in Austria. The Dutch were drawn into the war when they sent troops to help England, which favored Maria Theresia.

8

The Colonies

NEW NETHERLAND (NEW YORK)

The discovery of the New World was nothing more than a mistake made by Europeans trying to make their way to the riches of India. That is why the natives of North and South America are called Indians. The first Europeans to reach the New World thought that they had arrived in the outer reaches of the East Indies.

In 1609, Henry Hudson—an English captain working for the Dutch—failed to find the Northeast Passage around Russia to India that he had been sent to locate. His way to the east was blocked by ice, so he decided to look for a western passage. Instead of India, "Wrong-Way Hudson" found what today is known as New York. Because Hudson was working for the Dutch-owned VOC at the time, Holland claimed the land there.

It was not until 1621, when the Dutch West India Company was formed, that the first permanent Dutch colony was established, New Netherland. The WIC governor of the colony, Peter Minuit (1580–1638), was the one who officially bought the entire island of Manhattan from the Indians for 60 guilders worth of trade goods in 1625. The WIC's goal in the New World was not so much to expand the Dutch Empire as to expand Dutch trade. Sending settlers to establish a colony cost money, and the WIC was focused on the bottom line. That meant that it sent only the minimum number of people needed to support its network of trading posts. Beaver pelts—the central figure in the company's crest—was what the WIC was after.

There was little incentive at the time for people to emigrate from Holland, which was prosperous and had, compared to other European countries, a lot of religious freedom. According to the last WIC governor of the colony, Peter Stuyvesant (ca. 1610–1672), it was the scum of all nations who came to America. Stuyvesant's negative opinion of the colonists could only have been strengthened by one of the sources of Dutch settlers that was common for all Dutch colonies in those days: the poorhouses and orphanages of Holland. Orphans and the poor were unprepared for the hardships of life in the wilderness, and many of them died. Fortunately, the colony did not depend entirely on Dutch settlers. Though no records were kept of their nationalities, in 1644, Willem Kieft (1597–1647), the governor, noted that the settlers spoke eighteen different languages. Dutch, however, was the dominant language and culture of the colony. It survived the British takeover for over a hundred years. It continued in use in churches in New York until 1763.

The presence of the Dutch in New York can still be seen in the names of some of the boroughs of the city:

- Harlem—named for the city of Haarlem in the province of North Holland
- Brooklyn—named for the town of Breukelen in the province of Utrecht
- The Bowery—named for the seventeenth-century Dutch word for farm, *bouwerij*
- Wall Street (Walstraat)—a common street name in Holland, for it designates a street that follows the path of a city's old defensive wall. There is one in Deventer, Doetinchem, Emmen, Gorinchem, Groningen, Huissen, Oldenzaal, Oss, Rijssen, Sittard, Terneuzen, Venlo, Vlissingen, Wageningen, IJsselstein, and Zwolle. In Nijmegen—one of the Roman garrison cities—there is even an Eerste (First), a Tweede (Second), and a Derde (Third) Walstraat that mark the extent of the old defensive wall. Wall Street in New York has the same origin: It runs along the wall that Stuyvesant reinforced at his own expense to protect the Dutch settlement on Manhattan.

Much of what is known about the governors of New Netherland comes from Washington Irving's (1783–1859) famous (infamous, if you ask the Dutch) tongue-in-cheek *History of New York,* published in 1809. The pretended Dutch author of Irving's history, Diedrich Knickerbocker, lent his name to many things associated with New York. In the nineteenth century, it became a nickname for New Yorkers in general. Then there was the *Knickerbocker Magazine* (published 1833–1865), the Knickerbocker baseball club (which played the first official baseball game in America in 1846), and the New York Knickerbockers ("Knicks") basketball team.

While Irving's satire of the Dutch is undoubtedly not entirely without basis in fact, the Dutch governors could hardly have been the clowns or the idiots that Irving made them out to be. A more balanced view is provided by the American historian Charles T. Gehring (1939–   ), who has been working on the Dutch archives in New York for over twenty years. During that time, he has made more than 7,000 of the 12,000 archival documents from the Dutch period in New York available to scholars by transcribing and translating them in the New Netherlands documents series, published by Syracuse University Press.

In 1664—ten years after the end of the first Anglo-Dutch War—King Charles II (1652–1654) of England "gave" New Netherland to his brother James, the Duke of York. He sent an expeditionary force to the colony to make sure that his gift would be handed over as desired. While in the last year of Dutch control (1664) there were approximately 10,000 inhabitants in the WIC colony, the neighboring British Plymouth and Boston colonies numbered about 50,000 in 1660. The Dutch colony's population, then, was not sufficient in number to successfully defend the colony against the British. When peace was again restored in 1667, at the end of the second Anglo-Dutch War, New Netherland was officially surrendered to Britain in exchange for Surinam in northeastern South America.

If Holland could have held on to New Netherland, things would have been very different these days, and not just in present-day New York State. Given the Dutch policy on colonial settlement and interaction with the local population, there would have been many more Iroquois in this notional, modern-day New Netherland than there are now, and things would have been quite different in Holland as well. In 1975, following Surinam's independence, about one-third of Surinam's population emigrated to Holland. There's many a Dutchman—though few would admit it in public—who would have preferred that they had stayed in Surinam. The Dutch would probably not have liked the Iroquois any better, but it would be a big change in Holland's ethnic makeup.

SURINAM (DUTCH GUIANA)

The northeast coast of South America where present-day Surinam is located was first explored by the Spanish navigator Alonso de Hojeda (1466/1470–1515/1516) in 1499. The local Indians called this land Guiana. The first known Dutch settlement in Surinam dates to 1613, when fifty families tried to begin tobacco farming on the Corantijn River. The settlement was very short-lived. It was annihilated by the Spanish in 1614.

In 1650, Lord Francis Willoughby (ca. 1613–1666) sent an expedition to Surinam to look for more land on which to expand the successful sugar production taking place on Barbados. A year later, 100 English settlers—with their black slaves—arrived in Surinam to establish a colony. In 1667, the colony was conquered by Admiral Abraham Crijnssen at the head of a squadron of ships from the province of Zeeland. The Treaty of Breda (1667), which ended the second Anglo-Dutch War, transferred possession of Surinam to the Dutch in exchange for New Netherland.

The fighting war may have been over, but the economic war continued apace. Most of the English settlers were convinced to leave the colony and to take their slaves, machinery, and know-how with them. They were primarily resettled on Jamaica, and the colony that was handed over to the Provincial Council of Zeeland was only a shell of the profitable colony it had been under the English. Zeeland tried to return the colony to profit but found that it could not afford the investment needed to do so. In 1682, it succeeded in selling the colony to the WIC for 260,000 florins. It was not long before the WIC—which was heavily in debt and more interested in the short-term bottom line than in long-term investment—decided to sell one-third of the shares in the colony to the city of Amsterdam and to Cornelis van Aerssen, Lord of Sommelsdijk (1637–1688). Van Aerssen took the lead in reorganizing the colony and went out as its first governor in 1683. While his methods were autocratic and authoritarian, he managed to turn the colony around during the five years of his energetic rule. It is for this that he is often considered the true founder of the colony.

The colony reached its height of prosperity in the second half of the eighteenth century. There were more than 500 plantations growing sugar, cacao, cotton, tobacco, indigo, and coffee for export. In 1775, 64 ships sailed to Holland from the capital of Paramaribo, carrying 1,416,250 florins worth of goods. By 1787, the population of the colony had grown to over 49,000, of which 90% was made up of slaves—the labor force that made the colony profitable.

The readily available supply of investment funds from Holland began to dry up in the early 1770s, as native raids on the plantations shook investor confidence and a crisis hit the Dutch stock exchange (1773). Many of the plantation owners went bankrupt, and their properties were foreclosed on by the investors. (The Sommelsdijk family had been fortunate enough to sell its share of the colony to the city of Amsterdam in 1770.) Because the new owners of the plantations focused only on short-term profit, they did not invest in the colony's infrastructures, and the economy of the colony went into decline.

In 1792, the heavily indebted WIC was taken over by the States-General, but this new leadership of the colony did not last long. In 1795, when the French Revolution overflowed into the Netherlands, creating the Batavian Republic, William V fled to England. An English force, acting in his name, took possession of Surinam four years later. The Peace of Amiens in 1802 returned Surinam to the Dutch, but it fell under the English again in 1804 and remained there until 1816, when Surinam was returned to the new Kingdom of the Netherlands.

The treasury of the new Kingdom needed money. Revenues from the plantations in Dutch East India made it possible for the government to balance its books. Surinam, on the other hand, needed government subsidies. The government made them grudgingly with the understanding that the colony would exercise austerity.

Trade in slaves was prohibited in 1808. This did not mean that the slaves were free, only that they could not be sold. The result of this measure was that the slave owners began to treat their slaves better, because the slaves could no longer be replaced if they ran away or died. It also meant a further decline in the economy of the colony as the labor supply dwindled. By 1863—the year that the slaves were freed in Surinam[1]—the number of plantations had declined to 200.

The act that freed the slaves also compensated their owners for them at the rate of 300 guilders each. Some owners kept their plantations open only until they received their compensation for the slaves and then left. Deprived of the labor force that made the colony profitable, the economy continued to decline. Other plantation owners attempted to replace their slave labor with indentured workers from Bengal (beginning in 1873) and Java (beginning in 1890). They were no substitute for the economic power of the slaves, however, and the economy declined still further. When the contracts of these indentured workers expired, many of them chose to remain in Surinam. Their presence in Surinam was to become one of the fault lines of social unrest in Surinam in the twentieth century.

In 1955, Surinam and the Netherlands Antilles gained the right of equals in the Kingdom of the Netherlands. In the sixties and early seventies, however, pressure grew for complete independence from Holland.

Fears began to surface among the Hindu and Indonesian communities that the new government would be dominated by the Creoles (descendants of the black slaves brought to the colony). This led to an increasing stream of emigrants to Holland from among the better-educated Hindu and Indonesian segments of the population.

As independence from Holland came closer to being a reality, more people, fearing political and economic instability, left the country. After Surinam gained its independence in 1975, the reality of independence—despite growing Dutch foreign aid—failed to match people's expectations, and the stream of emigrants continued to grow. In 1972, there were only 55,000 Surinamese in Holland. By 1975, there were 130,000, or about one-third of the population of Surinam. This was the beginning of Holland's racial problems.

SOUTH AFRICA (THE CAPE COLONY)

Before the Suez Canal was opened in 1869, the trip around the Cape of Good Hope on the southern tip of Africa was no more than an inconvenient detour on the way to the Indies. The Portuguese and the British had both landed there, but neither had established a permanent settlement. In 1648, a Dutch ship was stranded in Table Bay for several months and its crew forced to live off the land. When they returned home, they recommended that the VOC establish a way station on the cape where they had been stranded.

In 1652, a fortified provisioning station was set up there under the command of Jan van Riebeeck (1619–1677). In 1657, the first "free burghers" arrived in the colony. They were discharged soldiers and sailors of the VOC. More settlers arrived, including a group of French Huguenots seeking religious freedom and a group of orphan girls from Amsterdam, orphanages and poorhouses being a regular source of settlers for Dutch colonies, as previously mentioned. These people were to become the Afrikaners of South Africa.

The Dutch colony at the cape, aptly termed the Cape Colony, did not belong to the United Provinces, but to the VOC, which controlled the colony for more than 140 years. In his account of life in the VOC colony, E. B. Watermeyer (1824–1867) criticizes the VOC for being purely despotic in all things political and purely monopolistic in all things commercial. It is a characterization that applies to the VOC's colonies no matter where they were. Their governors ruled with an iron hand and had their eyes fixed on the bottom line.

By the turn of the century, the colonists were agitating for more self-rule, but things were slow to change. The VOC refused their request, and the issue eventually came before the States-General in 1784. The States-General also refused the colonists. In February 1795, one month after the establishment of the Batavian Republic, the colonists in the districts of Graaff-Reinet and Swellendam renounced VOC control and set up an independent constitutional government under direct control of the Dutch state. Their independence did not last for long.

William V had fled to England. At his request, the British invaded the Cape Colony and the independent Afrikaner government came to an end. In 1803, the Cape Colony was returned to the Batavian Republic by the Peace of Amiens. In 1806, however, it was reconquered again by the British, who were then at war with both France and Holland. When the Dutch regained their independence from France, the British returned some of the Dutch colonies they had captured, but they kept the Cape Colony. The Dutch received £6 million in compensation.

The predominantly Dutch residents of the colony were not consulted by the British before they were made British subjects. This was to have a profound effect on the course of the history of the colony. Until 1870, Dutch settlers considerably outnumbered the English settlers, and the conflict between the Dutch Boers—the Dutch word for farmers, pronounced "boors"—and the British led to the expansion of European settlement in southern Africa as the Boers trekked inland to escape British control.

In 1834, the British passed the Slave Emancipation Act, which freed all the slaves throughout the British Empire. There were about 36,000 slaves in the Cape Colony at that time. The labor that they provided was what made the farms of the Dutch settlers a success. This was one of the issues that resulted in the Great Trek (1836–1840), during which the Boers crossed the Orange River and the great plains to enter the Transvaal, beyond the reach of British laws and regulations. The territory that they moved into eventually became two separate republics—the South African Republic and the Orange Free State—recognized independent of British rule by the Conventions of Sandriver (1852) and Bloemfontein (1854).

The British might have kept to the agreements of the conventions if Southern Africa had remained the economic backwater that it was in the first half of the nineteenth century, but the discovery of diamonds and gold changed not only the economic but also the political landscape. At that time, the world's monetary systems, primarily British, were dependent on gold. The paper currency that governments issued was backed by gold deposits. In 1868, the British annexed the diamond fields that had been found in the South African Republic and the Orange Free State. In 1877, they annexed the Lydenburg goldfields in the South African Republic. This led to the first Boer War of 1881, in which the two republics redeclared their independence from England and made it stick—at least temporarily.

Following the discovery of gold in Witwatersrand in 1885, C. J. Rhodes (1853–1902)—the benefactor who established the Rhodes scholarships to Oxford University—tried to subvert the republics by inciting an uprising against the government of Paul Kruger (1825–1904) among the *uitlanders* (foreigners), who had come from all over the world to work the gold but who had next to no political rights under Kruger's government. The plan was for Rhodes's friend L. S. Jameson (1853–1917) to take in a detachment of English–South African troops under the guise of restoring order in the wake of the uprising and take over the South African Republic. The *uitlanders* balked at the uprising. Despite the fact that he had been notified that the uprising would not take place, Jameson crossed the border anyway in 1895 just before New Year's. Without the pretext of an uprising, the Jameson raid was a political disaster. Openly implicated in the plot, Rhodes was forced to resign as prime minister.

The raid was followed by a period of contentious diplomacy, which ended in the second Boer War (1899–1902). The heavily outnumbered Boers resorted to guerilla tactics, but the British resorted to a scorched earth policy and placed all the Boer noncombatants in concentration camps. Over 26,000 Boers—mostly infants and toddlers—died in the camps. The abominable British treatment of the Boers adversely affected Anglo-Dutch relations, the Dutch, naturally, siding with the Boers against their longtime adversaries, the British.

The two Afrikaner republics—the South African Republic and the Orange Free State—eventually did win their independence; but in 1910, the two British republics—Natal and the Cape Colony—joined together with the two Boer republics to form the Union of South Africa.

There was another wave of Dutch emigration to South Africa in the period after World War II. It was a part of the general wave of government-sponsored emigration that took more than half a million Dutch out of war-ravaged Holland to seek their fortunes elsewhere. The end of apartheid in South Africa, however, is now reversing the flow. Dutch emigrants are coming back to Holland from South Africa, because, as F. H. Kuijs, who repatriated to Holland after forty years in South Africa, stated in an interview in July 1996 in the newspaper *Trouw*,

The abolition of apartheid has created another sort of apartheid. Blacks are now being given preference for appointments to positions that had previously only been open to whites. In concrete terms, for me that means that I couldn't say for certain if I would have a job next year or not. The uncertainty, an economic situation that is already lousy, and decreasing safety are what made me decide to come back to the Netherlands.

DUTCH EAST INDIES (INDONESIA)

The first Dutch voyage to what is now known as Indonesia was made by Cornelis de Houtman (ca. 1540–1599), who arrived there in 1596. Before his voyage, Houtman had gone to Portugal in 1592 to learn the "secrets" of trading with "East India," as the area was then called. This was not without danger, because the Portuguese kept their knowledge of the trade route to East India secret, so as to preserve their monopoly. Houtman and his brother Frederik (1571–1627) were taken prisoner by the Portuguese and were released only after paying a huge ransom.

The Portuguese had first reached "East India" in 1511. They conquered the island of Malacca and monopolized the lucrative trade in spices, which were much sought after in Europe. After 1580, when Portugal was annexed by Spain, all the profits of the monopoly went to Spain. For the Dutch, entering the spice trade made sense for two reasons. Practical and profit-loving businessmen that they are, they wanted a piece of the action for themselves. Being at war with Spain (the Eighty Years' War), they wanted to deprive Spain of the profits, which it was using to pay for the war.

In 1602, the Dutch established the VOC. The VOC expanded its control of the East Indies, driving out the Portuguese, and appointed its own governor for Dutch East India. The VOC managed to maintain its monopoly on trade with East India for almost 150 years (ca. 1630–1780). The monopoly finally began to break down as the partners in the VOC began trading independently and the French and British managed to skirt the prohibition on the export of seeds, so as to start their own spice colonies. The VOC completely lost its monopoly position at the end of the fourth Anglo-Dutch War (1780–1784). The peace that concluded this war gave the British the right of free navigation in East Indian waters.

In 1795, when William V fled to England following the establishment of the Batavian Republic, he called on the VOC in Dutch East India to open up the colony to his British allies. The VOC, however, found that its hatred of the British was stronger than its distrust of the French, and the VOC recognized French rule. In 1796, the VOC had to give up most of its administrative rights in the colony to a committee of the new government. In 1799, when the charter for the VOC expired, it was not renewed, and the French-inspired government took over the entire administration of the colony.

Shortly thereafter, the British captured all the Dutch possessions in Dutch East India. The Peace of Amiens, however, returned everything except Ceylon to the Dutch in 1802. The Dutch authorities in Batavia tried to remain neutral in the struggle between France and England, but shortly after France annexed Holland in 1810, the British retook the colony. When Holland became independent of France again (1813), the British returned all the Dutch colonies, except for Ceylon and the Cape Colony (South Africa).

The new Kingdom of the Netherlands—created after the French had been driven out—needed money. The revenues from the plantations in Dutch East India made it possible for the government to balance its books. Though the governor-general sent to East India during the period of French rule had tried to eliminate most of the excesses of the VOC's administration of the colony, the new government's need for money pushed developments in the other direction again. Private enterprise was prohibited, and the populace was obligated to produce coffee, sugar, indigo, and a few other crops for the government to help fill the state treasury.

Toward the end of the nineteenth century, however, protests against Dutch colonial policy began to surface. The book *Max Havelaar* (1859) had the same effect on Dutch policy as *Uncle Tom's Cabin* had on the issue of slavery in America. It is an indictment of the corruption among the native princes who worked with the Dutch and the European colonial administrators who ruled the colony. It was written by Eduard Douwes Dekker (1820–1887) under the Malaysian-sounding pseudonym of Multatuli, which is actually Latin for "I have suffered much," a pun that would not have been lost on the educated Dutch of that time, who were required to study Latin in school.

In 1870, a more liberal business policy, expressed in the new agricultural law, permitted private enterprise. In 1891, Dutch Minister of Colonies Baron Willem Karl van Dedem (1839–1895), for example, put forth the revolutionary idea that Dutch East India's own interests should be considered in making policy and that these interests should be represented in the government. The monarch's throne speech of 1901 outlined the direction that colonial policy was to follow toward the elimination of colonial rule. The Decentralization Law (1903), the Law on the People's Council (1916), and the Law on Administration Reform (1922) all moved in the direction of local rule. At first the People's Council was only an advisory body, but by 1925, it had legislative powers and had broken the stranglehold of the bureaucracy on administrative power.

During World War II, Dutch East India was occupied by Japan. When the war was over, Indonesia declared its independence. The Dutch tried to reestablish their sovereignty over the area, but it took four years of hard fighting and considerable international pressure for them to accept Indonesia's independence. It was December 1949 when the fighting finally stopped.

The number of Europeans and Eurasians in Dutch East India in 1940 was only a small minority (roughly 290,000) in a country of 70 million. Yet they controlled almost all of the business sector and the civil service. After the war, between 1945 and 1968, more than 330,000 people fled Indonesia, the majority of them to Holland. Most of them had been born and raised in Indonesia, and their families had lived there for generations. Many of them wanted independence as much as the indigenous population did, but they were driven out by the locals, despite their desire to stay and their feeling that they too were Indonesians.

The exodus left its mark on Holland. Not only did Indonesian restaurants spring up everywhere, just as Indian restaurants did all over England, but it also gave the Dutch their first taste of minority relations problems, as they tried to absorb the refugees who were Dutch but whose habits and accents were just different enough to make them strangers in a familiar land. As Tjalie Robinson (1911–1974), a Eurasian Dutch writer, put it, they were somewhere in between their two homelands and welcome in neither:

> You are always an outsider for both. In the Netherlands, because you have far too many strange habits and do not exactly fit in to the closed social system, and in Indonesia, because—despite hundreds, perhaps thousands of personal friendships—you are not wanted officially.

THE NETHERLANDS ANTILLES

The Netherlands Antilles is an autonomous part of the Kingdom of the Netherlands. Until 1986, it was comprised of six diverse islands in the Caribbean. There are the "ABC islands"—Aruba, Bonaire, and Curaçao—part of the chain called the Leeward Islands off the coast of South America; and there are the "SSS islands"—Saint Martin, Saint Eustatius, and Saba—the part of the chain called the Windward Islands to the east of Puerto Rico. In 1986, the continuing animosity between Aruba and Curaçao finally led

Aruba to leave the Netherland Antilles to become a separate autonomous part of the Kingdom with status equal to the Netherlands Antilles.

The islands were colonized in the seventeenth century by the WIC, which was also responsible for the colonies of New Netherland, Surinam, and Brazil. After the dissolution of the WIC in 1791, the islands remained Dutch possessions until 1954, when they gained autonomy within the Kingdom of the Netherlands. The Dutch, however, retained responsibility for foreign affairs and the defense of the islands.

Aruba (73 mi^2/190 km^2) lies only 30 kilometers from Venezuela. It was most likely discovered—together with Bonaire and Curaçao—in 1499 by Alonso de Hojeda on the same voyage as the one on which he discovered Surinam. Until the three islands were taken over by the WIC in 1634, Aruba was a center for pirates operating in the Caribbean. It was hardly of any economic importance until 1924, when the discovery of oil in Venezuela brought prosperity to the island. The Lago Oil and Transport Company—a daughter company of Standard Oil of New Jersey—built a transshipment harbor and refinery there to handle crude oil from Venezuela.

Bonaire (11 mi^2/28.8 km^2) was a plantation island. As with the other plantation colonies, when the slaves were freed in 1863 production was no longer profitable, and the island's economy went into decline. The island was divided into plots and auctioned off. Because of a lack of employment opportunities, many residents emigrated to Venezuela and Surinam and later, in the 1920s, to Aruba and Curaçao, where the oil industry had established itself. Bonaire is home to one of the transmitting antennas for the shortwave service of Dutch Radio International.

Curaçao (182 mi^2/472 km^2) is the largest of the Leeward Islands. It was occupied by the Spanish in 1527 and used as a cattle ranch. After the loss of Brazil (1654), the WIC established slave depots on Curaçao and Saint Eustatius for trade with the Americas. The economic decline brought on by the abolition of slavery was not stemmed until the Venezuelan oil boom. It was the establishment of the Royal Dutch Shell refinery there in 1916 that marked the beginning of the turnaround.

Christopher Columbus (1451–1506) entered Saint Martin—as well as Saint Eustatius and Saba—on the maps for his second voyage (1493). The Dutch were attracted to the uninhabited island by its rich salt pans and set up a settlement there in 1631. They were driven out by the Spanish in 1633. Only the southern part of the island (14 mi^2/34 km^2) returned to Dutch control with the Treaty of Westphalia at the end of the Eighty Years' War. The northern part of the island (20 mi^2/51 km^2) belongs to the French, by virtue of their settlement there in 1624. Strangely enough, the principal language of the island is neither Dutch nor French, but English.

This is due to a large influx of British settlers who began arriving after 1735 to set up sugar plantations there.

The uninhabited island of Saint Eustatius (12 mi^2/31 km^2) was first settled in 1636 by colonists from Zeeland. They began by planting tobacco but quickly switched to sugar. The island established itself as a center for trade with the British and French colonies. Prosperity began increasing in the mid-eighteenth century and continued to improve with the outbreak of the American War of Independence. Saint Eustatius was the main transshipment point for military materiel for the rebels in America. A cannon salute fired from the fort there was the first official recognition of the U.S. flag by a foreign nation. In the course of the fourth Anglo-Dutch War, the British captured the island in 1781 and sacked Oranjestad, the capital, in revenge for the "first salute."

The island of Saba (5 mi^2/12.8 km^2) was first settled by Dutch colonists from Saint Eustatius in about 1640. It was used primarily for plantations that grew cotton, sugarcane, and coffee. The difficulty of reaching the island by sea, plus the rugged terrain and its small size, kept the island from becoming a major economic success.

During the twentieth century, most of the employment opportunities on the islands were those created by tourism and the oil industry. When mechanization downsized the oil industry in the fifties, the islands found themselves with high unemployment and a large guest-worker population on Aruba and Curaçao. By 1965, the unemployment level had climbed to around 23%. This led to some emigration to Holland, but on a much smaller scale than was the case for Surinam. In January 1996, there were only 93,000 Antilleans in Holland, compared to 282,300 Surinamese.

BRAZIL

Brazil is another colony in the Americas that the Dutch lost due to the WIC's shortsighted focus on the bottom line. It had been discovered by the Spanish earlier than by the Portuguese, but the Spanish were prohibited from claiming it by the Treaty of Tordesillas (1494), which divided the world between Spain and Portugal. Pedro Alvars Cabral (1467/1468–1520) claimed it for the Portuguese in 1500, and Portuguese is still spoken there today. Sugarcane was the main product of the plantation colony. Its success, and the success of the plantations throughout the New World, depended on slave labor and large numbers of African slaves. By 1600, Pernambuco had a population of about 2,000 whites and approximately twice as many slaves.

When Portugal was annexed by Spain in 1580, the Dutch viewed Portuguese possessions as fair game for attack and conquest. After the Twelve Years' Truce ended, the WIC occupied the coast of Brazil near Olinda and Recife (Pernambuco). The Dutch ruled the colony from 1630 to 1654.

The statesmanlike Johan Maurits van Nassau (1604–1679)—a Brazilian—served as the WIC's governor from 1636 to 1644. He managed to achieve reconciliation with the Portuguese population and introduced religious tolerance. Competition with the Portuguese in Brazil overflowed into West Africa, where Johan Maurits ordered attacks on Portuguese possessions to take over their slave-trading activities there. When Portugal became independent of Spain in 1640, it tried, unsuccessfully, to retake the Dutch colony. Peace was not restored with Portugal until 1642.

Despite Johan Maurits's successes in leading the colony, the WIC, as always, focused only on bottom-line profits. It thought Johan Maurits's costs were too high and did not provide him the support that he needed. Johan Maurits resigned to return to Holland in 1644. Ten years after he left, in 1654, the Portuguese retook the last Dutch stronghold at Recife. In 1661, a payment of 8 million guilders was made to the Dutch in exchange for their rights there, closing the curtain on the Dutch sojourn in Brazil.

THE SLAVE TRADE

On the west coast of Africa, beginning in 1585, the Dutch built a series of fortified trading posts. From these outposts, they traded for slaves. Holland was not the only nation that dealt in slaves. Portugal had been doing it long before, working in close cooperation with local native chiefs. The Dutch simply followed the example of the Portuguese. Once the war with Spain ended in 1648, the WIC took up slave trading as its main activity.

The Dutch were actively involved in the slave trade only from about 1630 to 1795. During the peak of Dutch activity, they carried approximately 10% of the total volume of slaves. All told, the number of slaves landed by the Dutch was 460,000, only about 5% of the total. England, Portugal (together with Brazil), and France accounted for 90% of the slaves landed, or about 8.6 million.

The Dutch slave trade was a three-point barter arrangement. European and Asian goods were taken by ship from Holland to Africa, where they were traded for slaves. The slaves were then shipped across the Atlantic to the Americas, where they were traded for agricultural commodities or silver, which were shipped back to Holland.

The WIC had a monopoly on the slave trade from 1621 to about 1734, after which Dutch slave traders not aligned with the WIC took over part of the market. Dutch slave trade came to a halt following the financial crisis that rocked the Dutch economy in 1773. Its fallout was felt in the colonies, where the reduced ability of colonial customers to pay for slaves undermined the market. The outbreak of the American Revolution and the international crisis that surrounded it put a further damper on the slave trade.

NOTE

1. The slaves had been freed in neighboring French and British Guiana several years before—1848 and 1834, respectively.

9

Constitutional Democracy

THE BATAVIAN REPUBLIC (1795–1806)

When the fourth Anglo-Dutch War ended badly for the United Netherlands, Joseph II of Austria (1741–1790) took advantage of the beleaguered position of the Dutch to press for concessions as well. The United Netherlands was in no position to go to war with Austria and was forced to concede to Joseph's demands in the Treaty of Paris. A civil war seemed imminent as Patriot movement militias clashed with Orange supporters among the lower classes. The Dutch Patriot Movement formed the backbone for the federalism of the Batavian Republic that swept away the stadholdership. The Patriots were proponents of the novel idea of democratic government, in which the people could influence the composition of government bodies and exercise control over their actions. They were not alone in their thinking. The late eighteenth century was a period of change, ushered in by the American (1776) and the French (1789) Revolutions.

A pamphlet published anonymously in 1781 by the influential Joan Derk van der Capellen tot den Pol (1741–1784), titled "Aan het volk van Nederland" (To the People of the Netherlands), is a landmark document for the Patriot Movement. It deftly details the shortcomings of the stadholdership, blaming it for all the ills afflicting the Union at that time, especially the fourth Anglo-Dutch War. It advanced the idea of a democratic state, based on the sovereignty of the people, defended from the excessive power of the stadholder by armed citizen militias and an independent and uncensored press. His reasoning was obviously influenced by the American Revolution, as he was a leader in the presentation of the petition to the States-General calling for official recognition of the United States. Holland recognized America in 1782.

Despite his advocacy of armed militias, van der Capellen tot den Pol was not in favor of an armed overthrow of the government. He favored gradual reform, maintaining existing laws and traditions where possible. In particular, he supported the creation of citizen councils with powers to balance those of the regents, who depended on the stadholder for their appointments to local government, and thus were under his influence. Van der Capellen tot den Pol's was the majority view among the Patriots. Initially, only a small minority of them supported the abolition of the stadholdership.

Stadholder William V, who was deposed to make way for the Batavian Republic, was an indecisive leader of limited vision. His father William IV died when he was three, and his mother was appointed regent for him. When she died in 1759, the Count of Brunswick-Wolfenbüttel became William's guardian. Even after William reached the age of majority and could have taken up the stadholdership, Brunswick-Wolfenbüttel managed to retain his power by concluding the secret Act of Consultancy (May 3, 1766) with William, in which William essentially abdicated power to Brunswick-Wolfenbüttel.

Brunswick-Wolfenbüttel's pro-English sentiments during the fourth Anglo-Dutch War, which centered on issues of the American Revolution, sharpened opposition to his de facto stadholdership. When a Patriot newspaper (*De Post van Neder-Rhijn*) broke the story of the Act of Consultancy in 1784, Brunswick-Wolfenbüttel was forced to leave the Republic. Deprived of his adviser, William was left without a clue.

Both the Patriots, led by Pieter Paulus (1754–1796), and William's in-laws, who were like-minded, attempted to get William to consider democratic reforms, but he disregarded their advice. This led to heightened opposition to William, especially in the province of Holland, where the Provincial Council gradually stripped him of his powers and positions. When, in 1785, they took away William V's rights as commander of the garrison of The Hague, he and his wife—Princess Wilhelmina of Prussia (1751–1820)—left The Hague. He spent more than a year on the campaign trail in the other provinces before finally settling in Castle Valkhof in Nijmegen.

Wilhelmina was more energetic and insightful than William. She sought support for William from both the English House of Hanover—William's mother was Anna of Hanover, daughter of George II (1683–1760)—and from her uncle, the king of Prussia, Frederick the Great (1712–1786). The English promised moral support, but her uncle advised her to seek accommodation with the Patriots or to leave the Netherlands and, if necessary, her husband as well.

In 1787, after her brother—Frederick William II (1744–1797)—had succeeded Frederick the Great, Wilhelmina left for The Hague, to try to exploit the divisions in the Patriot Movement to restore her husband to power. Before she got there, she was detained by the Gouda Patriot militia and forced to turn back, when the Provincial Council failed to give her permission to continue her trip. Frederick William II took offense at the affront to his sister and demanded satisfaction. The Provincial Council refused, mistakenly counting on French support.

In September 1787, a Prussian force of 20,000 entered the country, quickly conquered the province of Holland, and reinstated William V as stadholder. The rights of the House of Orange and the Union of the Republic were thereafter to be guaranteed by England and Prussia. The Prussian restoration of the stadholdership was only a hollow victory. It cost William V what little respect and support he did have. It set the stage for the French intervention in 1795 that put an end to the stadholdership and started the period of democratic change that is the basis for the modern Dutch government.

In the wake of the Prussian restoration, thousands of Patriots left the United Netherlands for the Austrian Netherlands (Belgium) and France. Even though the Dutch Patriot émigré community in France was very much influenced by the events of the French Revolution, the Patriots continued to try to reach a negotiated settlement of changes in the government of the United Netherlands. William V and the regents—despite advice to the contrary from their friends and advisers—clung firmly to the old ways.

In 1792, war broke out between France on the one side and Austria and Prussia on the other. The Austrian Netherlands (Belgium) was immediately embroiled in the war, which soon overflowed into the United Netherlands. The cold winter of 1794–1795, which made a water defense impossible (it froze), and an uprising by the Patriots in the United Netherlands made it easier for the French under Jean-Charles Pichegru (1761–1804) to capture the country.

William and his family fled to England in January 1795. The States-General repealed the stadholdership and declared the Batavian Republic on January 26, 1796. The new political leadership bent over backward to appease the French to keep them from annexing the northern Netherlands the way they had already done with the Austrian Netherlands. In May, the Republic concluded an unfavorable treaty of alliance with France. The treaty required territorial and financial concessions. The Republic gave up Maastricht, Venlo, Limburg, and Flanders. It also had to pay 100 million guilders and finance the maintenance of 30,000 French troops on Dutch soil.

England, now at war with the Netherlands, began to paralyze Dutch trade and to conquer the Dutch colonies. The war was concluded by the Peace of Amiens in 1802. The Republic got all its colonies back (except Ceylon), and the House of Orange received 5 million guilders as compensation for the properties and offices it had held in the old Republic in exchange for recognition of the new Republic. The peace was short-lived. War broke out between England and France again in 1803, and the French forced the Batavian Republic to join them against the English.

In the ten years that it existed, the Batavian Republic barely managed to start the process of building the constitutional democracy of the Patriots' ideals, which would regulate the areas of taxation, education, health care, agriculture, trade, and industry by law. The politicians at the head of the new Republic were too divided among themselves to lead the country effectively. The creation of the new constitution, which was to be the foundation of the new Republic, dragged on and on, with the opposing political forces becoming more and more polarized. This political stagnation ended in the first of the three coups that took place during the brief term of the Batavian Republic's existence.

The first coup took place slightly less than two years after the declaration of the Republic, on January 22, 1798. A new constitution, based on the French constitution of 1795, was approved three months later (April 23) by the constitutional convention that had been purged of anyone who opposed it. The newly constituted government continued to purge its way to compliance even at the local level. This quickly reached such an extreme that General Herman Willem Daendels (1762–1818), who had helped to bring about the first coup, returned to Paris to seek support for the second. It took place on June 12, hardly five months after the first.

The first session of the States-General, elected under the constitution, convened on July 31. The balance of political power swung quickly to those who advocated unlimited democratic sovereignty, resulting in a coup by new constitution. In 1801, under the influence of R. J. Schimmelpenninck (1761–1825), Napoleon instructed his ambassador to present a proposal for a new constitution to the States-General. This

"French" constitution was rejected by the First Chamber, but it was reworked and presented to the voters anyway. The voters rejected it, but the report of the vote gave only the number of votes against, saying nothing about the number of voters who did not come to the polls. The new constitution was adopted.

In 1805, Napoleon, still unsatisfied with the way that the Dutch government was working, called for change again. The new Schimmelpenninck constitution was approved by the emperor in February, by the voters in April. Only 4% of the eligible voters (14,000 of 353,000) came to the polls. There were only 136 votes against it. Schimmelpenninck became the new head of government, replacing the committees that had previously headed the government. The power of the States-General was also weakened. The concentration of power in the hands of one man resulted in a wave of new legislation that had profound effects on the Dutch state long after the Batavian Republic ceased to exist.

The administration of the departments (provinces) was strictly organized, the finances of the Republic were centralized, and taxation was regulated at the national level. A law on lower education was passed that was highly regarded by foreign experts. The practice of health care was regulated and clinical; medical teaching schools were established. Dutch spelling and grammar were codified.

THE KINGDOM OF HOLLAND (1806–1810)

Schimmelpenninck did not remain in office for long, however. In May 1806, Napoleon changed the rules yet again. The Batavian Republic was replaced by the Kingdom of Holland. Napoleon thought that a monarchy that was dependent on him would be more reliable in his struggle with England, so he appointed his brother Louis king, a practice he followed in other countries as well. In 1806, Joseph Bonaparte became the king of Naples; in 1807, Jérôme became the king of Westphalia.

Louis had other ideas, though. He chose to follow Dutch interests instead of his brother's instructions. He kept all but two of Schimmelpenninck's ministers, which meant that the laws passed under Schimmelpenninck were actually put into practice. Under Louis, the judicial system was reorganized along French lines, but with Dutch conditions in mind.

FRENCH DOMINATION (1810–1813)

When King Louis renounced the throne in 1810 as a result of the conflict with his brother, Napoleon annexed the Netherlands. It was only after that that many of Napoleon's plans were fully implemented. The Continental system of trade restrictions destroyed all Dutch trade except for smuggling with England. Conscription for service in the armies of France became mandatory. The stricter Napoleonic legal code was introduced.

French rule united the provinces and put an end to many of the former abuses of government power. It insured uniform governance throughout the country, equality before the law, and freedom of religion. The people, nevertheless, felt a strong loss of political, spiritual, and commercial freedom. In the end, the Dutch had had enough of the French. Trade was in ruins. Debts were mounting, and everyone was trying to avoid obligatory service in the French army. Of the 15,000 Dutchmen who went to war in Russia with the Napoleonic army, only a few hundred returned. News of the victory of the allies over Napoleon in the "Battle of the Nations" near Leipzig (1813) was greeted enthusiastically.

The northern Netherlands were declared liberated on December 1, 1813. Adherents of the old Orange Party formed a temporary government. William V's son was declared the new king—William V had been named so because he was the fifth William to be stadholder; his son became William I (1772–1843) because he was the first William to be king. Prussian troops, together with the newly formed Dutch army, cleared the Netherlands of French forces.

THE KINGDOM OF THE NETHERLANDS

Because the English wished to have a strong country to the north of France to keep it in check, the London Articles of July 1814 united Belgium and Holland in the Kingdom of the Netherlands. The new country included present-day Belgium and Luxembourg, as well as the seven northern provinces that had made up the United Netherlands. The Kingdom covered 6,000 square kilometers and had 5.5 million inhabitants.

A new constitution was presented to the States-General and the Belgian Notables. Even though the majority of the Belgians were opposed to it, the new constitution went into force on August 24, 1814. The States-General were divided into two chambers in which Belgium and Holland each had an equal number of delegates. This put the Belgians at a relative disadvantage to the Dutch, for the Belgian population was seven times larger than the Dutch population. To have been truly fair, the ratio of Belgian to Dutch delegates should have matched the ratio of the Belgian to the Dutch population.

William I had a hard job to do in holding the new Kingdom together. The two parts of the Netherlands had been apart for too long and had developed along different lines. The northern provinces wanted to fund the government with high taxes. The southern (Belgian) provinces, which depended on industry, wanted high tariffs. The Belgians supported the heavy debt of the north only reluctantly. In 1815, the north had a debt of around 1,250 million guilders, most of it a result of Napoleon's exploitation. In the south, the debt was only 25 million. The benefit from the colonies was slow in coming, and the northern provinces viewed the little that went to the trading cities in the south jealously.

William I wanted to make the Netherlands a strong Continental power. His policies concentrated on industrialization. Many of the northern merchants, however, resisted his policies. They wanted to return to the old way of doing things that had made their fathers rich. The world balance of power, though, had shifted to the industrialized nations: The north was still underdeveloped; the south was already industrialized.

In addition, the southern (Belgian) provinces were Catholic. They felt that the Protestant north was discriminating against them, even though the Dutch had tried to be accommodating about religion. The constitution of 1814, which applied only to the northern provinces, had stipulated that the monarch be a member of the Dutch Reformed Church. This article was repealed in the constitution of 1815, which applied to both Belgium and Holland. The government concluded a concordance with the Pope in June 1827 that established three new episcopates in Amsterdam, Bruges, and 's-Hertogenbosch. Nevertheless, the powerful Belgian Catholic clergy remained distrustful of the Protestant north.

At the same time, the Belgian liberals, primarily Walloons (francophone Belgians), were displeased with the government's efforts to make Dutch the primary language of the country. They were also displeased with the king's arbitrary style of ruling. They were more in favor of French rule than of Dutch. As a result of a coalition between the liberals and the clerics, the July Revolution in France (1830) overflowed into a revolution in Belgium against the union with Holland.

Initially, it looked as if King William I would be able to preserve the union by force of arms. He fought successfully against the Belgian forces, but the great powers, who had united Holland and Belgium, declared themselves for their separation in the London Protocol of June 26, 1831. With the permission of the great powers, French forces pushed William's troops back, and by Christmas Eve 1832, they had taken the fortress at Antwerp. Together with the English, the French also blockaded the

Dutch coast. The hostilities ended with the London Agreements of May 21, 1833.

William long refused to recognize the independence of Belgium, exhausting the treasury in the process, but at last, in 1839, the separation was made official. The Belgian share of the debt of the Netherlands was reduced to 5 million guilders. The province of Limburg was united under Dutch rule. This left the Kingdom of the Netherlands with eleven provinces, which had a common history and language. Luxembourg remained joined with Holland via a bilateral union.

In 1840, William I renounced the throne so that he could marry the Countess d'Oultremount (1792–1864). She had been a lady-in-waiting for his wife, who had died in 1837. The countess was unacceptable to the Dutch public because she was Catholic and Belgian. Prodded by the crown prince—William II (1792–1849)—the press was especially critical of her.

As the new king, William II had fewer powers than his father, and opposition to his rule grew rapidly. Separated from the industrialized south, Holland went through a recession in the 1840s. The mood in the country was for more freedom in economic affairs and more say in government.

In 1848, when more violent revolution was sweeping through many European countries, the Netherlands peacefully became a democratic, constitutional monarchy. After the February Revolution in France, William II decided that it was time for constitutional reform. The new liberal constitution gave more power to the middle class and made the government's ministers responsible to the States-General instead of to the king.

Crown Prince William III (1817–1890) was opposed to the new liberal constitution. When it was adopted, he abdicated his right of succession and demanded that news of his abdication be made public. William II forbid publication of the news, and William III ascended to the throne a year later when his father died. He ruled for forty-one years. Clearly no friend of political liberalism, in November 1849, William III found himself forced to accept a liberal cabinet headed by Johan Rudolf Thorbecke (1798–1872). Thorbecke was the spiritual father of the liberal constitutional reform of 1848. William II had selected Thorbecke to head the commission charged with writing a new constitution, and it clearly bears Thorbecke's stamp. It was well ahead of its time in the conservative political climate of mid-nineteenth-century Holland. The most significant changes of the 1848 constitution were:

- the introduction of direct elections to the Second Chamber and Municipal Councils by those who paid a certain amount of taxes
- deputies to the Second Chamber were to be elected for four years, with half of the chamber to be replaced every two years
- deputies to the First Chamber were appointed by the Provincial Councils for nine years, with one-third of the chamber to be replaced every three years
- the introduction of the right of the States-General to question ministers
- the introduction of ministerial responsibility to the States-General

These changes increased the powers of the States-General at the expense of the king's. Before, he had appointed members to the First Chamber for life; the ministers had been responsible to him, and the electorate that he had to deal with had been smaller.

During the term of Thorbecke's first government, laws were passed on the right of assembly, the organization of provincial and municipal government, and the reorganization of the courts. The country's economic position improved due to a rejuvenation of maritime trade and of the merchant marine as a result of the repeal of trading privileges, the conclusion of new trade treaties, the construction of canals, and the expansion of the railways. Thorbecke's government also oversaw the reduction of governmental expenditures, postal reform, and the conversion of the debt.

Thorbecke's first government fell in 1853 on the issue of the removal of governmental control over the Catholic Church, which had been guaranteed in the new constitution. The announcement by Pope Pius IX that the Church would open five new bishoprics in Holland was poorly received by the Protestants, who collected over 250,000 signatures opposing the return of the Catholics and presented the petition to the king. William III's sympathetic reaction to the petition prompted Thorbecke to submit his resignation, which William happily accepted.

Even while heading the opposition in the States-General, Thorbecke continued to exercise considerable influence over domestic policy. In 1862, he was again called on by William III to form a new government. During the term of this government, he pushed through the abolition of slavery in the West Indian colonies, but when, in 1866, he tried to repeal the feudal system of forced labor, which had been introduced on Java in

1830, the radical wing of the liberals sided with the opposition against him, and Thorbecke stepped down again.

Thorbecke headed the government for a third time between 1871 and 1872, serving as minister for domestic affairs. He died shortly after the government had handed in its resignation in 1872. His third government fell over the issue of compulsory military service in the face of a growing German military threat.

THE BATTLE OF THE SCHOOLS

The question of public versus private schools was a defining issue in Dutch political debate for more than 100 years (1806–1917). The issue first centered around the right of religious schools to exist alongside public (secular) schools and later shifted to equal state funding for both.

In 1806, during the Batavian Republic, the Van den Ende Law on Education created a public school system run by the municipalities, based on Christian principles but favoring neither Catholicism nor Protestantism. While the law allowed for the establishment of *bijzondere* (special; read confessional) schools run by private persons or organizations, permission to operate a special school was required from the municipalities. The municipalities rarely granted permissions, and the result was a de facto state monopoly on education. This virtual monopoly remained unchanged until the new constitution of 1848, which is viewed as the beginning of modern democracy in Holland.

The Catholics were at the forefront of the struggle for special, denominational schools, which was, in essence, a nonviolent continuation of the struggle between Catholics and Protestants for religious dominance that had been waged by force of arms in the Eighty Years' War. The first verbal shot in the Schoolstrijd (Battle of the Schools), as the Dutch call it, was fired by Catholic Member of Parliament Leopold van Sasse van Ysselt (1778–1844) in a speech in 1825, which called for freedom in education. By "freedom," he meant the freedom to teach not just Christian principles, but Catholic principles to Catholic children in Catholic schools.

The new constitution of 1848, which removed the restrictions on running private schools, had been drafted by the liberal politician Thorbecke. His formulation of the article on schools in the constitution was contested by most other liberal politicians, who wanted to maintain the state monopoly on education. Their goal was a united Dutch people, and allowing denominational schools served only to perpetuate the split that existed in the populace along religious lines.

Dutch liberals of the mid-nineteenth century were not populists, but intellectuals. Their policies were aimed at promoting the general good, placing national above local interests. The liberals wanted secular schools in which students of all faiths were taught in the same classroom. They wanted the schools to provide each individual with the intellectual tools to make up his or her own mind about religion without having religion imposed on them by the school.

Most Protestant politicians sided with the liberals, because they were opposed to the establishment of Catholic schools. They wanted a public school system with a Protestant tint, but one that did not explicitly teach Protestant dogma. Their leader, G. J. Mulder (1802–1880), a professor at the University of Utrecht, exercised his influence on William III to have William approve the Van der Brugghen Law on Education in 1857. This was, in essence, a continuation of the education policies of the Van den Ende Law of 1806. It tasked public schools with instilling pupils with "Christian and social virtues," but excluded special (denominational) schools from receiving any type of support from the state.

With the passage of this law, the Battle of the Schools entered its second phase. The focus of the debate shifted to state funding for private schools. The papal encyclical "Quanta Cura" of 1864 and the pronouncement of the Dutch bishops in 1868, advising Catholics not to use the public schools, made the question of state subsidies for special schools a question of conscience for Catholics. The Protestant Anti-Revolutionary Party also saw that a clearly Protestant-Christian education without state support was impossible and made the Battle of the Schools a part of its platform under Abraham Kuyper.

The 1878 Kappeyne Law on Education set new standards that raised the cost of running a school considerably. This new law increased the fierceness of the struggle to put the special schools on an equal financial footing with the public schools and brought the Protestants and Catholics—historically bitter enemies—together in a coalition that survived the issue it was formed to promote. Together in this coalition, they were able to control the government from 1885 to 1925.

The Protestants and the Catholics wanted their children to be educated in the spirit of the faith of their parents and instilled with their moral values. They considered the right to choose the type of education that their children received to be a basic human right. Article 23 of the Dutch constitution, which defines state policy on education is in the first chapter, titled "Basic Rights."

The first Protestant-Catholic coalition cabinet formed under Aeneas Mackay (1838–1909) managed to pass an amendment that granted limited state subsidies to the special schools. The following coalition cabinets under Kuyper and Theodorus Heemskerk (1852–1932) managed to increase subsidies for the special schools a number of times. In the end, it took an amendment to the constitution in 1917 to fully legitimize financial equality for public and private schools. With the passage of the De Visser Law on Education in 1920, the state became responsible for funding the education of all children, regardless of the type of school they attend.

The state sets standards for facilities, class size, subjects taught, teacher certification, and tests that all students must pass. The state cannot, however, specify teaching materials or influence the appointment of teachers, and all regulations must take the religious beliefs of the special schools into account. The state can say that you have to be able to read and write Dutch, but not what textbook you have to use to do it. Prayer in school is a matter of individual school policy, not state policy. With state funding for all schools, parents have the right to send their children to any school they wish. This brings the mechanisms of the marketplace to the operation of state-funded schools. Schools that cannot attract the minimum number of pupils to stay open lose their funding and are closed.

Later, schools using progressive teaching methods also took advantage of the law to gain state funding as well. Today, the state funds not only Catholic, Protestant, Muslim, Hindu, and Jewish schools, but also the specialized Montessori, Dalton, Jenaplan, Freinet, and Free Schools.

VOTING RIGHTS

Universal suffrage was the plank in the liberal parties' political agenda that served as the counterpoint to the key item in the religious parties' political agenda: equal state funding for secular and religious schools. These two issues entirely dominated domestic politics in Holland from 1857 to 1914. The passage of each of these programs into law was the result of a political peace settlement between these two groups while World War I raged outside the borders of neutral Holland. In exchange for the liberal parties' votes for school funding, the religious parties voted for universal suffrage.

The achievement of accommodation between these two groups in 1917 was really a considerable accomplishment just fifty-three years after the "Quanta Cura" of 1864 made the question of state subsidies for special schools a question of conscience for Catholics and denounced liberalism as un-Christian. Nor were the liberals great friends of the Christian Church. Early liberal support of the expansion of voting rights had an anticlerical tint to it. The liberals wanted to confine voting rights to urban residents, whom they saw as better educated and "not on the leash of some cleric."

The constitution of 1798 had extended voting rights to everyone over the age of twenty who met certain requirements, like having sworn an oath of allegiance to the office of stadholder. The constitution of 1814, however, turned back the clock to "census-based" voting rights. Under this system, voting rights are based on the amount of taxes a citizen pays and his educational level. Only those who paid enough taxes and who were educated could vote. This system was a holdover from Roman law. The Romans held a census every five years, whereby the names, ages, and wealth of all the citizens were recorded. The rights that a citizen had were tied to the amount of wealth that he had. This was the arrangement in use in all the Western parliamentary democracies for most of the nineteenth century. It ensured that the well-to-do maintained control over the political life of the country. Thorbecke's constitutional amendment of 1848 retained this system, but it did expand the electorate. During Thorbecke's first ministry, the number of voters nearly doubled, from 55,000 to 100,000—almost 3.5% of the adult male population.

Opposition to universal suffrage was very strong. In expressing his opposition to it in 1878, Prime Minister Kappeyne van de Coppello (1822–1895) pointed to what had happened in America, where universal suffrage had been granted. It seemed to him to be "a rich source of bribery, violence and deceit."[1] He hoped that he would not live to see the day that it came to Holland. He did not.

The constitutional amendment of 1887 expanded the number of voters to 29% of the adult male population. The constitutional amendment of 1896 increased it further to 49%. Improvements in the educational system and the country's economic welfare automatically increased the number of voters, but by 1916, still only 70% of adult Dutch men had the right to vote. It was only the constitutional change of 1917 that granted universal suffrage to men, that removed the barriers to voting for women— women did not get the vote, however, until 1922—and that fully legitimized financial equality for public and special schools. The amendment of the constitution on these two points was possible only because of the political peace concluded by the religious right and the liberal left.

Though the liberals were the chief proponents of expanded suffrage, they were the ones who lost the most at the polls when suffrage was expanded. They suffered a clear defeat in the election of 1888, and following the introduction of universal suffrage in 1917, the religious parties (today combined in the CDA) came to power and remained there until political dissatisfaction with the status quo prompted the formation of the *paars* (purple) cabinet in 1994.

NOTE

1. Quoted in Klaas Jansma and Meindert Schoor, eds., *10,000 jaar geschiedenis der Nederlanden* (10,000 Years of the History of the Netherlands) (Lisse: REBO Productions, 1991), p. 339.

10

War, Crisis, and Recovery

WORLD WAR I

King William I stubbornly refused to acknowledge Belgian secession from the Kingdom of the Netherlands and held the Dutch army on a war footing between 1830 and 1839. Slowly but surely, the high costs of keeping the army at this state of readiness cost William the enthusiastic support of the Dutch public for his actions against Belgium, which had been inspired by the successes of the Ten-Day Campaign (1831) and the heroism of Jan Carel Josephus van Speijk (1802–1831). In 1839, William finally recognized Belgium, became the archduke of Luxembourg, and annexed the eastern part of Limburg, quite against the wishes of its citizens. With that, Holland entered a period of isolationism that would last for almost a century. The Ministry of External Affairs became the stepchild of the cabinet. Holland followed a policy of neutrality, and the military was very much neglected.

When the Great War—they had not decided to number them at that point—began in 1914, Holland was much relieved that the Germans decided not to move troops across Dutch territory to invade Belgium. Germany respected Holland's neutrality, in part because it was guaranteed by England, and in part because the German Command Staff recognized that a neutral Holland would be the best defense for Germany's western frontier and would also offer a certain economic advantage. In any event, the Belgian army was weak, and crossing Dutch territory just to take out the fortress at Luik was not worth the effort. The English likewise had no desire to bring Holland into the war. They recognized that the Germans could easily occupy Holland, cutting off their access via the Scheldt to the Belgian coastal harbors, where they eventually landed troops.

The greatest problem of the war for the Dutch was refugees. The first wave arrived on August 4, 5, and 6, 1914. Sixty to eighty thousand refugees, primarily Germans who had to leave Belgium, entered the country. For the most part, these initial refugees did not pose much of a problem, because they only transited Holland on their way to Germany.

The second wave was made up of Belgians fleeing the advancing German armies. When Antwerp fell, over a million Belgians crossed into Noord-Brabant and Zeeland. As the situation in Belgium stabilized, the refugees began to return home. By November 1, 1914, there were only 320,000 left. Eventually this number was reduced to about 100,000.

The third wave of refugees came in October 1918, when at least 40,000 refugees, primarily from northern France, came to Holland, fleeing the retreating German armies. These refugees were quickly repatriated with help from the French government. It was February 1919, however, before the refugee camps were completely cleared. All told, the cost to the Dutch government for its hospitality to the refugees was ƒ37 million.

Holland continued its policy of strict neutrality even as World War II began, but the German attack on Holland in May 1940 put an end to it.

THE GREAT DEPRESSION

During the second half of the nineteenth century, the Dutch policy of neutrality and isolationism helped Holland avoid many of the tensions that surfaced elsewhere in Europe during that time (the Franco-Prussian War of 1870–1871, for example). The Dutch even experienced considerable economic success.

Much progress was made in the late nineteenth century, and a period of prosperity began in Holland after 1870. The Dutch made reconstruction loans to the Southern U.S. states after the Civil War. Capital began to accumulate and was invested in the Indies, in Russia, and in Central Europe, but particularly in the expanding economy of the United States. By the turn of the century, industry and agriculture were completely modernized. Dutch wheat farmers found that they could not compete with the farmers of the American Midwest and turned instead to dairy farming (cheese) and horticulture (bulbs) for export. Shipping canals and railways were built. The great ports were modernized. The Dutch merchant marine became one of the largest in the world.

The economic crisis of 1922 and the Great Depression, which started in America with the stock market crash of 1929, brought an end to this period of prosperity. In Holland, the economic crisis of the thirties was more severe and its effects were noticeable longer than in surrounding countries. The Dutch economy, which had negotiated World War I relatively well, was caught up in the political instability that followed. Dutch exports suffered drastically from German and Japanese competition. The prevailing low prices for agricultural commodities depressed profits from this sector as well. Germany's new policy of food self-sufficiency further deprived Dutch farmers of their markets there.

This was the period that saw the introduction of electricity, the internal combustion engine, the airplane, the radio, and the movies. The Dutch economy was changing from an agricultural one to an industrial one. Between 1899 and 1930, the percentage of people employed in industry climbed from 33.8% to 38.8%, and the percentage of people employed in agriculture declined from 29.6% to 20.6%. Dutch heavy industry lacked the natural resources (except for coal) to be competitive. Light industries—like the production of rayons, chemicals, and fertilizers and the manufacture of radios and electrical appliances, for example—were, however, successful.

The higher standard of living based on prewar prosperity, together with wages that had risen faster than inflation, made Dutch products uncompetitive on the international market. The subsequent currency devaluations in France, Belgium, England, Scandinavia, and the United States priced Dutch goods even further out of the market. Dutch financiers, like those in other Western nations, experienced losses on their reconstruction loans to Germany, which defaulted on its foreign debt. The large amount of Dutch money invested in U.S. stocks made the Amsterdam Stock Exchange very sensitive to events on Wall Street.

The Dutch government felt itself forced into a policy of protectionism. Beginning in 1933, the government followed a policy that made adjustments to world price levels via wage reductions and economy moves. Six-time Prime Minister (1925 and 1933–1939 in five successive governments) Hendrikus Colijn's (1869–1944) steadfast adherence to the gold standard prolonged the economic crisis in Holland, while other countries had already begun to notice economic improvements. His were clearly the wrong policies. Unemployment climbed to peak at almost 400,000 people. In September 1936, Holland—the last European nation to do so—

took the guilder off the gold standard, and it devalued by 22%. Exports and business in general improved immediately. Government orders for armaments, as the threat of war became clearer, also aided in reducing unemployment.

The same conditions that led to Franklin D. Roosevelt's (1882–1945) New Deal in America were present in Holland. The political will to make those kinds of changes, however, was missing in Holland. The Reich Commissioner for occupied Holland, Arthur Seyss-Inquart (1892–1946), was quite right when he made his first report to Adolf Hitler (1889–1945) in 1940: "The Dutch have come to a halt politically, and economically have fallen into lethargy." The writers Jan and Annie Romein characterize the primary reason for this as "the perception of economic factors as independent of social factors. People could not imagine a type of prosperity in which entrepreneurs did not maximize profits. People did not see that economic policy ultimately has to be guided by the prosperity of the nation as a whole."[1] For all the harm and damage they did, the Germans did manage to reenergize the Dutch politically during the occupation. When the war was over, the Dutch rebuilt their country politically and economically in the image of the New Deal. The war was a political watershed. Protectionism was replaced by European integration, and the welfare state was born.

WORLD WAR II

On May 10, 1940, the Netherlands was invaded by the ground forces of Nazi Germany, bringing an end to Dutch neutrality. On May 14, Rotterdam was bombed by the German air force. Most of the facilities of the city's port, as well as ships docked or being built there, were destroyed. Over 40% of the city was leveled in the raid. After the bombing of Rotterdam, the Dutch were forced to surrender. Queen Wilhelmina (1880–1962) fled to England with the royal family and the government. The Dutch government-in-exile operated from there for the five years of German occupation.

Arthur Seyss-Inquart, a trusted friend of Hitler and the Reich Commissioner for occupied Holland, was the highest civilian authority in the country during the occupation. Seyss-Inquart was eventually tried at Nuremberg for crimes against peace and humanity. He was found guilty and hanged.

The Germans considered the Dutch a fellow Germanic people and treated them differently than they did the Slavs (e.g., Russians, Poles, Ukrainians). They hoped that they would be able to persuade the Dutch

into taking the German side in the war. The Dutch, however, proved un-
receptive to the ideas of National-Socialism. After early 1941, the friendly,
"fraternal" approach was abandoned altogether. In February 1941, the
Dutch went on strike to protest the Germans' anti-Semitic actions. The
strike began in Amsterdam and spread to other cities: Weesp, Hilversum,
and de Zaanstreek. It was initiated by the Communistische Partij Nederland (CPN; Dutch Communist Party). As great as the distrust of the CPN
had been among the Dutch—Stalin and Hitler were allies who had attacked and divided Poland—the clear anti-German position taken by the
CPN overcame that distrust, and people who would never have associated with the CPN before the war joined the strike. The first to stop
working were railroad workers in Amsterdam. They were followed by
both blue- and white-collar workers. Schools were empty. Streetcars that
left the depot were stoned. The police took little or no action. In Zand-
voort the Germans had to deploy the SS Death's Head–battalion to suppress the strike.

Dutch support of the Jews during the occupation did not, unfortunately, remain at this level for the rest of the war. The journalist Herman
Vuijsje calculates the death toll in his recent book.

> Seventy-five percent of the Dutch Jewish populace was murdered
> by the Germans; the highest percentage of all the Western-European
> countries, including Germany. In Belgium and Norway forty per-
> cent lost their lives, in France, twenty-five percent; in Italy twenty
> percent and in Denmark two percent. The percentage of those who
> hid out was higher in Germany itself and in Poland than in the
> Netherlands. Both in Belgium and in the Netherlands, 25,000 Jews
> managed to hide out, but at the beginning of the war, there were
> only 66,000 Jews in Belgium, against 140,000 in the Netherlands.[2]

Nevertheless, the country is the setting for the well-known story of a
young Jewish girl who, together with her family and some friends, hid
from the Nazis in a secret room behind a bookcase in a house in Amsterdam. *The Diary of Anne Frank* has been translated and published in a
number of languages. Just before the war ended, she was discovered and
taken to a concentration camp from which she never returned. The question of who betrayed the Frank family remains a topical issue in Holland,
as does the question of who was "right" and who was "wrong" (read col-
laborated) during the war.

In the summer of 1944, the tide of battle turned. The Allies landed on
the beaches of Normandy on June 6, ironically, the birthday of the wife of

Field Marshal Erwin Rommel (1891–1944), who was in charge of the German coastal defense of France. By September, the first areas in the south of Holland had been liberated. The Allied push stalled, however, when "Operation Market Garden" failed to take the strategic bridge over the Rhine at Arnhem. For the people living to the north of the Rhine, liberation had to wait until May of 1945. The intervening winter is now infamous as the *hongerwinter* (famine winter).

In support of the Allied advance, at the request of the government-in-exile, Dutch railways went on strike in September 1944. The strike paralyzed the rail system and the Germans had to rely on their own personnel and equipment during Market Garden. Unfortunately, the strike also meant that the people in the occupied areas suffered too. Supplies of food and fuel for them had to be moved by train, but the trains were not running in occupied Holland.

Strong resentment of the Germans and their part in World War II has lasted a long time in Holland. It is still markedly noticeable. Liberation Day is still actively celebrated on May 5. The Dutch still tell jokes about the Germans that poke fun at them because of their part in the war. There are still movies and books coming out about the war. The argument about whether those who cooperated with the Germans during the war should get a pension from the Dutch state was actively contested in the 1980s. As the generation that lived through the war dies out, the negative attitude toward Germans is becoming weaker, but it is held by enough members of the younger generations that it will not completely vanish even when the war generation is gone.

RECONSTRUCTION

The arrival of Allied troops brought not only freedom, but also a feeling of well-being. Whenever troops were in an area, there was plenty of bread, and the soldiers always seemed to have lots of chocolate and cigarettes—virtually unknown luxuries during the war—that they were willing to share. But this feeling of well-being left when the troops did. Rationing continued into the 1950s. The Dutch economy was devastated. The national debt had risen from *f*5 to *f*23 billion during the war.

The infrastructure of the country was in ruins. The Germans had taken everything that they could to Germany. Machinery and sometimes whole factories had been dismantled for removal to Germany. Metal of every kind, including church bells and train rails, had been taken to support the German war effort. The rail network was wrecked. The ports of Amsterdam and Rotterdam were a shambles. Canals and waterways were filled with boats, barges, and ships, which had been scuttled to hamper the Germans. Many of the bridges, which cross Holland's large number of canals and rivers, had been destroyed. Half a million people were homeless, and one and a half million lived in homes that had been damaged by the war. One person in eight had only the clothes on their back to wear. Cars were few and far between. Plows were pulled by horses, not by tractors.

When the war ended, Holland entered a period of political and economic reconstruction. Political reconstruction meant tracking down and punishing the collaborators, holding elections, and reestablishing government at all levels. Economic reconstruction meant repairing the damage inflicted on Holland by the war and housing the homeless.

HOLLAND'S WAR IN THE EAST INDIES (INDONESIA)

The Dutch East Indies (Indonesia) had been occupied by the Japanese during World War II, ending Dutch colonial rule. When the Japanese surrendered on August 15, 1945, they turned power over to the Indonesian nationalists A. Sukarno (1901–1970) and M. Hatta (1902–1980), who immediately declared Indonesia a republic. The Dutch, however, wanted to resume colonial rule of the islands. The colony had been an important factor in the economy before the war, and many people were convinced that if they lost the East Indies, that would be an end to prosperity.

Between 1945 and 1949, the Dutch sent more than 120,000 regular army troops to the Dutch East Indies in support of their efforts to restore the status quo antebellum. Hostilities lasted from October 14, 1945, through May 7, 1949, and cost the Dutch 4,751 military casualties. The Dutch finally gave in to international pressure—especially from the United States, which threatened to cut off Marshall Plan funds—and acknowledged the independence of Indonesia on December 27, 1949.

The military action in the East Indies had two unforeseen side effects in Holland: First, the thousands of young men serving in the East Indies were kept out of the domestic labor force during the immediate postwar years, which slowed the postwar recovery; second, their return to Holland after serving in the East Indies gave an extra push to the Dutch postwar baby boom, helping it last longer than it did in other countries.

THE MARSHALL PLAN

At the end of World War II, the United States did not make the same mistake that England made at the end of the Napoleonic Wars. America helped to rebuild the economies of war-ravaged Europe. England did not. England's inaction after the Napoleonic Wars meant that there was no market in impoverished Europe for English exports, which resulted in an economic crisis in England. But America instituted the Marshall Plan in 1948, which provided Western Europe (the countries of Eastern Europe declined to participate) with over $11.6 billion in credits and grants. Between 1948 and 1954, the United States gave Holland $1.127 billion, or $109 for every man, woman, and child in the nation. Great Britain and France received more ($3.17 billion and $3.42 billion, respectively), but on a per capita basis, it was less. Great Britain got only $62 per capita, France only $71. The Germans got $1.38 billion—more than Holland, but on a per capita basis, only $29. During the great floods of 1953, the United States picked up the tab for ƒ400 million of the ƒ1.1 billion worth of damage.

The Marshall Plan had not only an economic but also a political and social impact. It strengthened the ties between the United States and Western Europe as international tensions grew into the Cold War. It increased the people's economic well-being, which reduced the political appeal of communism for Western Europeans. It was the reason for the foundation of the OEEC (Organization for European Economic Cooperation), which, in a certain sense, is the predecessor organization to the EEC, which itself grew into the EU. It also helped to spread U.S. cultural values in Holland.

These cultural values were part of the "mental Marshall aid" to the recipient countries. "Productivity teams," consisting of workers, managers, and trade union members, were sent to the United States to attain American scientific and technological know-how. The combination of economic and mental aid was very effective. Industrial production rose 56% in Holland between 1947 and 1953, and by 1952, Holland was regarded as the most pro-American country in Europe. Not only did the productivity teams see how Americans worked, but they saw how they lived as well, and those impressions had an effect on Holland both at home and in the factory. What were then considered luxury goods, inspired by the rich life in America, began to appear in Dutch households. Washing machines, vacuum cleaners, electric irons, and refrigerators—in 1950, only 0.7% of all Dutch households had an electric refrigerator—were being made in Europe, using American production techniques and technology. In the fifties, Albert Heijn (1927–   ) opened the first self-service supermarkets, based on the U.S. model, and revolutionized the grocery business in Holland.

On the political front, the social democrats and trade unions were impressed by the social legislation of the New Deal. President Roosevelt had introduced Social Security for some groups in America as early as

1935, twelve years before it became law in Holland. The Dutch built on American ideas and gave them a distinctive Dutch flavor.

There were, however, voices that warned against becoming over-Americanized. Prime Minister Willem Drees Sr. (1886–1988), who introduced the first government old-age pension in 1947, admired the optimism and great generosity of the Americans, but he did not like the American "spendthrift" style of life. He thought that the Americans relied too much on their cars at the expense of public transportation. His wife was appalled by novelist Henry Miller's (1891–1980) description of the heat of winter and the cold of summer indoors in America, in his book *The Air-Conditioned Nightmare* (1945). The Dreeses' view was that America was too wasteful with its energy resources and that Holland should not try to imitate that.

There had been complaints about the American cultural way of life in the interwar years as well. In the twenties and thirties, Dutch intellectuals such as Johan Huizinga (1872–1945) and Menno ter Braak (1902–1940) dismissed American culture as superficial and banal. The Dutch interest in the United States then had been stimulated by the tales of family members who had immigrated there around the turn of the century. In the postwar period, interest was stimulated by the aforementioned mental aid of the Marshall Plan. In both periods, the criticism stemmed primarily from the intellectuals.

THE AMERICANIZATION OF HOLLAND

Marshall Plan mental aid had a clear cultural mission: It was America's European public relations program. This portion of the Marshall Plan was overseen by the United States Information Service (USIS). The USIS provided inexpensive translations of American literature, especially literature that gave an "accurate picture" of life in the United States. The USIS supplied material for the newsreels shown in movie theaters (a major source of news before television became common). It arranged trips to the States for journalists and feeds of material to the electronic media. When Holland decided not to buy U.S. films due to a lack of hard currency, part of the Marshall Plan funds were earmarked specifically for that purpose, and Holland got a minimum quota to buy. The first color photos that appeared in the ladies' magazine *Margriet* were of American film stars. The Donald Duck comic strip was introduced in Holland in 1952. It grew to a circulation of 300,000 and is still in production, though it is no longer in print in America. This was also the period that saw the first *Reader's Digest* reach Holland.

The generation gap appeared in Holland in the sixties just as it did in America. The protest generation of the baby boomers saw themselves in American and British rock music. The civil disturbances of the sixties and seventies took place to the accompaniment of American rock music. The civil rights marches and race riots in America were brought directly into Dutch homes via the brand-new medium of television. The Vietnam protests followed. "Anti-Americanism" became the label for what was just a copy of what was happening on American streets and campuses. In reality, it was antiestablishmentism. Young people in Holland liked to wear Levis—the ultimate American fashion statement—and listen to Bob Dylan (1941–   ), whose lyrics capture the cynicism, anger, and alienation of American youth of that day. During the demonstrations against the stationing of the cruise missiles on Dutch territory, polls showed that 75% of the populace supported Dutch membership in NATO, and almost as many said that they were pro-American.

Today, everybody has Microsoft software on their computer. American movies dominate the theaters. Commercial television networks like SBS6, RTL4, and RTL5 are hardly distinguishable from American television fare. The talk shows cover the same topics. You can watch *Oprah* with subtitles and then see a domestic talk show on the same theme.

Americans who visit Holland will come across all sorts of familiar artifacts: commercials that are literally translations of ads in the United States; American television programs that are shown in English with Dutch subtitles; products like Old El Paso taco shells and Coca-Cola (the Dutch name for chocolate chip cookies is "American Cookies"); American businesses like Compaq, Pizza Hut, and McDonald's.

For many in Holland, McDonald's is the symbol of the encroachment of American culture into Holland. The Dutch view the spread of McDonald's restaurants with a mixture of disgust and admiration. For them, the chief characteristic of the McDonald's experience—and almost everything else American—is convenience. It is fast, inexpensive, and you don't have all that fuss with a knife and fork and table manners. Indeed, there are 154 McDonald's restaurants in Holland (as of May 1997), but the chain has not always been so successful there. In the seventies, some McDonald's were closed due to a lack of business. People viewed eating there gracelessly as too American. Albert Heijn, the supermarket chain, which is always on the leading edge of innovation, withdrew its investment in the American corporation. It was not until the early eighties that business began to pick up. During that time, McDonald's began organizing charity campaigns to support good causes: McLibrary, McDonald's

House, and McTree all helped to bring about public acceptance of Mc-
Donald's in Holland.

The McTree campaign in Arnhem was run to collect money to plant
trees to commemorate the 750-year anniversary of the founding of Arnhem. Then–Prime Minister Dries van Agt (1931–   ) together with Joris
Voorhoeve (1945–   ) and Erica Terpstra (1943–   ), members of Parliament at the time, stood behind the counter for hours, selling hamburg-
ers so that sponsors would contribute to the cause. That helped to make
it more acceptable to eat at McDonald's. Today, McDonald's serves spicy
peanut butter sauce—the ultimate Dutch fast-food experience—with
french fries. No matter how familiar it looks, there is always a Dutch
twist to it. America may have been the source of the idea, but it is not
100% the same after it takes root in Holland.

NOTES

1. Jan Romein and Annie Romein, *De lage landen bij de zee: een geschiedenis van
het Nederlandse volk* (The Low Countries by the Sea: A History of the Dutch People) (Utrecht: W. de Haan, 1949), p. 636.

2. Herman Vuijsje, *Correct weldenkend Nederland sinds de jaren zestig* (The Politically Correct Netherlands since the Sixties) (Amsterdam: Contact, 1997), p. 117.

11

The Rise and Fall of the Welfare State

THE RISE OF THE WELFARE STATE

The Dutch word for welfare state is *verzorgingsstaat*; literally, it means "caretaking state." Besides protecting its citizens against economic difficulties, the Dutch welfare state also attempted to redistribute national income so that everyone would share in the increased prosperity of the nation. At its height, its goal was that no one should have to worry about paying for the necessities of life. The Dutch welfare state was born in the minds of the politicians who had lived through the Great Depression and World War II. It was nurtured by the economic successes of the forties, fifties, and sixties, only to fall victim to the excesses of the "me" generation that followed the generation of the Depression and the war.

The decade of the 1950s introduced Holland to the concept of economic prosperity. After the war, consumer goods had been scarce. Rationing had continued into the fifties. Coffee, for example, which the Dutch like ever so much, was rationed until 1952. From that time on, economic well-being improved in Holland. The Dutch soon discovered that they were rich. Postwar reconstruction had succeeded beyond their wildest dreams. There were things to buy, and there was money with which to buy them. The consumer society had been born.

The politicians who came to power at the end of World War II had a conservative outlook. Their original goal for postwar reconstruction had been to restore the economic, political, and social structure to the status quo before the Depression and the war. The success of economic restoration made change possible. That change resulted in the welfare state.

Willem Drees Sr. is the personification of Dutch politics in the fifties. He was prime minister from 1948 to 1958, when the basis of the welfare state was laid. Drees was an old-style socialist with a Calvinist upbringing. He did not drink. He did not smoke. He biked to work. He was very scrupulous. He is often characterized as a strict, but just, father figure. The party leader of the PvdA, he became the prime minister of the great postwar Catholic-Socialist coalition of the PvdA and the Katholieke Volkspartij (KVP; Catholic People's Party). A pragmatic idealist, Drees built up the basis for the Dutch welfare state piece by piece, striving for a solid system of Social Security for everyone, based on full employment. He realized that it was impossible to do everything at once and worked slowly toward his goal.

Drees is perhaps most famous as the father of the Dutch Social Security system of old-age pensions. The system began in 1947 with the Noodwet-Drees (Drees Emergency Act). In 1957, it evolved into the Algemene Ouderdomswet (AOW; General Old Age Pensions Act) under PvdA member J. G. Suurhoff (1905–1967), the minister of health and social affairs. While young people today have written off the AOW as a dying social program and are looking to finance their own old age, for the generation of the Depression and the war the introduction of the AOW was a monumental change in social policy. It became the cornerstone of the welfare state.

Optimism and faith in progress continued to grow, fed by the improving economy. Between 1948 and 1962, industrial production doubled. There was also a great feeling of consensus in society. There were no resources to fight over as long as the economy continued to grow. That made it very easy to reach a consensus. Everybody could have what they wanted. The problems for the Dutch welfare state began when resources became scarce.

The pillars, with their separate but equal everything, were the building blocks of society then, and consensus was the mortar that held society together. The pillars kept society compartmentalized into small groups, in which the pressure of the group could maintain a certain order. In larger groups this pressure weakens and can disappear altogether.

The breakdown of the pillars in the early sixties changed the size of the groups to which individuals belonged. The larger the group, the less each individual member of the group feels responsible to it. The less the members of the group feel responsible for the group, the less the group feels responsible for its members. When the group becomes so large that its individual members are anonymous, the power of group pressure to control an individual's behavior disappears. The result is a change in the dynamics of society from maximizing the good of the group (the pillar) to maximizing the good of the individual.

In Holland, this effect was compounded by the reaction to the protests of the sixties and seventies. The protest of that period was directed against the powers that be, who made and enforced the regulations, which are the hallmark of Dutch society. While strict regulation may sound like a contradiction in terms for a country where things like "soft drug coffee shops," gay marriages, and euthanasia are possible, Dutch society is nevertheless one of regulations. All these things are regulated; the key difference is enforcement.

The result of the protests of the sixties and seventies was that the authorities became less confrontational; however, the myriad regulations are still there. The authorities have the same sense of self-preservation as the rest of society and cannot be expected to wither away as the communist philosopher Karl Marx (1818–1883) predicted. If the powers that be do not write regulations, they are out of a job. To keep their job, they continued making regulations; but the way regulations were enforced changed. Active enforcement by the central authorities changed to self-enforcement. Wherever possible, the authorities took the attitude that individuals should police themselves. If the authorities found that a law or regulation was not being obeyed, it was changed to match what the people were doing, rather than trying to get people to comply with it.

The premise that society could be counted on to police itself gave rise to removing the conductors from public transportation as an economic measure. Public transportation became less expensive to operate without all those "extra" salaries to pay. The result was that illegal—nonpaying—ridership on public transportation rose to new heights. Revenues fell. In the early nineties, the pendulum of regulation began to swing the other way. Enforcement returned to public transportation. Teams of controllers, drawn from the ranks of the unemployed, began to "raid" trams and buses, blocking off all the exits, checking everyone's ticket, and issuing citations to those who did not have one. Because it was so easy to avoid paying the fine by giving a false name and saying that you did not have identification with you, the Wet op Identificatieplicht (Obligatory Identification Act) was introduced in 1995. Holland was the last European country to introduce this requirement of being able to positively identify yourself with a legal document.

Changing the rules to match public behavior is very Dutch. It is the obvious corollary to a self-policing society. The result is that there is an exception to almost every rule. Enforcement is much easier if everyone obeys the rules or can be exempt from them. It is the premise behind Dutch "soft" drug policy.

When a Dutch person encounters a new rule, the tendency is to exclaim, *"Het zou toch moeten kunnen"* (This should really be possible). They all know that there is an exception to every rule. You only have to look at traffic signs as you go about the city to see how rampant it is: NO ENTRY! (except for bicyclists), says one, NO PARKING! (except for permit holders), says another.

In Holland, the ultimate explicit statement that there is no exception is a physical barrier to make it impossible to violate the rule. If you really are not supposed to drive up a small country lane for any reason, then there is a post in the middle of it that blocks your way and below the NO ENTRY! sign a warning that there is a "post in the road." If you really should not park somewhere for any reason, then there are posts along the curb half a car's length apart and the road is wide enough for only one lane of traffic. If you really are not supposed to walk on some wall, then the top is built on a 60-degree angle. If you really are not supposed to sit on a railing, then the rail is lined with very uncomfortable spikes. These types of barriers and automatic enforcements are nonconfrontational. If the individual wants to argue about the rule, he or she can do it with the barrier, and the person who made the rule avoids a confrontation.

The hyperindividualized society of the 1970s, 1980s, and 1990s, where anything goes, is the exact opposite of the pillarized society of the first half of the century—when rules were nonnegotiable—which gave birth to the welfare state. This change in society lies at the heart of the problems of the Dutch welfare state.

In 1956, the good of the individual began to take the upper hand over the good of the group. That was the year in which wages went up more than was justified by the increase in production. Prices followed wages, and inflation was the result. The consensus had started to break down.

When consensus broke down and inflation raised its head, the PvdA and the KVP began to disagree about how and how much government expenditures were to be reduced to deal with the problem. The Great Postwar Catholic-Socialist Coalition of the PvdA and the KVP finally collapsed in 1958, when a motion entered by C.P.M. Romme (1896–1980)—the party leader of the KVP—caused the Drees government to fall. At age seventy-two, Drees decided to withdraw from politics. The era of consensus politics that had given birth to the welfare state was coming to an end. Writing after he left office, Drees showed great insight into the cause of the fall of the welfare state: "We were, in general, cautious fiscally. I have always pleaded that people should be careful when overseeing the government's finances. There are many who are too easily inclined to act as if they were inexhaustible."[1]

For a number of reasons, welfare programs usually end up costing more than originally planned. The economic conditions that made the program possible change; the economic predictions that made the program seem possible do not work out. Benefits and eligibility are expanded by politicians seeking to gain favor with the voters by taking out their checkbooks, rather than making the hard choices that would lead to the affordable common good. Unscrupulous recipients learn how to take advantage of the system.

The discovery of natural gas near the town of Slochteren in 1959 must have made the government finances seem inexhaustible. Profits from the sales of the gas went directly into the state treasury. As the timeline of the complete construction of the Dutch welfare state below clearly illustrates, the money went toward building the welfare state, not toward building an infrastructure that would help the economy grow.

1962   Algemene Kinderbijslagwet (AKW; General Children's Benefit Act) introduced

1964   Ziekenfondswet (ZFW; Health Insurance Act) introduced

1965   Algemene Bijstandswet (ABW; National Assistance Act) introduced

1967   Algemene Wet Bijzondere Ziektekosten (AWBZ; General Act on Exceptional Medical Costs) introduced

        Ziektewet (ZW; Sickness Benefits Act) introduced

        Wet op de Arbeidsongeschiktheidsverzekering (WAO; Disability Benefits Act) introduced

The prosperity of the fifties and sixties gave way to the economic crisis of the seventies and eighties, beginning with the oil embargo of 1973. Unemployment shot up to unimagined levels. The number of people drawing social benefits grew with it. The second oil crisis in 1979, the result of a steep price rise for crude oil, made the bad economic situation worse. Individual consumption dropped, inflation and unemployment climbed. Interest rates were set high to combat inflation. The high interest rates of the early 1980s resulted in a climbing number of business bankruptcies, which produced more unemployment.

In the seventies, price compensation clauses began to appear in labor contracts. These clauses insured that automatic wage increases would be granted to workers to compensate them for the effects of inflation. On the social front, this mistake was compounded by coupling social benefits (and civil service salaries) to rises in wages. When new contracts were negotiated between management and labor in the private sector, government costs went up automatically. Increased government costs translated to increased tax rates and social insurance premiums, which in turn pushed wage costs up even further. The result was an automatic wage spiral that fed on itself.

THE FALL OF THE WELFARE STATE

In 1953, social insurance premiums amounted to only about 5% of the net national income. In the following decade, premiums more than doubled to almost 11%. From 1965 to 1975, ABW payments increased eightfold from ƒ440 million to ƒ3.7 billion.

In the eighties, the Dutch finally realized that the welfare state was too expensive and began taking action to reform it. In 1995, the Dutch spent ƒ189 billion on both social insurance and social services. Insurance payments took ƒ129 billion, and social service payments took ƒ21 billion. Civil service pensions received ƒ7 billion, and ƒ32 billion went to pension insurance. Together, the first three expenditures take up about one-quarter of the GNP. This is down from the early 1980s, when it was about one-third, but up from 1970, when it was only little more than one-fifth. The government's share of the economy is one of the highest in Europe, surpassed only in the Scandinavian countries.

The growing size of the government's share of GDP in the early eighties brought about calls for change. Much of the increase in the government's share of GDP was due to social insurance programs. Tax and social insurance premium revenues fell short of the amounts required to fund the programs, resulting in budget deficits. When the CDA-VVD coalition came to power in 1982, Prime Minister Ruud Lubbers (1939–   ) announced that this would be a "no-nonsense" government, committed to the reduction of the role of the state in the socioeconomic arena. The coalition lasted almost seven years.

The no-nonsense government introduced a series of reforms to the welfare state, aimed at reducing both the number of people entitled to receive benefits and the amount of the benefits. One of the first measures taken was to uncouple benefits and civil service salaries from wage rises in the private sector. This measure was particularly unpopular with the PvdA, which saw coupling as the way toward a fair and just distribution of the national wealth. When the PvdA replaced the VVD in the third Lubbers cabinet, it insisted that coupling be reinstated.

Civil service salaries were not just uncoupled, but were subjected to a 3% cut. The benefits for sickness, disability, and unemployment were reduced from 80% of the last salary/wage that the worker earned to 70%. The duration of unemployment benefits was adjusted downward. The level of benefits for those at the minimum levels fell about 10% in terms of real disposable income.

One of the major precursors to change in the welfare state was the recognition of welfare fraud as a major issue of concern in the late eighties and early nineties. This is certainly a blow to one of the cornerstones of the collective socially secure state, which requires that the profits, produced by society as a whole, be reallocated, taking from each according to his or her abilities and giving to each according to his or her needs. The system works only if the participants can trust one another to take only what they need.

When that system of trust breaks down, and people cheat to get more than they need, it encourages some to withhold their contributions to the common good, by entering the shadow economy, where taxes and social insurance premiums are not paid. It encourages others to see if they can take advantage of the system too. The Dutch attitude became: "You are only stealing from your own pocketbook if you don't." Those who remain true to the ideal eventually become disillusioned and are no longer as resistant to changes that reduce benefits to those who they feel do not deserve them. The nineties have seen benefits in the Dutch welfare state continue to fall and eligibility requirements continue to tighten. Even the PvdA is now supporting cuts in benefits and restrictions on eligibility requirements.

PORTRAIT OF THE DUTCH WELFARE STATE

The Dutch welfare state guarantees everyone a minimum income, whether they work or not. In 1998, that income was ƒ2,033.34 per month for couples, ƒ1,423.34 for a single head of household, and ƒ1,016.67 for a person living alone. There are two kinds of welfare entitlements: social insurance and social services.

Social insurance is for people who are employed, and social services are for the populace as a whole. Social insurance is funded by premiums paid by both the employer and the employee. It is an additional cost of labor that is passed through to the consumer. The cost of social insurance premiums is limited by only taxing wages and salary below the inflation-adjusted *loongrens* (income boundary), which, in 1998, was ƒ62,200 before taxes per year. Social services are funded out of general tax revenues. People who are employed are covered by the following:

- WAO
- Werkeloosheidswet (WW; Unemployment Benefits Act)
- ZFW
- Wet Uitbreiding Loondoorbetaling bij Ziekte (WULBZ; Act on Expanding Continuing Salary Payments during Illness)

The populace as a whole is covered by:

- Algemene Arbeidsongeschiktheidswet (AAW; General Disabilities Pensions Act)
- AKW
- Algemene Ouderdomswet (AOW; General Old Age Pensions Act)
- Algemene Nabestaandenwet (ANW; General Survivors' Pensions Act)
- AWBZ
- ABW

The National Assistance Act

The most important social service is the ABW, introduced in 1965. Everyone in Holland who does not have enough money to cover their own cost of living is entitled to an ABW benefit. For couples, it is 100% of the minimum wage. For heads of household, it is 70%. For singles, it is 50%. High school graduates who cannot find a job, for example, are entitled to an ABW payment. There are some strings attached. For the unemployed high school graduate to get an ABW payment, he or she has to have looked for a job but not found one; then, after six months, he or she has to accept a temporary job through the Jeugdwerkgarantiewet (JWG; Guaranteed Jobs for Young People Act). For those between the ages of eighteen and twenty-one, the payment is not particularly generous. It is the same amount that their parents received as an AKW benefit before the child turned eighteen. The base AKW benefit in 1998 was ƒ449.51 per quarter.

The General Old Age Pensions Act

The AOW replaced the Drees Emergency Act in 1957. It is the basis for the Dutch Social Security system. Benefits begin at age sixty-five and are set at the minimum wage level. Pension payments were individualized in 1985 so that even nonworking spouses are awarded a pension. About 60% of the Dutch think that the AOW has passed its prime and are beginning to look at what they need to do to finance their own retirements.

The Unemployment Benefits Act

The WW was introduced in 1949. When the program first began, benefits were set at 80% of the last salary/wage that the worker earned, but climbing unemployment and spiraling wages put an end to that in the eighties. Payments now are made to those who have worked at least twenty-six of the thirty-nine weeks before they lost their job. For six months, benefits are set at 70% of the minimum wage, unless the recipient has worked in four out of the last five years, in which case they can receive 70% of the last salary/wage that they earned, with a maximum of the income boundary. For those who have worked longer, benefits can continue longer, to a maximum—with forty years' work credit—of five years.

The General Survivors Pension Act

The ANW replaced the 1959 Algemene Weduwen en Wezenwet (General Widows and Orphans Benefits Act) on July 1, 1996. The ANW provides a pension for widows, widowers, surviving children under eighteen, and ex-spouses receiving alimony. For surviving spouses without children, the ANW pays 70% of the net minimum wage. Surviving spouses with children receive an additional 20% of the net minimum wage for the children. For ex-spouses, benefits are limited to the amount of alimony. For widows, payments terminate upon remarriage, upon cohabitation with a new partner, or upon reaching the age of sixty-five, when they qualify for AOW benefits. To reduce costs, beginning on January 1, 1998, the government introduced means testing. ANW benefits are reduced if the survivor earns wages or salary.

The General Children's Benefit Act

The AKW was introduced in 1962, amending the earlier 1939 act, under which benefits had been limited only to the children of those who were employed. It provides quarterly payments to parents and others who are bringing up children. Benefits continue until the child reaches age eighteen. At that time, the child either becomes eligible for a scholarship, goes to work, or becomes eligible for ABW benefits.

In 1995, the AKW was amended. The amount of the benefits still depends on the age of the child, but family size is no longer a factor in the size of the payment. The quarterly base amount of the AKW in 1998 was ƒ449.51. For children born after January 1, 1995, those birth to six receive 70% of the base amount, those aged seven to twelve receive 85%, and those from thirteen to eighteen receive 100%. The parents of children born before October 2, 1994, continue to receive AKW benefits on the old scale: birth to six years get 70% of the base amount, seven to twelve, 100%, and thirteen to seventeen, 130% (ƒ584.36).

The Health Insurance Act

The ZFW was introduced in 1964. Ziekenfonds (Medicare) is the state health insurance program for those whose income falls below the inflation-adjusted *loongrens* of ƒ62,200 before taxes per year (in 1998). Enrollment is compulsory for everyone whose salary falls below this boundary. Those who have an income higher than the limit have to buy their health insurance from a private insurer. Ziekenfonds premiums are automatically deducted from the individual's salary or ABW benefits. The average premium for an adult was ƒ230 per year (in 1997).

Ziekenfonds enrollment provides for basic health care, but benefits are being reduced to cut costs. The introduction of co-payments for services occurred in 1997. Only visits to the family physician, dentist, and maternity services are excepted. Co-payments are 20% of the service cost, up to a yearly maximum of ƒ100. The total expected savings for 1997 were ƒ110 million.

The number of covered services has been gradually reduced to keep costs low. The state offers Ziekenfonds enrollees a supplemental package of benefits at an extra cost to cover services that are no longer part of the Ziekenfonds package.

The General Act on Exceptional Medical Costs

The AWBZ was introduced in 1967. It insures against medical costs that are not covered under the compulsory state health insurance program or a private health insurance policy. This includes hospital care after one full year of hospitalization, plus various kinds of rehabilitation, outpatient, and mental health services. Co-payments for those confined to an institution or a nursing home were capped at ƒ1,350 and ƒ2,220, respectively (in 1996).

The Disability Benefits Act

The WAO was introduced in 1967. It makes payments to workers who become disabled and are unable to work for more than a year. The amount of a WAO benefit depends on the degree of the disability (at least 15%) and the employee's age. Originally, WAO payments continued until age sixty-five, when the recipient was moved to the AOW. Beginning on August 1, 1993, the WAO benefit has to be recertified every five years. Persons who were already receiving WAO benefits on July 31, 1993, were grandfathered under the old program. The AAW is the same program for the self-employed and those who become disabled at an early age, before they begin to work. It was introduced in 1976.

When the WAO was first enacted, benefits were set at 80% of the last salary/wage that the worker earned. In 1987, they were reduced to 70% as an economy measure. In 1994, the benefit for those permanently disabled was set at the minimum wage plus 2% of the difference between the minimum wage and the last salary/wage that the worker earned for each year that the worker was older than fifteen when the WAO benefit took effect.

Upon the program's inception, it was predicted that the number of persons receiving benefits under the WAO would only rise to between 150,000 and 200,000. Within four years, the number of recipients was above 200,000 and still growing. When the AAW was introduced in 1976, the number of recipients climbed to 500,000. By 1988, it was over 800,000 and still climbing. One reason behind this was that the WAO was being used as an early retirement program to eliminate older employees from the workforce.

The Sickness Benefits Act

The Ziektewet (ZW) of 1967 was the forerunner to the WULBZ. It made payments to those who were too ill to work or were disabled. Benefits were set at 70% of the last salary/wage earned, but not less than the minimum wage. On March 1, 1997, the government shifted ZW payments—except in cases of pregnancy and maternity—to employers under the WULBZ. Now employers have to pay sick or disabled workers 70% of the last salary/wage that they earned for a maximum of one year. (Some politicians are discussing making it three years.) At the end of the year, the worker qualifies for the WAO program. The government still covers maternity leave under the ZW. The benefit is sixteen weeks at 100% pay.

The unforeseen side effect of the shift of responsibility from the government to the employer has been a tendency for employers not to hire people with health problems. Employers do not want to take the chance of having to pay someone to be sick. When the government carried the risk, it was shared across the whole of the workforce. Now that the employers carry the risk directly, they can see a clearly tangible cost involved in hiring people who are likely to be out of work a lot with health problems. The result for the government is that people with health problems are having trouble finding work, so they end up drawing some other kind of benefit and do not pay social insurance premiums because they do not work.

The change from the ZW to the WULBZ has also prompted a huge political debate over the proposal from the Stichting van de Arbeid (Association of Labor) to give priority health care to those who are employed. The Dutch health-care system does not operate on free-market principles, but it is a planned system. This results in waiting lists for certain services, which the Association of Labor wants to avoid for its members.

In this case, time really is money while an employee is waiting for a medical service that will return him or her to work. Under the WULBZ, the employer has to continue to pay the employee's salary while the employee waits for the service. The employers' view of the proposal is that they want to control this new cost that has been imposed upon them. Public reaction to the proposal has been devastating. The public does not seem to mind waiting for medical services, but the decision of who gets treated first should be a medical, not a political or economic, one.

Toeslagenwet (Supplementary Benefits Act)

This act provides supplemental benefits to WW, ZW, or AAW/WAO recipients, if their benefit is less than the minimum guaranteed income.

Leuke Dingen

Finally, the welfare system of Holland offers Leuke dingen, the "Fun Things" supplement for people who live at the minimum income level for a year or more. The Dutch recognize that a minimum income is only just adequate for existence, but existence does not necessarily permit you to have a life. Thus the Fun Things supplement covers the actual cost of cultural, educational, and recreational activities, such as joining a music or theater group or a choir, joining a sports club or a hobby association, taking a course, paying the membership fees for a library or buying a year's museum pass, going to a play, subscribing to a magazine, and so forth. Those who participate are reimbursed 100% for their costs up to a maximum of ƒ125 per year, per person.

NOTE

1. Quoted in G. Puchinger, *Nederlandse Minister-Presidenten van de twintigste eeuw* (Dutch Prime Ministers of the Twentieth Century) (Amsterdam: Sijthoff, 1984), pp. 217–218.

12

The New Society:
The Pillars Collapse

THE ELECTRONIC MEDIA

Radio

The first radio broadcast in Holland was on November 6, 1919, making Holland the first country in the world to have scheduled radio broadcasts. Scheduled radio broadcasting did not begin in America until 1920. In Germany and the United Kingdom, it was 1922. In the decade that followed, radio developed along the lines of the print media. Each pillar of society developed its own source of radio programming content.

Initially, there was only one radio station, located in Hilversum. In 1924, the Protestants established the Nederlandsche Christelijke Radio Vereeniging (NCRV; The Dutch Christian Radio Association) to get airtime to broadcast religious programs one night a week. The Catholics could not lag behind and thus established the Katholieke Radio Omroep (KRO; Catholic Broadcast Radio). The socialists followed in 1925 with the Vereeniging van Arbeiders Radio Amateurs (VARA; Association of Labor Radio Amateurs). In 1926, the liberal Protestants started the Vrijzinnig Protestantse Radio Omroep (VPRO; Liberal Protestant Broadcast Radio). In 1928, the KRO and the NCRV set up their own transmitter in Huizen. The airtime that became available on the Hilversum station was taken over by the Algemene Vereeniging Radio Omroep (AVRO; General Association of Broadcast Radio), which did not represent any particular religious or social order.

The first broadcast law was passed in 1930. At that time, there were forty to fifty hours of airtime per week available on the two transmitters. All the airtime was divided into five parts. The NCRV and the KRO got to keep their transmitter, AVRO and VARA got equal time on the Hilversum transmitter, and the VPRO got a smaller, fixed amount of airtime on the Hilversum station as well.

After World War II, radio reached the peak of its popularity. By 1949, there were 1,337,000 radios in Holland. As radio's popularity increased, the programming presented by the broadcast associations became less didactic and more popular. Radio, however, was soon replaced by television.

Television

The first television broadcast in Holland was on October 2, 1951. It was not until 1960, however, that television could be seen all over the country. The millionth television set was bought in 1961. In 1962, there were only thirty hours per week of television airtime, but there were two million licensed sets. It was October 1964 before a second channel was added. The third television channel was not added until 1988.

Dutch television was organized along the lines of Dutch broadcast radio. Airtime was made available to the broadcasting associations (the NCRV, KRO, VARA, VPRO, and AVRO) based on the number of members that each association had. There was one key difference, though: People who had always turned off the radio as soon as "our" program was over stayed tuned to the television no matter whose program it was. Writing for the *NRC*, Raymond van den Boogaard recalls how his grandfather watched television: from the test pattern to sign-off. When a politician or priest or pastor who represented another political view than the one his grandfather held came on the screen, his grandfather would make a gesture with his hand as if he wanted to sweep the speaker from the screen. But the set remained on.

This pattern was repeated in most Dutch households. That meant that the Dutch got to know more and more about one another's views and ideas, and the pillars became weaker. Today, while each association is still connected to its past constituency through its name and history, the connection is not as strong as it used to be, because each has moderated the views expressed in its content to reach a larger audience to get more airtime.

In 1989, commercial broadcasters operating from Luxembourg took their place alongside the noncommercial public channels. In 1992, they were joined by domestic commercial broadcasters. Today, there are two dominant market leaders. The noncommercial public channels (NL1, NL2, and NL3) have a budget of over 1.1 billion guilders. The Holland Media Group—a commercial broadcaster (RTL4, RTL5, and Veronica)— does well over 700 million guilders' worth of business. These two media giants hold a combined market share of about 80%. They keep each other in balance, each holding about a 40% share. The remainder of the market is split between the three smaller channels—SBS6, TMF, and TV10—and home video, which has a larger market share (6.2%) than both SBS6 (5.4%) and RTL5 (5.1%).

The introduction of commercial television channels sped up the erosion of the ideological base of the broadcast associations. Revenues from advertisements on noncommercial public television dropped as the commercial broadcasters took ever-larger market shares of the viewing audience with their more popular, less ideological programming. To counter this process, the broadcasting associations had to further popularize their programming and abandon their ideological underpinnings.

Two processes led to a convergence of political and religious views and the slow dissolution of the pillars: the programming associations' moderation of their ideological content; and the tendency to watch everything that was on television. Society in Holland today is more easily characterized by a polarization of conservatives and liberals, just as in the United States or the United Kingdom.

The pillars were, however, the mainstay of the Church's authority in Holland. As television dissolved the pillars, it also took over the Church's moral authority. In an editorial in the *NRC*, Herman Wigbold, the former editor in chief of *Het Vrije Volk* (The Free People) characterizes the impact of television in modern-day Holland as being the same as the Church had before the advent of radio and television: "Then the Church set the values that people had to abide by, and those who did not abide by them were sinners. Now for many, television is the point of reference."

WOMEN AND THE FAMILY

During the interwar years, after women's suffrage had been introduced, progress on women's rights slowed and was brought to a standstill in the Depression. In 1934, the government prohibited women who were living with a man from holding a civil service position. In 1935, marriage became a cause to fire a woman from a civil service position. In

1937, a draft bill was presented to the States-General that would have prohibited women from taking any paying job outside the family. The bill did not pass, but it shows the intensity of the feelings about working women at the time.

In the postwar period, the political treatment of the family in Holland was for a long time dominated by a decision made in 1947 to set the minimum wage at a level that would support a married man and his family (a wife and two children under sixteen). In 1950, the Katholieke Arbeiders Beweging (Catholic Trade Union) ran an advertising campaign with the slogan "Mother in the family and not in the factory!" This "breadwinner" system, which freed married women from the necessity of taking a paying job, formed the basis for many of the decisions made in reconstructing Dutch society after World War II. Still today, women who have never had paying jobs but who have always been wives and mothers get pensions of their own. The schedule of the Dutch school day is set up so that only a nonworking mother can get her children back and forth to school twice each day as the schedule demands. Dutch schoolchildren go home for lunch, and their mothers come and get them.

The fifties, nevertheless, marked a change in the political tide in favor of women. In 1953, Anna de Waal (1906–1981), was appointed the first female state secretary of education, arts, and sciences. In 1956, she was followed by Marga Klompé (1912–1986), who became the first minister of social services. The following year, the prohibition on married women in the civil service was abolished; 1957 was also the year in which married women gained the legal right to conclude contracts. By 1990, affirmative action had brought the number of women to 26.3% of the civil service.

Nowhere in Europe was the postwar baby boom as big or as long lasting as in Holland. Birth statistics shot up immediately after World War II and stayed up for almost twenty years. In the early sixties, the average number of children per woman was 3.2—the highest in Europe, except in strictly Catholic Ireland. The high birthrate was a result of religious pillarization. When the pillars fell apart in the sixties, the birthrate dropped like a rock. By 1985, the average number of children per woman had fallen to 1.5. This was one of the sharpest drops in the birthrate anywhere. At present, the average age at which Dutch women have their first child is 28.6, the highest in the world.

In the late sixties, the changing tide turned into a wave. This was the beginning of the period known as the "second wave" of women's emancipation. The first wave was the period around the turn of the century, which saw Queen Wilhelmina ascend to the throne in 1898 as the first woman head of state in Holland. It was during this period that Wilhelmina Drucker (1847–1925), Alleta Jacobs (1849–1929), Betsy Perk (1833–1906), and Mina Kruseman (1839–1922) were active, promoting not only voting rights, but also women's admission to high school, universities, and the States-General. This wave crested as World War I ended. The constitutional change of 1917, which granted universal suffrage to men, removed the legal barriers to votes for women, but women did not actually get the vote until 1922. In 1918, Suze Groeneweg (1875–1940) became the first woman member of Parliament, where she served until 1937.

The beginning of the second wave of women's emancipation was marked by an article written by J. Kool-Smit (1933–1981) titled "Het onbehagen bij de vrouw" (Woman's Discomfort), which was published in *De Gids* (The Guide) in 1967. In 1968, the action group Man, Woman, Society was set up with the goal of achieving equal rights for women. In 1969, the organization De Dolle Mina (Crazy Mina) was founded. With the slogan *"Baas in eigen buik"* (The boss of your own belly), this group advocated birth control and abortion rights. The group's showy actions were intended to focus public awareness on women's issues, and indeed they gained both national and international attention. After 1972, most of De Dolle Mina's members left the organization to join the mainstream political parties. Since 1973, there has not been even one cabinet without at least one woman in it. In 1995, the cabinet had four women ministers and five women state secretaries. In 1975, the government began making money available to finance projects for and by women. In 1981, the Emancipation Council was set up to advise the government on women's rights.

Despite the changes in the position of women in Holland, less than 30% of the populace feels that women must work to contribute to the family's income. This is much lower than the average in Europe, where 69% think that a woman has to work to contribute to the family's income. Indeed, this notion—that women need to work to help support the family—is coming under attack as new sociological studies show the negative effects of growing up in day care and as calls are being heard for children to be raised at home. The CDA is the primary proponent of "familyism," as the philosophical counterweight to "extreme" individualism, economism, and feminism that form the basis for the social policies of the "purple" coalition of the VVD, D'66, and PvdA. In Holland, 40% of the women still support traditional family values and feel that their contribution to society as mothers is undervalued today.

In 1997, the Central Labor Bureau took women off the list of the "problem" unemployed. That year, the number of women seeking employment for more than twelve hours per week fell 12% to 176,000. The

Ministry of Social Affairs credits this drop to its program of broader financial support for day care. Unemployment among women, however, is still higher than among men: 6.5% compared to 4.8%.

Nevertheless, the two-income family is gaining ground. The number of one-income and two-income households is about equal. Households with two children under sixteen and two incomes made up about one-fifth (ca. 1.3 million) of all the households in Holland in 1995. Their modal disposable income then was ƒ65,000.

MINORITY PROBLEMS

The problem of minorities was the issue most often named (52%) when the respondents to a 1994 poll of voters were asked to create a list of urgent political issues. Of those polled, 20% were in favor of a complete halt to the admittance of asylum seekers. When the respondents were given a list of six issues and asked to arrange them in order of importance, however, unemployment and crime became the most important issues.

While the responses to the two items would seem to contradict each other, unemployment and crime are minority issues. Minority unemployment was running at 21.9% in 1996, three times the unemployment rate among the ethnic Dutch. Minority youngsters take part in criminal activity—particularly drug trafficking—three to six times more often than ethnic Dutch youngsters in the same age group, according to a parliamentary report issued in 1997.

Many ethnic Dutch ignore or are unaware of the fact of high unemployment among minorities and concentrate instead on the idea that the minorities are taking jobs that the ethnic Dutch could have. Even though the mainstream media try to be politically correct in their crime coverage, the ethnic Dutch see press reports about minorities and crime or about state sponsorship of drug trafficking in the home countries of Holland's most populous minorities, and they generalize that most members of minorities are criminals. The international indictment of Desi Bouterse—the leader of the military coup in Surinam in 1980—for drug trafficking only served to increase this perception to the detriment of all the Surinamese living in Holland.

Holland's present minority problems are the result of immigration. The first wave of immigration was postcolonial. When Indonesia was finally declared independent, roughly 300,000 Eurasians were "repatriated" to Holland, a country that many of them had never seen before. After that, the flow of immigrants was more like a trickle than a wave. Highly skilled and well-educated immigrants came from the remaining colonies looking for a better life. At the same time, unskilled guest workers, who were not really immigrants but were only working in Holland "temporarily," added to the numbers of foreigners. The most recent wave followed the end of colonial rule in Surinam. When Surinam became independent, almost one-third ot its population emigrated to Holland.

Dutch expectations were then, and still are, that immigrants will assimilate completely into Dutch society. The earliest immigrants understood that they would be accepted by the ethnic Dutch only if they acted as Dutch as the Dutch. The integration of the immigrants from Indonesia into Dutch society is often recounted as a "success story," because they did just that.

While cultural differences between the ethnic Dutch and the Eurasians still occasionally lead to misunderstandings on both sides, most Eurasians are hardly considered minorities by the ethnic Dutch, nor does the government classify them as such. The Ministry of Internal Affairs lists the ethnic minorities in Holland as: Turks, Moroccans and other North Africans, Cape Verde Islanders, southern Europeans, Surinamese, Antilleans and Arubans, Moluccans, refugees, and asylum seekers.

The immigrants who came to Holland from Surinam before it became independent were well-educated Surinamese searching to improve their lives for themselves and their families. The parents of writer Ingrid Baal (1951–   )—a second-generation immigrant, born in Holland—were typical of this group. Her father was one of many Surinamese doctors who came to Holland during that time. In 1968, there were 168 Surinamese doctors practicing in Holland but only 150 in all of Surinam. Baal's parents made a clear choice that they would assimilate into Dutch society. Her father was thankful that he had the chance to come to Holland and never complained about the heavy mental price he and his wife had to pay for their better life. He was conscious that, if Holland had not colonized Surinam, he would never have had the status and position that he obtained in Holland. Their assimilation, like that of the Eurasians, can be considered a success from the Dutch point of view.

One of the main characters on the liberal Dutch television sitcom *Zeg 'ns aaa* (Say Aaah, Please) is typical for this type of immigrant. Dr. John Wijntak is a well-assimilated black doctor from Surinam. He is almost as Dutch as the whites on the show. The writers have done their best to have the minority characters—not just the Surinamese, but also the Turks and Moroccans—on the show play positive roles that break down the typical negative stereotypes of minorities. The roles are positive because the characters have been assimilated. Diversity is shown only by a slight foreign accent and some interesting but delicious food.

The wave of Surinamese immigrants that followed independence was different. It consisted primarily of people from the slightly less well-educated layers of society. "Assimilation" is a dirty word in the Surinamese community in the Bijlmer, a sprawling, high-rise apartment complex in southeast Amsterdam that is (in)famous as a ghetto filled with postindependence Surinamese immigrants. Surinamese who have made it in Dutch society, like Patricia Remak—the first black VVD alderman in Holland—are ridiculed with the name "Bounty" (the name of a candy bar), because they are brown on the outside and white on the inside. The farther you are from the ghetto, however, the less strident the name-calling and the more recognition that assimilation is the key to success in their adopted country.

Guest workers began arriving in Holland in the forties and fifties, when industries in Western Europe were having trouble finding enough workers. They were recruited from southern Europe, primarily from Italy, the former Yugoslavia, Spain, and Portugal, which had high unemployment. These guest workers were meant to be just that: guests. It was never expected that they would remain in Holland, and no thought was given to their assimilation into society. Most of this first group did, in fact, return to their home countries.

In the sixties, the European economy improved. Competition for guests workers increased among the Western European countries, and the employment situation improved in the home countries of the original guest workers. Holland found itself forced to recruit guest workers from farther afield. In 1964, Holland concluded an official agreement on recruiting guest workers with Turkey. An agreement with Morocco followed in 1969. The expectation was still that these workers would return home. The official view was that heavily overpopulated Holland could not afford to become a host country for immigrants.

Guest-worker recruitment hit its high point in 1970 and 1971. It continued after that, despite climbing unemployment among the ethnic Dutch, brought on by the economic downturn marked by the oil crisis of 1973. The Dutch may have been out of work, but not enough of them were willing to do the heavy and dirty jobs that the guest workers took.

In the seventies and eighties, more and more guest workers decided to stay in Holland rather than return to their home country. As they stayed longer, they brought their families to Holland to join them. It was not until the early eighties, however, that the Dutch government finally recognized the fact that the guest workers had turned into immigrants. Before that, there had been talk of setting a two-year limit on guest-worker stays to ensure that they stayed only temporarily, but it had never become policy.

There had, likewise, never been a policy on helping the guest workers assimilate into Dutch society. There had been no need to formulate one. The guest workers were only in Holland temporarily, and the previous waves of immigrants, who had come from the old colonies, all spoke Dutch and were at least somewhat familiar with Dutch customs. Despite improving efforts on the part of the government to help former guest workers—now immigrants—assimilate, the Turkish and Moroccan minorities in Holland remain more separate than integrated.

Dutch efforts to assimilate former guest workers and the postindependence wave of Surinamese immigrants, are hampered by modern technology. In the modern age, immigrants have the choice of living physically in one country and mentally in another. It was not all that long ago, though, that the second of the two choices did not exist. There were no airplanes for quick trips, or inexpensive phone connections, or e-mail for talking with loved ones, or satellite television for keeping up with developments in your "mental" home. Before these technologies came on the scene, the physical and mental distances that needed to be overcome in order to live in two places were too great.

Ingrid Baal talks about the impact on her parents of not being able to attend their parents' (her grandparents') funerals. For them, just as for the Eurasian repatriates from Indonesia, there was no turning back. The gap was not as wide as it was for emigrants to the New World in the seventeenth century, but they had to make a mental break with the old country and assimilate in their new home country. There was no other choice.

Living in an immigrant ghetto provided a sense of community for the newcomers, but staying in the ghetto was not the path to success; assimilating was. Before airplanes and satellites, these ghettos fell apart by the second or third generation. Now they are longer lived, as second- and third-generation Turkish and Moroccan immigrants attend ethnic schools (called "black schools" by the ethnic Dutch) and marry partners arranged for them from the old country. The composition of the ghettos is nevertheless changing. It is primarily the second- and third-generation males who remain in the ghettos and enter arranged marriages with partners from their home country. The second- and third-generation females are leaving to gain the status they see Dutch women hold, one that women in the ghetto and the old country do not.

The modern immigrants to Holland can now catch a plane to go home for the type of family events that Baal's parents missed. They can watch television direct via satellite and keep up with events in their mental home, ignoring things in their host country. Baal was pleased that her parents made the choice to live in Holland both mentally and physically.

It saved her from what she describes as a "schizophrenic situation . . . physically and mentally commuting between the Netherlands and [in her case] Surinam,"[1] a situation in which many modern immigrants find themselves.

The same idea was presented in an interview with a group of young Turks that appeared in *Het Parool*—a socialist newspaper—in April 1997. Necati, twenty-one years old, feels that young Turks get into trouble because they have fallen into a crack between the Dutch culture and the Turkish culture and cannot choose one or the other: "Guys who have had a good Turkish upbringing at home are OK. You have to know where you belong. I belong in the Turkish culture." All five of the young men interviewed would just as soon go back to Turkey, but they realize that it is not realistic. Their jobs and their friends are in Holland.

The Moroccans say the same thing. "When you are brought up in the old tradition, it is hard to survive in Amsterdam," says Amin El Mouaden, the coordinator of a Moroccan young people's center in Amsterdam. Fatima, whose father tried to marry her off on her last trip to Morocco, clearly suffers from the cultural schizophrenia from which Baal's parents saved their daughter. "We are living a lie now. You always have to lie and be deceitful when you are home," Fatima says. "I'm not going to do that to my children."[2]

This is the key to Holland's current minority problems. The Dutch still expect people who choose to come to their country to assimilate, but the immigrants are remaining foreigners in their adopted country. The Eurasians, who were returned to Holland against their will, had a right to contest assimilation as a condition of acceptance, but most did not. The other new immigrants came to Holland by choice, and the Dutch do not understand why they do not want to pay the price of admission, like the older immigrants did. The Dutch do not want to change their whole lifestyle just to be accommodating to the people who came to Holland by choice. They still expect the newcomers to take on more Dutch habits and customs than they keep from their foreign homelands.

AGE DISCRIMINATION

From the 1980s, when postwar unemployment reached its peak, until 1994, older (read: past forty) Dutch employees were always the first to be shown the door during downsizings, "right-sizings," and reorganizations. It was in 1994 that the older-employee guidelines, which had permitted this, were abolished. The reasoning behind establishing the guidelines in the eighties was that if a younger employee was let go, then he or she would remain unemployed for a very long time, with little prospect of finding a new job. The same was true of older workers. Most of them would not ever return to the workforce. It was felt, however, that they had already worked most of their lives and had earned the right to stop working.

There was little resistance to the guidelines for a number of reasons. The workers who were being let go were supported by the Dutch welfare safety net, made up of alphabet-soup names like VUT (Vervroegde Uit-treding [Early Retirement]), WW, and WAO, which made it possible for older workers to stop working with little or no impact on their standard of living. The people being let go were the generation of the postwar reconstruction era. They felt themselves responsible for the economic success of postwar Holland, which they had worked hard to achieve. The offer of early retirement, made possible through the liberal VUT, WW, and WAO rules, was viewed as a reward for their efforts. Early retirement was also presented as a way for them to give younger workers a chance. Cooperation and compromise have long been a hallmark of Dutch society, and this approach was a typical Dutch consensus solution. It was a way out of the unemployment crisis.

The employers supported the older-worker guidelines, because younger workers are less expensive and are more productive. This reasoning was first applied to blue-collar jobs but soon came to affect the whole job market. Employers ignored the value of experience, the loyalty to the firm, and the cost of training replacements. Advertisements for jobs all stated age ceilings (most often in the twenties). Discrimination against older workers became part of the corporate culture. While the guidelines were abolished in 1994, change is slow in coming. The ads may not carry age ceilings anymore, but older workers still have more difficulty finding a job than younger workers.

Nothing demonstrates the continuing nature of this problem more clearly than the reaction to a 1997 television interview with Crown Prince William Alexander. In this interview, the prince said that he is in no hurry to succeed his mother on the throne, because "she is in the prime of her life." Many commentators reacted to this statement, pointing out how difficult it is for people over fifty-five to find a job. Queen Beatrix turned sixty in January 1998.

The abolition of the older-worker guidelines in 1994 came about because the government and employers realized how much the program actually cost. The guidelines had done what they had been intended to do. Only about 25% of those over fifty-five work in Holland. To put this in perspective, in France, about 33% of those over fifty-five work. In the

United States and the United Kingdom, it is about 50%. In Sweden and Japan, it is 66%. The percentage of Dutch workers over fifty-five is one of the lowest in the world.

Costs for keeping these older workers out of the job market will continue to climb until the year 2030, when the last of the Dutch baby boomers enter retirement and the number of people retiring begins to decline. The Dutch social safety net is a pay-as-you-go system. The demographics that mean fewer people will be retiring after 2030 also mean that there will be fewer active workers to pay for those retirees. This is not only a problem for the WAO, the VUT, and the WW; it is a problem for the Dutch health-care system as well.

The government is not trying to get those who took early retirement to return to the workforce. It recognizes the fact that most of them will never work again. (Those over 57.5 do not have to look for work to qualify for WW benefits.) The government is instead aiming at those aged between thirty-five and forty-five. For those in this age group, retirement at fifty-five can no longer be as commonplace an occurrence as it was for those who are in their fifties now. The goal of government policy is to return to the employment levels of the early seventies, when as many employees in the fifty-five to sixty-five age group worked as did in the forty-five to fifty-five age group.

The political discussion that is now taking place in the media is helping to change corporate attitudes, by pointing out the business advantages of older workers: experience, loyalty, continuity. It is also advancing another typical Dutch consensus solution: having older workers switch to part-time employment instead of retiring. The results of this change are that their cost to the firm decreases, they continue to pay into the Dutch welfare system, and their experience, loyalty, and sense of corporate culture are preserved in the workplace.

Holland is an international leader in part-time work. Part-time status is not, however, the same in Holland as it is in the United States. In Holland, part-time workers have benefits and accumulate credit toward retirement.

DRUG POLICY

The total cost of the drug problem to the Dutch economy is approximately ƒ1.44 billion per year. This consists of approximately ƒ160 million spent on the treatment of addicts, plus about ƒ270 million for combating drug trafficking and about ƒ370 million on combating crimes (primarily against property) committed by addicts. Property losses from addict crime add about another ƒ640 million to the cost. In addition, in the last decade, the number of prison cells in Holland has grown from 5,000 to over 12,000, due, in large part, to the increasing number of prison terms being handed down for drug trafficking.

Dutch drug policy treats the issue as a health problem rather than as a moral one. The Dutch approach is best characterized as "harm reduction" or "damage control." Drug consumption is not illegal in Holland. Drug use, instead, is treated as a health issue, stressing prevention and treatment. The almost ƒ160 million that Holland spends on the treatment of addicts includes both in- and outpatient treatment, as well as methadone maintenance and needle exchanges. The definition of drug use as a health issue instead of a legal one is reflected in the distinction between "hard" drugs (XTC, heroin, and cocaine)—"drugs presenting unacceptable risk"—and "soft" drugs (hashish, marijuana). It is an evaluation of the health risks associated with the use of each type.

The possession, sale, transport, trafficking, and manufacture of narcotics, on the other hand, are illegal. In addressing this side of the problem, the differentiation between "hard" and "soft" drugs becomes a matter of enforcement priority. The Dutch do not have enough police resources to combat both classes of drugs equally; therefore, they have chosen to focus their domestic police resources on hard drugs. Combating international drug trafficking, however, rates the highest priority. Holland is a signatory of a number of international counternarcotics agreements and a member of the UN International Drug Control Program and the UN Commission on Narcotic Drugs.

It is the Dutch policy on soft drugs, however, that receives the most international attention. The tolerant Dutch soft drug policies are in conflict with the policies of total prohibition that exist in other countries such as the United States and Sweden. In Holland, while, de jure, the possession of user quantities of both hard and soft drugs is illegal, it is only a misdemeanor—not a felony as it is in many other countries—and is seldom prosecuted. The Dutch prefer treatment to imprisonment for addicts.

The Dutch policy of turning a "blind eye" to the open sale of soft drugs in so-called coffee shops is the primary target of international criticism. The Dutch view this policy as compartmentalizing hard and soft drug users from each other to prevent soft drug users from "stepping up" to hard drugs.

The Dutch recognize that in a certain phase of their lives, young adults will want to experiment with soft drugs. The de facto legalization of soft drug use makes this possible without forcing these young people into contact with the drug underworld, which is what would happen if both hard and soft drugs were treated equally. With soft drug sales essentially confined to coffee shops, the Dutch are able to regulate the market much the same way as they regulate prostitution and the sale of alcohol.

The success of the policy of harm reduction for drug use can be seen in the statistics for drug-related deaths. While precise statistics on the number of addicts are impossible to collect, especially in countries where drug use is illegal, statistics on the number of drug-related deaths are readily available and generally reliable. In 1993, a comparison of the number of drug-related deaths for seventeen industrialized countries placed Holland seventeenth, with two deaths per one million inhabitants. Switzerland led the list with fifty-three deaths per million. Denmark (forty deaths) and Luxembourg (thirty-five) took second and third place. The United States and the United Kingdom tied for fifth place, with twenty-four per million. France, the harshest European critic of Dutch drug policy, was fifteenth, with eight deaths per million inhabitants.

Dutch drug policy is under pressure both internationally and domestically. People in Holland are becoming tired of drug-related crimes against property and of the antisocial conduct of addicts. In some neighborhoods, the fabled Dutch consensus and tolerance, the foundation of Dutch drug policy, have broken down, and the inhabitants of the neighborhood have formed vigilante groups to run the addicts out of the area.

Soft drug coffee shops are also coming under pressure from neighborhood groups, primarily for the same reasons that bars selling alcohol are not welcomed everywhere, but also because they attract foreign drug tourists. In some communities, two-thirds of the sales of soft drugs made by coffee shops during the weekends are to foreigners. This is one of the reasons that Holland's neighboring countries are not pleased with the Dutch drug policy. Holland's neighbors, who have stricter drug policies, view soft drug coffee shops as a readily available source of illegal drugs for import into their countries.

Because border controls have been eliminated as a part of European integration, drug tourists run little risk of being stopped as they return home with their purchases. To accommodate their neighbors, however, the Dutch have lowered the amount of soft drugs that can be sold at one time to a single individual from 30 grams to 5 grams. This limit is aimed at reducing the amount of soft drugs that the tourists take back home with them.

The same geographic features that make Holland the "Gateway to Europe" for legitimate international trade also make it the gateway for illegitimate drug trafficking. Location is everything. Dutch police estimate that there are about 100 criminal organizations active in Holland, the majority of which are trafficking in drugs. The Dutch are actively engaged in combating them.

In describing the composition of these organizations, the Ministry of Health, Welfare, and Sport does its best to provide a politically correct formulation, avoiding the use of the pejorative word *allochtoon*, but the definition of the problem is nonetheless drawn along racial lines:

> Residents of foreign extraction, who have close contacts with criminal organizations in their countries of origin, are over-represented in criminal organizations that contribute to the trade in hard drugs. Organizations, which are made up chiefly of *autochtoons* [ethnic Dutch], are primarily active in the trade in soft drugs.

This fact does not do anything to improve Dutch race relations, but the carefully worded statement does show that the Dutch are well aware of the problem.

While Dutch drug policy is not entirely free of problems, it should not be dismissed out of hand on strictly dogmatic grounds. It is clearly worth a closer look for other countries, as the world community tries to come to grips with this thorny problem.

HOLLANDITIS

Pacifism, antimilitarism and neutrality have long been a part of Dutch history. Simon van Slingelandt (1664–1736), appointed the *raadpensionaris* (grand pensionary) of Holland in 1727, worked closely with Robert Walpole (1676–1745), the first de facto English prime minister, toward the goal of "European peace." T.M.C. Asser (1838–1913) was a proponent of compulsory arbitration as an alternative to armed resolution of international conflicts and was chief of the Dutch delegation to The Hague Peace Conferences of 1899 and 1907. For 125 years (1815–1940), Dutch foreign policy was one of neutrality.

Between the two world wars, in a time of economic austerity, when the government proposed to allocate funds for expansion of the fleet in 1923, the Sociaal-Democratische Arbeiderspartij in Nederland (SDAP; Social Democratic Workers' Party in the Netherlands) and the Nederlandsch Verbond van Vakvereenigingen (NVV; Dutch League of Trade Associations) organized massive demonstrations against the Vlootwet (Fleet Act). The act failed to pass by one vote, and the government fell as a result of it.

After World War II, in the fifties, communist-inspired peace protests—not just in Holland, but all over Europe—comprised one factor in the U.S. decision to implement the Marshall Plan. The Drees government sanctioned the placement of American nuclear weapons in Holland in 1957 without even a parliamentary debate on the matter. Nuclear weapons were cheaper, after all, than troops.

Until late in the sixties, Holland was a pillarized society, primarily concerned with rebuilding the economy. Dutch foreign and military policy were formed by the political elite without much media coverage or parliamentary and public debate. That changed when the baby boomers began to come of age and the pillars began to break down. Television brought the world into people's living rooms. Issues and decisions had to be explained and defended. They even became important for elections.

The changes of the sixties and seventies started with questions of the economy and domestic politics, and as those things changed, the foreign policy elite also found themselves dealing with public opinion. The questions of the Vietnam War, membership in NATO, and the stationing of nuclear weapons on Dutch soil were subjected to public debate that dominated the front pages of the Dutch and international press. Between 1979 and 1985, the debate took to the streets, and the U.S. historian and commentator Walter Laqueur (1921–   ) coined a name for it: Hollanditis.

In 1979, NATO decided to base cruise and Pershing II missiles in Europe. Holland's share was to be forty-eight Pershing IIs. The center-right government of Prime Minister van Agt at first agreed, but the decision was unpopular. In November 1982, a new center-right government was formed by Ruud Lubbers. In typical Dutch fashion, rather than confront the issue head-on, Lubbers—who supported deployment—put forth a number of compromise proposals. These included:

- accepting the missiles in installments to allow more time for negotiations between the Americans and the Soviets
- taking on other NATO tasks in exchange for not deploying the missiles
- starting construction of the missile bunkers without accepting the missiles themselves
- reducing the total number of missiles to be based in Holland

The prominence of the protest in the European media made Holland a test case for deployment. Antinuclear forces in other European countries watched Holland closely. If the Dutch could keep the missiles out, so could they. This greatly increased the international and domestic pressure on Dutch decision makers to resolve the issue.

Lubbers skillfully avoided a cabinet crisis on the issue in 1985 by offering to stop deployment if the Soviets would reduce the number of SS-20 missiles to 378. The offer successfully shifted the focus of attention away from NATO and the United States to the Soviet Union. When the Soviets ignored the offer, Lubbers was able to get the parliamentary support for deployment that he needed. The official Dutch acceptance of the missiles, which came just before President Ronald Reagan and Soviet leader Mikhail Gorbachev met in Geneva, undoubtedly strengthened the Americans' negotiating hand at the talks.

Hollanditis had an effect on domestic politics as well. The PvdA painted itself into a corner politically, trying to turn the issue of nuclear weapons to its advantage against the CDA. It declared that it would not take part in any cabinet so long as the American missiles were not categorically rejected or removed from Dutch territory. The PvdA's self-exile from government continued until Reagan and Gorbachev made the question a moot point by concluding the Intermediate Range Nuclear Missile Treaty in 1987.

After 1985, the peace movement in Holland lost its massive character. Subscriptions to the quarterly newsletter published by the Interkerkelijk Vredesberaad (IKV; Interfaith Peace Consultative Committee) peaked that year at 20,000. After that, the number of subscribers dropped sharply. Protest against Dutch participation in the Gulf War (1991)—especially when compared to protests in Germany—only served to demonstrate how marginalized the peace movement had become. So few protesters came out in Amsterdam that it did not even make the papers or the television news. In the post–Gulf War period, Dutch antiwar organizations complained that people are not interested in their issues, that people are not politically active, and that political ideals have fallen by the wayside.

It is not so much that the people have changed but that the issues have. Pax Christi (Peace of Christ)—one of the oldest, religious, antiwar organizations in Holland—has focused its efforts on helping refugees from the Sudan; on land-mine clearance and prohibition; on military cooperation in Europe; and on violence on television, in videos, in computer games, in music, and in toy weapons. The IKV supports sending Dutch troops to the former Yugoslavia as peacekeepers. Pax Christi and the IKV are organizing in the former Yugoslavia, trying to start a dialogue between the two sides to expand mutual understanding. They are also organizing aid programs in Holland and supporting asylum for Yugoslavs who refuse service in the armed forces.

The placement of U.S. nuclear missiles on Dutch soil made the Dutch targets for a preemptive or a counterstrike. That got people's attention. The new issues are nebulous and far from home, and the government handles them better. Hollanditis is not cured, however; it is just in remission. Pacifism, antimilitarism, and neutrality are still part of the Dutch character.

NOTES

1. Ischa Meijer, "Het tussentijdse uitstellen" (The Intermediate Postponement), *Het Parool* (October 22, 1993): 15.

2. Frans Bosman, "Slachtoffers tegen wil en dank" (Victims Whether They Want To Be or Not), *Het Parool* (April 19, 1997): 22–23.

13

The New Post–Cold War World

THE MONARCHY

The word "royalty" with all the trivialities of sex and money that have become attached to it in English, hardly seems to apply to the present Dutch royal family. There have, of course, been scandals like the time that Prince Bernhard (the present queen's father) was involved in the Lockheed bribery scandal, but nothing on the order of the Windsors. In Dutch, the word for royal is *koninklijk* (kingly), and it is full of pomp and circumstance. Every year on the third Tuesday in September, the queen rides in a golden coach drawn by horses to deliver her speech at the opening of the States-General. This carefully choreographed anachronism reminds the public (perhaps only subconsciously) that the queen's right to rule stems from another time that—for most—has the feeling of a glorious myth rather than the feeling of history.

Maintaining this sense of glamor and pomp for the subjects of the Kingdom of the Netherlands is also part and parcel of the job of being the royal family. It is indeed a family business. Once per quarter, the Dutch royals have a family business meeting to discuss the public role and duties of each. The illusion that the royal family presents to its subjects is part of what makes the monarchy work in Holland. Foreigners have trouble understanding this sometimes, because the power of a kingly image can be fully felt by only the people who grow up with it. Even though the media plays a key part in projecting the royal image to the public, they also have the power to destroy it. That is why the Dutch royal family keeps the press at a distance. One cannot be "on duty" all the time; and one has to have some time to call one's own. Still, compared to the Windsors, Beatrix is quite outgoing.

The queen keeps a close watch on what appears in the press. An interview with Crown Prince William Alexander for the *NRC*, for example, could not be published in 1995, because the queen wanted parts of it rewritten. Similarly, a 1997 television interview with the Crown Prince, conducted by Paul Witteman, had 12 seconds cut out of it, and after it had been broadcast, the producer was prohibited by the Rijksvoorlichtingsdienst (State Information Office) from making copies available to the public. In addition, all the Web sites with the full text of the interview were forced to remove their content.

The year 1998 marked the eighteenth anniversary of Queen Beatrix's ascension to the throne. When she took over from her mother, she brought her own style of royal rule with her. The Queen Mother (Juliana) had been seen as the mother of her country. Beatrix introduced a new businesslike atmosphere. She is a perfectionist with a no-nonsense style of leadership, an exceptional memory, and seemingly endless reserves of energy.

In trying to come to grips with the queen's duties, the description of the rights of a constitutional monarch given in 1867 by the English writer Walter Bagehot (1826–1877) is often quoted in the Dutch media: "the right to be consulted, the right to encourage and the right to warn."[1] The journalist Harry van Wijnen puts it in a more modern perspective: Her job is to be "a constitutional counterweight to the government . . . really nothing more than a live-in shadow government."[2] While the shadow government in England is formed by the opposition party, in Holland, no matter which party is in power, the shadow government is always the same. Prime Minister Wim Kok, with whom the queen meets every Monday to discuss the current issues, says that she knows the limits of her power but takes "full advantage of the possibilities and responsibilities that she has."[3]

When the queen meets with a minister, she is well informed on the issues, and the minister had better be too. Former Prime Minister van Agt, who served both Queen Juliana and Queen Beatrix, recalls that "tough questions—if you did not have all the data at hand—could not be avoided in a fog of words. Because both were not only quick-minded, but had a phenomenal memory besides."[4] Queen Beatrix takes copious notes and draws on them in subsequent discussions, reminding her interlocutor of what was said before, sometimes even several years earlier.

She really does read all the reports and decision papers that she gets. She writes notes in the margins and compiles long lists of questions. When a minister comes to discuss a major or controversial issue with the queen, he can expect questions like: "Have you considered this possibility?" "Have you already weighed this aspect of the issue in your decision?" "Would you take a closer look at that?" "Asking questions, endlessly asking questions. That is her weapon," says a politician who regularly visits Huis ten Bosch (the royal palace), but who would only speak to reporters about the queen on the condition that he remain anonymous because of the strict control of all information about the royal family going to the press.

Compared to her mother, Queen Juliana (1909–   ) who ruled from 1948 until 1980, Queen Beatrix is much more aloof, but this has not affected her popularity. Polls still show that support for the monarchy is as great as ever. A 1998 poll, for example, showed that over 66% of the populace believes that Holland will still be a monarchy fifty years from now. An opinion poll in 1997 found that two out of three of the Dutch think that Queen Beatrix should abdicate in favor of her son, Prince William Alexander, when she reaches retirement age. The queen will be sixty-five in 2003. If, however, Beatrix waits until age seventy-one to retire, as her mother did, William Alexander has a longer wait in store. He says he is ready to take on the job but does not mind waiting.

In the Witteman interview, which some commentators described as the crown prince's comprehensive examination for his degree in kingsmanship, William Alexander said that, as he prepares to become king, he wants to model himself on King William I (1772–1843), "the Merchant King," with his spirit of commercial enterprise, who strove to improve the welfare of Holland. When Witteman asked him with which of the three most recent queens he felt more affinity—"Wilhelmina, the strong stateswoman, Juliana, the social mother, or Beatrix, the perfect manager"—his answer was, "More with my grandmother." The change in style, when William Alexander becomes William IV, will be interesting to watch.

William Alexander is as yet unmarried, and his choice of a bride is the cause of considerable speculation in the press. Not only will the story of a royal romance and the glamor of a royal wedding sell newspapers and television commercials, but they are matters of state. William Alexander's choice has to be approved by the States-General. Once he makes his choice, however, it will be final, as he said in his interview with Witteman. If the States-General does not approve of her, then he will abdicate his right to the throne. "It is a fundamental decision. You can't change your mind after you've made it up," said the prince. At the same time, he is clearly aware that his wife will be taking on a job that brings with it responsibilities and costs: "I expect my eventual wife to make a huge effort in a job that is new for her. She will also have to give up a gigantic part of her private life." He has learned the lesson of Charles and Diana.

The majority of the Dutch think that he should follow his heart, and public opinion will undoubtedly have the same effect on the States-General in William Alexander's case as it did when Beatrix announced her betrothal to a German—still a very sensitive issue only twenty years after the end of the war—and over 75% of the populace supported her choice to the chagrin of certain members of the government. The States-General can hardly expect the crown prince to allow them to form a commission to interview candidates for the "job" of queen. While arranged marriages of political convenience were the custom in royal families in times past, they hardly seem appropriate in the twenty-first century.

THE ARMED FORCES

The New Mission

The end of the Cold War brought on a new era in the defense policy arena. The Dutch, always quick to disarm after a war, immediately cashed in their peace dividend and began to reduce the size of the armed forces. No longer was the main threat to security a single, readily identifiable enemy. After the Cold War, the threat came from multiple, nebulous "hot spots" around the globe. To counter this new threat, Dutch politicians gave the military a new dual mission: (1) defense of the Dutch homeland and of the territory of Holland's NATO allies; and (2) crisis prevention and control (i.e., peacekeeping).

Budget and manpower cuts, on the one hand, and a new dual mission, on the other, have caused considerable cultural and organizational change in the Dutch military. The discrepancy between the military's assigned missions and the resources available to accomplish them is beginning to show through and is prompting considerable political debate. This is further complicated by NATO expansion to the East, which is adding even more requirements to the military's already full, smaller plate.

The new dual mission has shifted the emphasis in training for Dutch military officers. Now, in addition to being officers and tacticians, they

also have to be diplomats. Crisis prevention and control operations require that the military not only be ready to fight, but also that it assist in:

- monitoring arms build-downs and troop demobilizations
- clearing land mines
- protecting and resettling refugees
- economic reconstruction
- humanitarian aid
- preparing for elections
- restoring national governing bodies

These tasks require extensive cooperation with both governmental and nongovernmental civilian organizations, which means that today's officers need skills that were not previously taught at military schools.

The political decision to commit Dutch troops to action has, consequently, also become more complex. The issue is no longer one of immediate national survival in the face of a direct enemy attack on Holland: fight or surrender? It is now a question of an indirect attack on long-term peace and security in the region: How will this situation affect Holland six months from now? A year from now? Will it overflow into a widerspread conflict?

In typical Dutch fashion, the decision process has been well delineated in a set of rules. It weighs the political issues against military considerations. Politically, the operation will be approved, if it supports the maintenance of international peace and security; advocates the maintenance of norms of international law; defends Dutch or European interests or the interest of alliances, like NATO, of which Holland is a member; and if it is a multilateral action. Militarily, the operation has to meet certain requirements:

- achievable political and military objectives
- widespread support among both politicians and society as a whole
- a clear command structure
- clear rules of engagement
- an acceptable risk factor
- financing

As with every set of Dutch rules, there are always exceptions. The Dutch are still debating whether the political considerations outweighed the military ones in the decision to commit Dutch troops to United Nations (UN) peacekeeping operations in the former Yugoslavia. In 1995, the UN safe haven at Srebrenica fell while under the protection of Dutch peacekeeping troops, and thousands of Muslim men there were massacred by the Serbs. DutchBat's handling of the situation has been a considerable embarrassment to the Dutch military.

Political Control and the Tendency to Disarm

Although Holland was at one time a great sea power, reductions in the size of the navy by the tightfisted States-General cost the Dutch dearly. The great naval heroes Maarten Harpertszoon Tromp (1598–1653) and Michiel Adriaanszoon de Ruyter paid with their lives when called on to meet challenges for which the navy was not prepared. The second half of the nineteenth century saw the Dutch navy no better off. When the great sea powers began to build armored, steam-powered ships of the line— France was the first in 1861—the Dutch Parliament voted against following suit. It was not until 1892 that the navy began to get modern naval vessels.

The king used to be the commander in chief of the army in more than just name. In the nineteenth century, he was still expected to be at its head in the field. William II, the hero of Quatre Bras (June 16, 1815) and Waterloo (June 18, 1815), had always had a weak spot for the army. On March 23, 1849, King William III stated in an order of the day that he saw it as a sacred duty to his father to look after the needs and interests of the military.

In the Kingdom of the Netherlands, however, it is not the monarch, but the politicians who hold the purse strings and who call the tune to which the military dances. The Dutch aversion to the military has a long history. Reductions in the military are popular with the public. As a cost-saving measure, the army underwent a reduction in force in the summer of 1849, the very year that William III declared his intention to look after the army's needs and interests.

As the threats to Holland increased, so did political interest in the army. No sooner was the Armistice declared in 1918, however, than the Dutch began to reduce the size of the army again. The Great Depression brought on another round of reductions in force, and in 1940, when it was time to mobilize against the threat imposed by Germany, the army had been neglected for so long that there was neither enough equipment

nor enough trained commissioned and noncommissioned officers to support the expansion.

After World War II and through the Cold War, the Dutch built up the military again. In 1986, the ground forces numbered about 66,200 men. The navy had 17,068 men, including 2,800 marines. The air force numbered 17,957. After the end of the Cold War, the Dutch cashed in their peace dividend. The draft was ended, and the strength of the armed forces was reduced. By 1998, the ground forces had been reduced to 33,735 and the air force to 13,334 men, but the navy stayed about the same: 17,450. The total size of the defense establishment (including civilians) was reduced by 40.9% to 74,017. The military's budget was reduced by almost 30% to ƒ14 billion.

The End of the Draft

In his book *Mijn jaren als bevelhebber* (My Years as Commander of the Ground Forces), Lieutenant General Hans A. Couzy (1940–   )—commander of the Dutch ground forces at the time of the greatest cuts (1991–1996)—says that the military is in part to blame for the severity of the changes it experienced in the post–Cold War period, because it did not try to lead the process but, rather, waited for politicians to impose change from above. He urges his successors to be more proactive not only to world events, but also to trends and events in Dutch society. This will be difficult, Couzy notes, because without the draft, which he characterizes as the military's "umbilical cord to society," the military will gradually lose its public support.

To illustrate the potential problems that the elimination of the draft poses for the military, Couzy points to the experience of the United Kingdom, which is now into its third generation of the all-volunteer military. In a conversation in 1996 with his British colleague General Sir Charles Guthrie (1938–   ), Couzy was told that public support for the British army was growing smaller. Couzy warns against letting the Dutch armed forces become isolated from society in the same manner. Without public and political support, an army loses its political and social legitimacy.

Prince William Alexander is a strong supporter of the military. The prince holds commissions in all three branches of service. He is a commander in the naval reserve, a lieutenant colonel in the army reserve, and a wing commander in the air force reserve. He has undoubtedly seen Couzy's book. During his 1997 interview with Paul Witteman, he too commented on how the army is losing contact with the people now that the draft has been eliminated. One of his goals is to serve as the bridge between the military and the public, because he believes in the continued need for the military and foresees a time when people will again begin to question the need for the military. As if to prove the prince right, some commentators attacked his performance in the interview with Witteman on just this point.

Peacekeeping

While cutting the military's budget and reducing its ranks in the post–Cold War period, Dutch politicians added international peacekeeping to the military's missions. Peacekeeping missions are very popular politically. Since the end of the Cold War, the number of peacekeeping operations has increased dramatically. At present, the UN has about 26,000 military and police observers active in peacekeeping missions around the world.

The UN has been involved in peacekeeping operations since its inception in 1945. The United Nations Truce Supervision Organization (UNTSO) has monitored the demarcation lines between Israel and its Arab neighbors since 1948. The Dutch military has been providing observers to UNTSO since 1956.

While the first armed military action taken under UN auspices was in 1950 in Korea, its protracted nature and unsatisfactory outcome discouraged further UN-led actions of this type. The success of "Operation Desert Storm" in 1990, on the other hand, marked a watershed in international thinking about UN-led peacekeeping operations. Since then, the Security Council has voted for a number of other UN peacekeeping operations.

The Stabilization Force (SFOR) in the former Yugoslavia is a NATO operation under UN mandate (Security Council resolution 1088). As of June 1997, the Dutch had 1,296 military members committed to this operation—more, by far, than are committed to strictly UN operations. If the number of Dutch troops committed to UN and EU peacekeeping operations peripheral to SFOR are counted, the Dutch have 1,661 military members supporting the maintenance of peace in the former Yugoslavia. Their total worldwide commitment of troops to peacekeeping operations is only 1,702.

In the Middle East, the Dutch have had military members on peacekeeping duties at the UN Interim Force in Lebanon (UNIFIL), and at the UN Disengagement Force (UNDOF) on the Golan Heights. There is also Dutch participation in the UN Special Commission (UNSCOM) monitoring the destruction of weapons of mass destruction in Iraq, as well as in the Multinational Interception Force (MIF)—the naval task force in the Persian Gulf to monitor Iraq's compliance with UN Security Council resolution 665.

In Africa, twenty-six Dutch peacekeepers are active in the UN Angola Verification Mission (UNAVEM). The Dutch also have two instructors at the land-mine school in Luanda, which is run under the auspices of the UN Office for Project Services (UNOPS). Over 2,000 Dutch soldiers served as peacekeepers in Cambodia, and now a small Dutch team is active in the UN Development Program's Cambodian Mine Action Center (UNDP/CMAC). Since 1993, the Dutch have had an observer attached to the Organization for Security and Cooperation in Europe (OSCE) mission in Moldova, monitoring the withdrawal of the Russian Fourteenth Army.

The Dutch Ministry of Defense is also responsible for police observers and advisers provided for international peacekeeping efforts. The Dutch have police advisers in Albania with the Multinational Advisory Police Element (MAPE), which functions under EU auspices. In the former Yugoslavia, the Dutch provide advisers to the UN International Police Task Force (UNIPTF), which provides training to and monitors the maintenance of law and order by local police.

In 1997, the Dutch expended ƒ205.5 million on peacekeeping operations. Of this, ƒ40 million was for UN contributions. The Dutch contribution of ƒ40 million represents 1.59% of the total of all the contributions of the UN member states.

Military Public Relations

As a result of its participation in the peacekeeping mission to the former Yugoslavia, the Dutch army is under a cloud of suspicion and has lost a lot of face. DutchBat was responsible for the protection of the safe haven of Srebrenica in 1995, when it fell to the Serbs, who subsequently massacred thousands of Muslim men who had sought shelter there.

The military's reputation was not helped by the strange statements made by the DutchBat commander immediately after the fall of Srebrenica. Colonel Karremans said he "honestly had not thought" to ask the Serbian General Mladic about the fate of the Muslim men who had been taken away. There was also the question of the refusal by DutchBat to render assistance to seriously wounded Muslim civilians. Even more troubling was Major Franken's signature on "Franken's list," which named local DutchBat employees without UN ID cards to be turned over to the Serbs. All of this was compounded by DutchBat's festive reception of visiting Dutch dignitaries, which was broadcast on television in Holland at the very moment that the men from Srebrenica were being murdered.

A poll taken after the fall of Srebrenica showed that only about one-third of the Dutch populace trusted the military. While this figure climbed back up to about 60% in 1997, Dutch trust in its military is still below the level of its neighbors. In the United Kingdom, 79% of the populace trusts the military; in France 73%; in Germany 71%

The behavior of DutchBat is somewhat less incomprehensible when viewed against the background of the culture of nonconfrontation that was discussed in Chapter 11. Maarten Huygen, reporter for the *NRC-Handelsblad*, compares the actions of DutchBat to those of the Dutch during World War II: "The military is not any different than the people of the Netherlands. . . . It has heard a lot about the Second World War, but it has not learned a lot from it." When push comes to shove, it reverts to "administering lists and reaching consensus with the occupier,"[5] just like the Dutch civil authorities did during the occupation by helping Germans round up the Jews.

The all-volunteer Dutch army is having a hard time finding recruits, partly because of Srebrenica, partly because of the improving job market, and partly because of the general Dutch dislike of the military. To address the problem, the government is considering allowing sixteen-year-olds to enlist. To help improve the image of life in the military, the army is cooperating with John de Mol Productions to create a television series called *Combat*. The show premiered in February 1998 on the Veronica network. Women will also have to form a bigger part of the military. The Dutch have set goals of women filling 12% of the ranks of the uniformed services and 30% of the Department of Defense civilians by the year 2010.

Shared International Defense Policy

Dutch politicians are looking for ways to further reduce military expenditures. They see a greater sharing of defense responsibilities as one way to do this. The "Memorandum for the Record" on the defense portion of the budget for 1998 states this clearly: "Dutch security policy can only be successful on an international level." This is nothing new for Dutch defense policy. The Dutch were just as interested in the League of Nations and an internationally shared defense policy on the eve of World War II as they are today.

In the post–Cold War period, the Dutch continue to see NATO as a cornerstone of their internationally based defense policy. They strongly support the expansion of NATO to include former nation-states of the Warsaw Pact. The cost of this expansion is calculated at ƒ270 million per year for ten years; the Dutch see their share as ƒ13 million per year.

At the same time, they strongly support a more active role for the UN in peacekeeping operations. In 1994, foreign minister and D'66 member Hans van Mierlo (1931–   ) suggested creating a UN brigade to provide the UN with a Quick Reaction Force of its own. While the political hurdles to his proposal could not be immediately overcome, its suggestion by the Dutch clearly underscores their intention to base their defense policy on multilateral, international military structure, rather than solely on their own military.

Outside of NATO and the UN, the Dutch already participate in a joint army corps with the Germans. The military union of Europe is only the next logical step after political and monetary union. The major European powers, however, do not share the Dutch desire for combined military operations, which would make them too dependent on others for their security.

THE EUROPEAN ECONOMIC AND MONETARY UNION

The treaty signed in Maastricht in 1992 set the members of the European Union on the road to the Economic and Monetary Union (EMU). The new Euro zone will be as large as the dollar zone of the United States. It will contain just under 300 million people and account for 19.5% of global GDP, as well as about 18.5% of world trade.

During the first weekend in May 1998, eleven countries—Austria, Belgium, Finland, France, Germany, Ireland, Italy, Luxembourg, Holland, Portugal, and Spain—were certified, in some cases (such as Belgium and Spain, where debt is running at 118.2% and 119.0% of GDP) through creative bookkeeping, as meeting the economic criteria to become the first members of the EMU. The meeting that set the process of the EMU in motion was marred by political infighting over the appointment of the chairman of the European Central Bank (ECB). All of the Central Bankers of the European Union—except the French—supported the Dutchman Willem Frederik Duisenberg (1935–   ) for the position. Duisenberg was already the president of the European Monetary Institute in Frankfurt and eminently qualified for the position. The French, however, wanted their Central Banker, Jean-Claude Trichet (1942–   ), to take up the post. An accord on this issue at the certification meeting was reached only when Duisenberg himself volunteered to step down after four years in favor of Trichet, instead of serving out the entire eight-year term of office. The question remains, however, if Duisenberg will indeed step down after four years or if he will demonstrate his independence by remaining longer as some political insiders are beginning to hint already.

The differences over the appointment are not merely a matter of national pride, but of philosophical differences over the monetary policy of Europe. Duisenberg represents a tight monetary policy and Trichet a more liberal monetary policy. The creative bookkeeping used to certify some members for participation and the disagreement over the appointment of the Central Banker (and the course of European monetary policy) do not bode well for Euro-politicians—those who hold positions in the European central government and bureaucracy—trying to make the hard choices necessary for the success of the EMU. To achieve the EMU, the eleven member states will have to overcome a number of problems. Their governments are decentralized, their economies are different, and their cultures are even more so.

On January 1, 1999, the Euro became a currency, but the banknotes of the eleven members will continue to circulate. After a three-year transition period, the Euro will begin to circulate on January 1, 2002. Six months later, on July 1, 2002, the schilling, the franc, the mark, the punt, the lira, the guilder, the escudo, and the peseta will cease to exist. Each nation will print and mint its own Euro currency with a national emblem on one side and a common Euro emblem on the other. Notes from one country will be accepted as currency in all the others.

After the Euro becomes a currency, the EMU member states will surrender their right to set interest and exchange rates to the ECB in Frankfurt am Main. Under the Maastricht Treaty, member states have to hold their budget deficits to 3% of GDP and outstanding government debt to 60% of GDP, while keeping inflation under control. National politicians in member states that adhere to the treaty requirements and give up their rights to set interest and exchange rates will lose their ability to set economic policy. Because the first indication of the Euro's success is its performance on the world's currency markets, Duisenberg and the ECB are likely to emphasize, as the German Central Bank does now, low inflation and currency stability. This type of conservative monetary policy will not be equally welcome in all member states, especially France. The shock absorbers that national politicians could count on to soften the impact of local economic problems—tax cuts or hikes, increases or decreases in public spending, interest and exchange rate adjustments—will no longer work on the local level. For the EMU to be successful, decisions of this type will have to be made for all the member states by the ECB.

One of the underlying assumptions for the EMU is that resources can move freely within the Euro zone to compensate for economic problems. Member states are still in the process of aligning their legislation and regulations to make this possible. Even after the laws and regulations of the member states have been aligned, one factor will remain a problem. Money and goods may be able to move freely within the zone, but the labor force is another thing.

Unemployment, while at historic lows in Holland, is at historic highs in other parts of Europe. In the United States, workers have the option of moving from one part of the country with high unemployment to another part where there is low unemployment. While not everyone takes advantage of that option, it is still a real option because of the uniformity of the United States. English taught in California is the same English in the schools of New York, Washington State, or Florida. In Europe, a three-hour drive takes you to another language zone with a distinctly different culture. The problems that Europe has had and is still experiencing with guest workers make it clear that labor-force mobility within the Euro zone will be extremely limited. This is the issue most likely to cause the EMU to fail. Overcoming labor problems will require unprecedented political cooperation among the member states.

The EMU can be a positive for Europe in the way that the introduction of a single currency was for the United States in the late nineteenth century. The United States did not have a single currency until the federal government began printing money to help pay for the Civil War. Before that, state banks issued their own currency. Many consider the institution of a single currency for the entire United States one of the main reasons that the American economy is one of the strongest in the world.

THE ENVIRONMENT

During the 1960s, environmental consciousness began to increase in Holland. The original Delta Works plan called for the Scheldt to be closed off completely from the sea. This would have meant that the Scheldt would have changed from a saltwater to a freshwater environment, just like the Zuiderzee became the IJsselmeer. This would have had considerable benefit for agriculture in the area. Less salt water seeping into the fields from the Scheldt would have meant increased crop yields. On the other hand, the change would have meant the end of a unique natural habitat, a saltwater tidal area with its characteristic flora and fauna. It would have also marked the end of mussel and oyster fishing in the Scheldt. The Dutch chose to preserve the original habitat and built a pier dam with movable barriers that can be closed as needed. The same type of environmental considerations stopped the draining of the Markerwaard Polder, which had been a part of the original plan for the IJsselmeer.

Mountains of Manure

In the nineties, environmental concerns are becoming even more important. Not only are water habitats, industrial pollutants, vehicle exhausts, and acid rain concerns, but also the growing mountains of manure produced by poultry farms and large herds of dairy cattle and pigs. Spraying more manure on a field as fertilizer than the crops on the field can use causes environmental damage. The excess nitrates not used by the plants get into the groundwater. If the manure is sprayed on the field in liquid form, the ammonia in it escapes into the atmosphere and becomes acid rain.

Animal husbandry is big business in Holland. In 1995, the export of milk and dairy products amounted to ƒ7.6 billion, or about 2.5% of all exports from Holland. Dealing with the manure surplus has become a big political issue. The source of the problem is the way cattle, pigs, and poultry are raised in Holland. Holland is a small country, and to meet its meat and dairy needs in the postwar period, farmers took to "intensive" animal husbandry. An intensive cattle farm has very little land but lots of cattle. That means that there is not as much land on the farm as there is manure to spread on it, so there is a surplus of manure on the farm.

When the problem was recognized in the early eighties, farmers began reducing their herds. Cattle account for 75% of the manure production, pigs account for 22%, and poultry for 3%. In the eighties, there were 5.2 million head of cattle and 14 million pigs. By 1997, the number of cattle had been reduced to 500,000, but the number of pigs had remained the same. In 1994, domestic livestock deposited 83 million tons of manure on farms in Holland. The amount of the surplus was estimated at 1% of the total. The Dutch have tried a number of approaches to deal with the manure surplus—shipping it to nonsurplus areas of the country for use as fertilizer, processing it into pellets for export as fertilizer, financial disincentives and manure bookkeeping requirements for farmers—but none has provided the ultimate solution. They are still wrestling with the problem

Even though the size of cattle and dairy herds was reduced, farmers found ways to keep production at the same level by better breeding, feeding, and housing techniques. In 1950, the average yield per milk cow was 3,300 liters per year. By 1995, the yield per cow had climbed to 6,500 liters. By the mid-1980s, production had overshot demand, and to avoid dairy surpluses, the European Union established a milk quota in 1984 to hold down milk production. Dutch farmers especially felt the impact of this regulation. They export about 30% of their milk and dairy products to EU countries.

Manure control is not the only environmental problem facing animal farmers in Holland today. Consumers are also beginning to show that they care about how the animals are raised. Free-range meat and free-range eggs, though more expensive, are becoming more popular, and intensive cattle, pig, and poultry farms are coming under pressure to change their method of production. This will be hard, given the limited amount of land available for animal farming.

A Foreign Relations Problem

Pollution of the Rhine River is a serious environmental problem. The Rhine is not only a transportation artery, but also a source of drinking water in Holland. Once the pollutants in the Rhine reach the North Sea, they contribute to pollution along the Dutch coast. For the Dutch, this is not just an ecological issue. On its way to Holland, the Rhine flows through Switzerland, Germany, and France, which all contribute to its pollution. The cleanup of the Rhine will require the cooperation of these countries, as well as action by the Dutch. This makes it not only an environmental problem, but also a foreign relations problem.

Regulation by Taxation

The Ministry of Health and Environment was established in 1971. Countrywide air pollution monitoring has been in place since 1975. Lead-free gasoline only came on the market in Holland in 1987. By 1990, it had gained about 49% of the market. By 1997, its share had grown to almost 80%. Lead-free gasoline and catalytic converters are not the only steps that the Dutch government is taking to reduce pollution from automobiles. An excise tax surcharge was imposed on gasoline and diesel fuel in 1981, earmarked for pollution abatement. The tax on gasoline was again raised in 1997 by 13 Dutch cents per liter, bringing the price of gasoline to ƒ2.30 per liter, or ƒ8.71 ($4.35) per gallon. About three-fourths of the price is made up of taxes. The primary purpose of the tax hike was to reduce pollution by increasing the cost of driving so that, in comparison, public transportation would be a viable alternative to individual cars.

Reducing the number of cars on the road reduces not only pollution, but also the pressure on politicians to expand Holland's overcrowded road system. Building roads in Holland is especially expensive because of the swampy nature of most of the land, and the Dutch government is becoming increasingly aware that it has to reduce expenditures.

Taxation is a favorite Dutch method of regulation. In 1996, the Dutch introduced an ecotax, the Regulerende Energie Belasting (REB; Energy Regulation Tax) on the energy used by individual households. The use of electricity and natural gas is taxed when the consumer uses more than 800 kilowatt-hours of electricity, or 800 cubic meters of gas. The tax is 3.5 Dutch cents per kilowatt-hour, and 9.53 Dutch cents per cubic meter for gas. The goal of this tax is to get the consumer to buy more energy-efficient appliances and to insulate their homes better, by making them pay more if they use more. In 1995, to help the consumer understand how much energy major appliances use, the Dutch introduced a requirement that all new refrigerators and freezers have an energy-consumption tag.

The funds generated by the REB go to energy producers who deliver energy from renewable sources, such as wind energy, water energy, or photovoltaics. In 1996, more than 1 billion guilders were collected in ecotax levies: ƒ649.8 million for electricity, and ƒ446.0 million for gas.

In addition to the ecotax, the design of all new buildings and major renovations of existing buildings must be accompanied by an Energy Use Factor (EUF) statement, showing that the energy use for the building will meet stated requirements. If the design does not meet the requirements, a permit will not be issued for the construction. The EUF is pegged to the average home's use of electricity and gas, with the electricity usage converted to an equivalent number of cubic meters of gas. It is based on the average home usage in 1993 of 1,500 cubic meters of gas per year. It is being introduced, in typical Dutch fashion, in steps. Building designs submitted in 1995 had to have an EUF of 1.4 (1,400 m³) or less. In 1998, they had to have an EUF of 1.2 (1,200 m³). By the year 2000, new buildings will have to have an EUF of 1.0 (1,000 m³).

It is up to the building contractor to decide how to achieve this goal. It can be any combination of new building techniques (more insulation) or technologies (roof-mounted, solar-assisted heating panels). The expectation is that the buildings' owners will recoup the extra costs of construction via the reduced energy costs for using the buildings. The increased demand for these construction techniques and technologies will also cause their prices to fall. As prices fall, the Dutch will examine requiring that existing buildings be retrofitted with them for the increased energy savings. Holland's total energy usage per year is 830 billion kilowatt-hours. It is estimated that up to 244 billion kilowatt-hours could be saved a year by the application of these modern technologies. That translates to a savings of about ƒ48 billion.

The Dutch also offer tax incentives to companies for investment in renewable energy sources through deductions for the cost of the investment. Consumers are offered the incentive of a lower BTW (6% instead of the normal 17.5%) on the energy delivered from these sources. These incentives help make the cost of energy from renewable sources competitive with energy derived from conventional sources such as fossil fuels. On the stock market, investments in the stocks of "green" companies that produce energy from renewable sources are given favored treatment. Dividends and profits from these stocks are not taxed.

Nuclear Power

Nuclear power, as is the case in many other countries, is on the way out. The country's two nuclear plants provide 5% of the electricity produced in Holland. After the Chernobyl nuclear accident near Kiev in 1986, it was decided not to build any more plants. The plant in Dodewaard was being closed in 1997, and the plant in Borsele will be closed in 2004.

NOTES

1. Walter Bagehot, *The English Constitution* (1867) "The Monarchy," quoted in Angela Partington, ed., *The Oxford Dictionary of Quotations*, revised fourth edition (Oxford: Oxford University Press, 1996), p. 47, item 8.

2. Harry van Wijnen, "Ze wil de regie in handen houden" (She Wants to Keep Her Hands on the Controls), *Profiel* (Profile; a weekly supplement to the *NRC-Handelsblad*) (January 29, 1998).

3. Wim Kok quoted in Grutterink, "BEATRIX ZESTIG: Beatrix praat zelfs met Kok niet over stoppen" (Beatrix Sixty: Beatrix Does Not Even Talk with Kok about Quitting), Algemeen Nederlands Persbureau (General Dutch Press Bureau) wire (January 31, 1998).

4. Andreas Antonius Maria van Agt, "Speurend als een buizerd" (Senses Like a Buzzard), *Profiel* (Profile) (January 29, 1998).

5. Maarten Huygen, "Goed en fout in Srebrenica" (Right and Wrong in Srebrenica), *NRC-Handelsblad* (November 2, 1995).

Notable People in the History of Holland

A note on Dutch alphabetical order for those who may later work with Dutch sources: the Dutch alphabetize last names that begin with de (the), van (of), or van de / van den / van der (of the)—often abbreviated as v.d.— by the first letter of the part of the name that follows the article or preposition. Van Heutsz, for example, is listed under the letter "H," not under the letter "V." That custom has been followed here.

Agt, Andreas ("Dries") Antonius Maria van (1931–   ). Politician, member of the CDA. Van Agt was trained as a lawyer at the Catholic University in Nijmegen. He was the vice prime minister and the minister of justice in Joop den Uyl's (see biography herein) cabinet (1973–1977). He was prime minister in the CDA-VVD cabinet (1977–1981) and the short-lived CDA-PvdA-D'66 cabinet (September 1981–May 1982), which fell over the issue of employment. In the CDA-D'66 cabinet that followed, he was the foreign minister. When the CDA-D'66 coalition fell as well (1982), van Agt withdrew from national politics, to be succeeded by Ruud Lubbers as party leader and prime minister. Van Agt later became the European Union ambassador to Japan (1987) and the United States (1990–1995).

Asser, Tobias Michael Carel (1838–1913). Winner of the Nobel Peace Prize in 1911 (shared with Alfred Fried). Asser was recognized by the prize committee for his work on international arbitration. A member of the committee called him a "practical legal statesman" and a "pioneer in the field of international legal relations." Asser was a noted negotiator and participated in the negotiations for almost every treaty Holland concluded between 1875 and 1913. As the chief of the Dutch delegation to The Hague Peace Conferences of 1899 and 1907, Asser was a proponent of compulsory arbitration as an alternative to armed resolution of international conflicts. Sitting on The Hague Permanent Court of Arbitration, which he helped plan and organize, he heard the first case before the court—a dispute between the United States and Mexico over payments to priests in California from the Mexican Pious Fund. The court ruled in favor of the priests in California.

Boerhaave, Hermann (1668–1738). Professor of medicine. He introduced the modern clinical method of instruction of medicine. In 1737, sixty of his ninety-seven medical students at the University of Leiden were foreigners. His students took his teaching methods to Vienna (Gerard van Swieten, Anton de Haen), Edinburgh (John Rutherford), and to a number of German universities (Albrecht von Haller). His influence was so great that more than thirty years after his death, in 1770, Frederick the Great declared that all professors of medicine must follow the Boerhaave method.

Broek, Hans van den (1936–   ). Dutch European commissioner in Brussels. His portfolio is in foreign affairs, dealing with Middle and Eastern Europe, the Commonwealth of Independent States (USSR), Mongolia, Turkey, Cyprus, and Malta, as well as the European Union's mutual foreign and defense policy. He was appointed to this position in 1993. Prior to that, he was the Dutch foreign minister from 1982 to 1993.

Court, Pieter de la (1618–1685). One of the most important Dutch political theorists of the seventeenth century. He defended the policies of the Provincial Council of Holland against those of the stadholders. His publications laid the foundation for the ideology of *Waare Vrijheid* (true liberty), which arose during the first Stadholderless Period (1650–1672), stressing the autonomy of the provinces. His *Het welvaren der stad Leyden* (The Welfare of the City of Leiden) defended the free market against the monopoly of the guilds. With the encouragement of Johan de Witt (see biography herein), he expanded this work to cover the whole Republic. In it, he defended the economic, religious, and governmental freedoms that were at the base of the ideology of the supporters of provincial rights, who opposed the stadholder. His *Historie der gravelike regeering in Holland* (History of the Reign of the Counts in Holland) was written to show that sovereignty did not emanate from the counts, but from the people.

Doorman, Karel Willem Frederik Marie (1889–1942). Naval hero. In 1942, at the outbreak of the war with Japan, Doorman had tactical command of the Combined Striking Force, made up of the ABDA (American, British, Dutch, Australian) fleet. As the Japanese prepared to make a landing on the island of Java, Doorman led his squadron into battle, signaling: "I am attacking. All ships follow me." The far-superior Japanese force easily destroyed nearly all of the squadron. Doorman went down with his flagship, the cruiser *De Ruyter*—named for Michiel Adriaanszoon de Ruyter (see biography herein)—together with most of her crew.

Drucker, Wilhelmina Elizabeth (1847–1925). Women's rights activist and journalist. The daughter of an unmarried mother (her real last name was Lensing), she had a difficult childhood. She was a self-made woman. In 1889, she set up the Vrije Vrouwenvereeniging (Association of Free Women), which was the first organization to work to remove the legal and political limitations placed on women. In 1894, she took the initiative—together with Alletta Jacobs (see biography herein)—in founding the Vereeniging voor Vrouwenkiesrecht (The Association for Women's Suffrage). From 1913 until her death, she was the editor of the women's movement magazine *Evolutie* (Evolution), which was published from 1893 to 1926. The militant women's rights movement of the early seventies, De Dolle Mina was named for her, as Mina is short for Wilhelmina.

Duisenberg, Willem ("Wim") Frederik (1935–). Financier. He holds a Ph.D. in economics from the University of Groningen, where he wrote his thesis on the economic effects of disarmament. He worked on the IMF staff in Washington, D.C., and later taught economics at the University of Amsterdam. Between 1973 and 1977, he served as PvdA minister of finance in the Joop den Uyl (see biography herein) government (1973–1977). Returning to the private sector, he worked with the Rabobank and the Nederlandsche Bank. During his tenure with the Nederlandsche Bank, he served in a number of international functions, such as chairman of the board of the "Central Bankers' Bank," the Bank for International Payments, in Basel; chairman of the Committee of the Central Bank Governors of the European Union; and Dutch representative to the IMF. In 1996, he was unanimously elected chairman of the European Monetary

Institute, and in 1998, amid a conflict between France and the rest of the EMU member states, he became chairman of the European Central Bank.

Einthoven, Willem (1860–1927). Winner of the Nobel Prize in medicine in 1924. Born in Semarang, the Dutch East Indies (now Indonesia), Einthoven was recognized by the prize committee for his discovery of the mechanism of the electrocardiogram. He concluded his acceptance speech with recognition of the efforts of others working in his field: "A new chapter in the scientific knowledge of heart disease has been introduced, not through the work of a single person, but through the labor of many talented men, who have carried out their investigation, unlimited by any political boundaries."

Erasmus, Desiderius (ca. 1466–1536). The greatest European thinker of the later Middle Ages. He was one of the most critical researchers of his time. He preached a tolerant, Christian humanism in a period when religious fanaticism was rampant everywhere. He espoused a philosophy of philanthropy and defended the absolute integrity of intellect. His written texts express the same sober Dutch view of life that is plainly visible in the paintings of contemporary Flemish artists. He represented the epitome of common sense and moderation. He was not, however, without a sense of humor. He said that his horse just had to be the smartest horse in Europe, since it had visited so many universities. Holland awards the Erasmus Prize to persons or institutions that have made an exceptionally important contribution to European culture or the field of social science. The Erasmus University in Rotterdam is named after him.

Groen van Prinsterer, Guillaume ("Willem") (1801–1876). Founder of the Protestant Anti-Revolutionary Party. From the Second Chamber, he vigorously opposed Johan Rudolf Thorbecke's liberalism. Suspicious of democracy, he supported more power for the monarch rather than for the Parliament. He was also very much opposed to the restoration of Catholic rights. In the Battle of the Schools, his ideal solution would have been a state school with a strictly Protestant character. In the Battle of the Schools, therefore, he initially opposed the funding of special (in his view, Catholic) schools, but when it became clear that the only way that schools could have a strictly Protestant character was to establish them as special schools, he threw his support behind the cause.

Groot, Hugo de (a.k.a. Hugo Grotius) (1583–1645). The most important Dutch political theorist of the seventeenth century, considered the founder of international law. His most important work in this area was *De Jure Belli ac Pacis* (On the Law of War and Peace), which was published in Paris in 1625. He was the pensionary of Rotterdam from 1613 to 1618, when he was ousted by Prince Maurits. Sentenced to life in Castle Loevestein, he escaped in 1621, hidden in a box meant to be full of books. After that, he lived in Paris, never to return to Holland.

Hein (Heyn), Pieter ("Piet") Pieterszoon (1577–1629). Naval hero. Hein was a privateer sailing for the WIC. In 1628, he captured the Spanish "Silver Fleet" in the bay of Matanzas (10 miles east of Havana) on the island of Cuba. This yielded a prize of 12 million guilders. Hein was extremely popular with the Dutch public. *Piet Hein* is the name of the royal family's yacht. It was a gift from the people of Holland to Princess Juliana (see biography herein) and Prince Bernhard on the occasion of their wedding in 1937.

Heutsz, Johannes Benedictus van (1851–1924). Military commander and colonial official. Commissioned as a second lieutenant in October 1872, he volunteered for assignment to the Dutch East Indies (now Indonesia) where the Atjeh Wars (1873–1877) had just begun. During the course of his career, he served tour after tour in the Dutch East Indies, in increasingly senior positions, ending as the civilian and military governor of Atjeh, in North Sumatra. In this position, he introduced a new military policy that finally led to pacification of the countryside in 1904. He returned to Holland in that year, only to be reassigned to the Dutch East Indies a few months later as governor-general. While governor-general, van Heutsz set up an educational program that was intended ultimately to lead to an independent national existence for Indonesia. The program was continued by his successors A.W.F. Idenburg (1861–1935) and J. P. van Limburg-Stirum (1873–1948), but it was suspended during the international economic crisis of the thirties. The Royal Dutch Indian Army (KNIL) was disbanded on July 26, 1950. To insure that the traditions of the KNIL would continue to live in the Dutch army, the Dutch designated an infantry regiment the successor of the traditions of the KNIL and gave this regiment the honorific title Regiment van Heutsz. A battalion from Regiment van Heutsz fought in Korea during the UN-sponsored police action there in the 1950s.

Jacobs, Alleta Henriette (1849–1929). Women's rights activist. The eighth of eleven children, she was the first woman admitted to high school and the first to graduate from a university in Holland. In 1878, she received her degree as doctor of medicine from the university in Groningen where she was admitted in 1871 only after Prime Minister Thorbecke interceded on her behalf. She practiced gynecology and pediatrics in Amsterdam, where, for two days a week, she offered free treatment for the poor. The "census-based" requirements for voting did not expressly exclude women, but no woman had ever met them before. Jacobs did. When she tried to register to vote in 1883, her application ultimately reached the Hoge Raad (Supreme Court), where it was refused. Subsequently, the constitutional amendment of 1887 expressly excluded women from the vote. This restriction remained in force until a new constitutional amendment removed it in 1917. Jacobs was one of the founders—together with Wilhelmina Drucker (see biography herein)—of the Vereeniging voor Vrouwenkiesrecht in 1894, and in 1903, she became its national chairwoman. In 1904, she helped found the Wereldbond voor Vrouwenkiesrecht (World League for Women's Suffrage), which later became the Internationale Vrouwenbond voor Vrede en Vrijheid (International Women's League for Peace and Freedom). Her sister Charlotte was the first feminine pharmacist, and her sister Frederique was the first woman certified to teach science in high school.

Klompé, Margaretha ("Marga") Albertina Maria (1912–1986). First woman member of the cabinet of ministers (1956). She was one of the cofounders of the Katholieke Vrouwendispuut (Catholic Women's Debating Society, 1948), which strove to encourage women to enter politics and to seek management positions in the social arena. She was also a proponent of greater influence for women and the laity in Catholic Church affairs.

Kruseman, Wilhelmina ("Mina") Jacoba Paulina Rudolphine (1839–1922). Women's rights activist, actress, singer, and author. One of the first and fieriest advocates of women's rights, together with Betsy Perk (see biography herein), she helped change the way that people thought about women. *De moderne Judith* (The Modern Judith, 1873) is a collection of her lectures from the tour that she and Perk made in 1872. Her novels attacked the lives of dependency that women of the time led. Under the name of Stella Oristorio di Frama, she made a singing tour of the southern United States in 1870.

Ockels, Wubbo Johannes (1946–   ). First Dutch astronaut. Flew on the space shuttle *Challenger* on its last successful mission (October 31–November 6, 1985) as a Spacelab mission specialist. After returning from the mission, he went to work at the European Space Research and Technology Center in Noordwijk.

Oldenbarnevelt, Johan van (1547–1619). First *raadpensionaris* (grand pensionary) of the province of Holland. Because of the dominance of the province of Holland, the office of the grand pensionary of Holland quickly evolved into a central position of power in Dutch politics. Oldenbarnevelt was also one of the major figures in the establishment of the VOC (1602) but opposed the foundation of the WIC. He was instrumental in the conclusion of the Twelve Years' Truce with Spain. The truce was vigorously opposed by the Volkspartij (People's Party), which did not want peace with Spain; by the Protestant clergy, who feared a resurgence of Catholicism; and by Prince Maurits and his brother William Lodewijk, who understood that they would not be as powerful in peace as they were in war. In 1619, van Oldenbarnevelt was put to death with the complicity of Maurits. He became a martyr for the supporters of provincial rights, who opposed the stadholder.

Oldenbarnevelt, William van (1590–1634). The third son of Johan van Oldenbarnevelt, planned the assassination of Prince Maurits in 1623. When the plot failed, he escaped to Brussels, where he was awarded an annuity by Archduchess Isabella (1566–1633), who ruled the southern Netherlands (Belgium). William's brother Reinier (1583–1623), who was also involved in the plot, was caught and beheaded.

Orange-Nassau, Constantijn van (1969–   ).   Third son of Queen Beatrix and Prince Claus. Entered the University of Leiden in 1988, completing his law degree in 1995. The title of his dissertation was "Asylum Procedure Provisions Examined in the Light of the Geneva Convention: A Legal Analysis." He works in the office of Dutch European Commissioner Hans van den Broek (see biography herein), in Brussels.

Orange-Nassau, Johan Friso van (1968–   ). Second son of Queen Beatrix and Prince Claus. Studied mechanical engineering at Berkeley (1986–1988) and aerospace technology at the Technical University at Delft (1988–1994). He worked as an intern at McDonnell-Douglas in California just before completing his degree in aerospace engineering management. Between 1990 and 1995, he also studied business economics at the Erasmus University in Rotterdam. In 1998, he completed his studies at the European Institute of Business Administration at Fontainebleau in France, after which he accepted a position with Goldman Sachs in "the City" financial district in London.

Orange-Nassau, Juliana van (1909–   ). Queen of the Kingdom of the Netherlands from 1948 to 1980. During her reign, she signed the documents that granted Indonesia its independence (1949) and that changed the status of Surinam and the Antilles from colonies to commonwealth partners (1954). It was also during her reign that the disastrous floods of 1953 killed 1,835 people in the provinces of Zeeland and South Holland. Her reign was characterized by her very great interest in social issues. Internationally, she was very much concerned with refugee problems and children's welfare. Politically, she was a fervent supporter of international cooperation and European union. She abdicated in favor of her daughter Beatrix in 1980. In her thirty-two years on the throne, she was served by the governments of Willem Drees Sr. (1886–1988), L.J.M. Beel (1902–1977), Jan Eduard de Quay (1901–1985), V.G.M. Marijnen (1917–1975), J.M.L. Cals (1914–1971), Jelle Zijlstra (1918–   ), P.J.S. de Jong (1915–   ), Barend Willem Biesheuvel (1920–   ), Joop den Uyl (see biography herein) and A.A.M. van Agt (see biography herein).

Orange-Nassau, William Alexander van (1967–   ). Crown prince: first son of Queen Beatrix and Prince Claus. He completed his International Baccalaureate at Atlantic College in Llantwit Major, Wales. Before going to college, he completed his military service with the Royal Dutch Navy. He studied history at the University of Leiden (1987–1993), where he wrote his dissertation on the Dutch response to France's decision under President Charles de Gaulle (1890–1970) to leave NATO's integrated command structure. In 1994, he attended the Dutch War College. Certified as a military and commercial pilot, he loves to fly: "It's a wonderful relaxation for me. It's the only place where I am not covered by ministerial responsibility, where I am responsible for the safety of the aircraft and of myself and of the passengers. It's a task where you can free your mind from everything else. Because you have to be one hundred percent concentrated. If I push the wrong button, there's nobody who's going to fix it for me."

Perk, Christine Elizabeth ("Betsy") (1833–1906). Women's rights activist, author, and playwright. She founded the weekly *Ons streven* (Our Goal) in 1869 but quickly lost editorial control. In 1870, she founded the publication *Onze roeping* (Our Calling), which advocated education for women. In 1871, she founded the first women's association Arbeid Adelt (Work Ennobles), which was intended to help improve the lot of well-mannered but poor women. In 1872, she joined Mina Kruseman (see biography herein) on a speaking tour to promote women's emancipation.

Ruyter, Michiel Adriaanszoon de (1607–1676). Naval hero. De Ruyter first went to sea at age eleven, serving as a common sailor. He sailed variously in the navy and in the merchant marine. With some reluctance, he returned to naval service in 1652 and fought with distinction under Maarten Tromp (see biography herein) in the first Anglo-Dutch War (1652–1654). In 1653, Johan de Witt (see biography herein) personally convinced de Ruyter to take on the post of vice admiral in permanent service at the Dutch admiralty. Here he served under Lieutenant Admiral van Wassenaer van Obdam (1610–1665), who had replaced Tromp as naval commander, after Tromp was killed. During this time, de Ruyter led numerous cruises against the Algerian and French pirates. After van Obdam was killed in the second Anglo-Dutch War (1665–1667), de Witt had de Ruyter appointed commander of the fleet, replacing Cornelis Tromp (1629–1691)—Maarten's son—who had initially been given a temporary appointment to that post. The change was politically motivated. Tromp was an ardent supporter of the stadholder, and de Ruyter was a moderate supporter of the Provincial Councils' rights. In August 1666, de Ruyter's brilliant withdrawal following the Dutch defeat at the battle of North Foreland saved the fleet. His raid up the Thames River as far as Chatham caused panic in London and brought a speedy end to the war. In the third Anglo-Dutch War (1672–1674), he led the expanded, well-trained, and disciplined Dutch fleet to victory over the English. After the war, the fleet underwent a reduction in force and fell into deplorable condition. Despite de Ruyter's protests about the condition of the fleet, it was sent to the Mediterranean (1675) to help the Spanish against the French, where de Ruyter was mortally wounded at Messina.

Slingelandt, Simon van (1664–1736). Statesman. He was the secretary to the Council of State (1690–1725). He favored a strong central government and in his *Discours over de defecten in de tegenwoordige constitutie der regering van den Staat der Vereenigde Nederlanden en over de middelen van redressen* (Discourse on the Defects in the Current Constitution of the Government of the State of the United Netherlands and on the Means of Correcting Them, 1716) criticized the political state of affairs. In 1727, he was appointed the *raadpensionaris* of Holland, but a condition of his appointment was that he give up his ideas of reform. During his term of office, his foreign policy made him a statesman of European stature. He worked closely with Robert Walpole (1676–1745)—de facto the first English Prime Minister—toward the goal of "European peace." His ideas were later taken up by the Patriots movement, which published his *Staatkundige geschriften* (Political Writings) in four volumes between 1784 and 1785.

Speijk, Jan Carel Josephus van (1802–1831). Naval hero. During the Belgian revolution, van Speijk was the commander of a gunboat taking part in the bombardment of Antwerp. When his ship was blown into the seawall during a storm, it was overrun by the Belgians. Van Speijk went below, pretending to get the ship's papers, but rather than surrender his ship, he lit a fuse to the ship's powder hold. He and most of the crew were killed in the explosion. In the northern provinces (now Holland), his action was viewed as heroic, and it encouraged the north to fight on against the Belgian secession.

Tinbergen, Jan (1903–1994).   Economist. In 1969, Tinbergen and Ragnar Frisch shared the first Nobel Prize for economics "for having developed and applied dynamic models for the analysis of economic processes." In 1929, Tinbergen received his doctorate from the University of Leiden in physics. When economics attracted his attention, he began applying the mathematical basis of physics to economics. Using statistical instruments, Tinbergen created a working model of the Dutch economy with over fifty variables. What is perhaps his best-known work—*Business Cycles in the United States, 1919–1932*—was published under the auspices of the League of Nations. When drafted into the Dutch army, for reasons of conscience, he chose alternate service rather than to bear arms. His brother Nikolaas (1907–1988) was awarded the Nobel Prize in 1973 for physiology (together with Konrad Lorenz and Karl von Frisch) in recognition of "their discoveries concerning the organization and elicitation of individual and social behavior patterns" in animals.

Tromp, Maarten Harpertszoon (1598–1653).   Naval hero. First went to sea with his father as a child and participated in the battle of Gibraltar (April 1607) aboard his father's ship. In 1637, with some reluctance, he accepted the appointment as the commander in chief of the naval forces of Holland and West Friesland. In 1639, his remarkable tactics led to the crushing defeat of the Spanish fleet in the Downs of the English Channel, which marked the end of Spanish sea power. He supported Stadholder Frederick Henry's policies for centralizing the fleet, which the Provincial Council opposed. Due to a lack of funding, the fleet was not prepared, when, in 1652, Tromp's refusal to lower the Dutch flag in deference to English Admiral Robert Blake (1599–1657) started the first of the four Anglo-Dutch Wars. Tromp won control over the channel in December 1652, but the inferiority of his fleet allowed the English to regain the upper hand. Tromp was killed in the last major conflict of the war, when the Dutch broke the English blockade of the coast off Scheveningen in August 1653.

Uyl, Johannes ("Joop") Marten den (1919–1987). Politician, member of the PvdA. Den Uyl was trained as an economist at the University of Amsterdam. Prime minister of the PvdA-D'66-PPR cabinet (1973–1977). During his premiership, den Uyl was faced with the Organization of Petroleum Exporting Countries (OPEC) induced oil crisis, the Lockheed bribery scandal surrounding Prince Bernhard (Queen Beatrix's father), and the hostage incident in which South Moluccan terrorists took over a school and a train. Even though his party won a plurality of the vote in 1977, he was unable to form a government, and the CDA under van Agt (see biography herein) took over the political leadership of the country with a minority government. When he withdrew from political life, he was succeeded as party leader by Wim Kok (1938–   ).

Waals, Johannes Diderik van der (1837–1923). Winner of the Nobel Prize in physics in 1910. Van der Waals was recognized by the prize committee for his work on the equation of state for gases and liquids, which was not of purely theoretical interest, but had practical applications as well. A member of the committee noted that "modern refrigeration engineering, which is nowadays such a potent factor in our economy and industry, bases its vital methods mainly on van der Waals' theoretical studies."

Witt, Johan de (1625–1672). The most prominent *raadpensionaris* of Holland. He was one of the intellectual fathers of the ideology of *Waare Vrijheid* (true liberty), which arose during the first Stadholderless Period (1650–1672), stressing the autonomy of the provinces. His opposition to the House of Orange stemmed from his view that their bellicosity was a threat to the commercial interests of the Republic. When William III (1650–1702) was returned to the stadholdership, de Witt resigned. He was murdered later that year. While it has never been proved that William III was involved in a plot to kill de Witt, the circumstantial evidence strongly supports his involvement. He took the prime suspects under his protection and gave them a reward. De Witt's fate made him a martyr of the Patriot Movement in the eighteenth century.

Appendix: Dutch Print Media Companies

Consolidation in the print media has considerably reduced the number of media companies. There are now five media companies, which control 96% of the country's daily papers:

- Perscombinatie Meulenhoff, with a total daily circulation of 1,460,363—31% market share—owns *Algemeen Dagblad, De Volkskrant, NRC-Handelsblad, Trouw, Rotterdams Dagblad, Het Parool, De Dordtenaar,* and *Rijn en Gouwe*

- Telegraaf Holdings, with a total daily circulation of 1,204,843—25% market share—owns *De Telegraaf, Noordhollands Dagblad, Limburgs Dagblad, Haarlems Dagblad, IJmuider Courant, Nieuws van de dag, De Gooi- en Eemlander Dagblad,* and *Leids Dagblad*

- Verenigde Nederlandse Uitgeversbedrijven (United Dutch Publishers), with a total daily circulation of 843,867—18% market share—owns *De Limburger, De Gelderlander, De Barneveldse Courant, Brabants Dagblad, De Stem, Brabants Nieuwsblad,* and *Eindhovens Dagblad*

- Wegener Arcade, with a total daily circulation of 756,326—16% market share—owns *Twentsche Courant, Tubantia, Haagsche*

Courant, Gelders Dagblad, Deventer Dagblad, Overijssels Dagblad, Apeldoornse Courant, Arnhemse Courant, Utrechts Nieuwsblad, Dagblad Rivierenland, Zwolse Courant, Nieuw Kamper Dagblad, Dagblad Flevoland, Provinciale Zeeuwse Courant, and *Goudse Courant*

- Noordelijke Dagblad Combinatie, with a total daily circulation of 314,736—7% market share—owns *Nieuwsblad van het Noorden, Drentse Courant, Groninger Dagblad,* and *Leeuwarder Courant.*

Bibliographic Essay

The suggestions for further reading below are confined to a selection of English-language books. Those who read Dutch will find extensive lists of Dutch sources in most of the titles listed in the bibliography, but especially in Jonathan Irvine Israel, *The Dutch Republic: Its Rise, Greatness, and Fall, 1477–1806* (Oxford: Oxford University Press, 1995).

TIMELINES AND DOCUMENTS

The first part (pp. 1–64) of Pamela Smit and J. W. Smit, *The Netherlands: A Chronology and Fact Book* (Dobbs Ferry, NY: Oceana, 1973) contains a highly-detailed chronology from 57 B.C. to A.D. 1971. A chronology of the period 1568 to 1795 is found in Charles Ralph Boxer, *The Dutch Seaborne Empire, 1600–1800* (Harmondsworth: Penguin, 1973).

For genealogical tables for the House of Orange (1748–1911), see Sydney W. Jackman and Hella Haasse, eds., *A Stranger in The Hague: The Letters of Queen Sophie of the Netherlands to Lady Malet, 1842–1877* (Durham, NC: Duke University Press, 1989). Genealogical tables for the House of Orange-Nassau and other prominent Dutch families can be found in Geoffrey Parker, *The Dutch Revolt* (Ithaca, NY: Cornell University Press, 1977). Genealogical tables for the House of Stuart (1567–1807) and the House of Orange (1475–1702) can be found in Pieter Geyl, *Orange and Stuart* (New York: Charles Scribner's Sons, 1969).

The second part of Pamela Smit and J. W. Smit, *The Netherlands: A Chronology and Fact Book* (Dobbs Ferry, NY: Oceana, 1973) is a collection of translations of major documents from the history of Holland: The Dutch National Anthem; Report on the Riots of Antwerp, 1566; William of Orange's Speech to the Assembly of the States-General, 1576; The Bill of Abjuration; The Itinerary of Jan van Linschoten, 1598; Diary of a Seaman, Arctic Voyage; Excerpts from Pieter de la Court's *The Interest of Holland*, 1662; Manifesto of the Democratic Movement, 1781; Lord Castlereagh's Memorandum to the Allies concerning the Netherlands, 1813; Proclamation Establishing the Netherlands, 1813; An English View of the Dutch Parliament in 1860; Queen Wilhelmina's Description of the Beginning of World War II, 1940; Description of Amsterdam's Anti-Persecution Strike, 1941; Queen Wilhelmina's Description of the Liberation, 1944–1945; The Damages of the Second World War, 1945; Documents concerning the Dutch-Indonesian Conflict, 1945–1949.

Another collection of translations of historically important documents is found in the second part (pp. 110–185) of F. Gunther Eyck, *The Benelux Countries: An Historical Survey* (Princeton, NJ: Van Nostrand, 1959): The Charter of Luxembourg City, 1244; The Treaty of Vienna, 1815; The Treaty of London, 1831; The Customs Convention between the Benelux Countries, 1950.

For translations of original documents on the slave trade, see Johannes Postma, *The Dutch in the Atlantic Slave Trade, 1600–1815* (Cambridge: Cambridge University Press, 1990).

NARRATIVE HISTORIES

An excellent overview of Dutch society can be found in William Z. Shetter, *The Pillars of Society: Six Centuries of Civilization in the Netherlands*, second revised edition (Utrecht: Netherlands Centrum Buitenlanders, 1997) and *The Netherlands in Perspective: The Organizations of Society and Environment* (Leiden: Martinus Nijhoff, 1987). Frank E. Huggett, *The Dutch Today* (The Hague: Staatsuitgeverij, 1973) is a more popular treatment done under contract to the Dutch Foreign Office. Though somewhat dated, the coverage of society in J. Goudsblom, *Dutch Society* (New York: Random House, 1967) and Adriaan Jacob Barnouw, *The Dutch: A Portrait Study of the People of Holland* (New York: Columbia University Press, 1940), *The Making of Modern Holland: A Short History* (New York: Norton, 1944), *The Pageant of Netherlands History* (New York: Longmans,

Green, 1952), and *The Land and People of Holland* (Philadelphia: Lippincott, 1972) are quite good. Max Schuchart, *The Netherlands* (New York: Walker & Co., 1972) and Gerald Newton, *The Netherlands: An Historical and Cultural Survey, 1795–1977* (Boulder, CO: Westview Press, 1978) are rather more up-to-date.

For a very scholarly study of popular culture, music, and the mass media in the latter half of the twentieth century and how they were influenced by American pop culture, see Mel van Elteren, *Imagining America: Dutch Youth and Its Sense of Place* (Tilburg: Tilburg University Press, 1994).

Though the information is not always the most current available, the Web site <http://www.BZ.MIONBUZA.NL/english/home.html> run by the Ministry of Foreign Affairs offers a general overview of life in Holland, as does the Web site <http://www.netherlands-embassy.org/nl-pca.htm> of the Dutch Embassy in Washington, D.C. For current statistics, see the Web site <www.cbs.nl> of the Central Statistical Bureau.

Frank E. Huggett, *The Modern Netherlands* (New York: Praeger, 1971) has a collection of statistical data from the 1940s, 1950s, and 1960s in the appendices.

On the geography of Holland, see A. M. Lambert, *The Making of the Dutch Landscape: An Historical Geography of the Netherlands* (New York: Seminar Press, 1971).

For more information on government in Holland, see Rudy Andeweg and Galen A. Irwin, *Dutch Government and Politics* (New York: St. Martin's Press, 1993). Marjolein 't Hart, Joost Jonker, and Jan Luiten van Zanden, eds., *A Financial History of the Netherlands* (Cambridge: Cambridge University, 1997) is a financial history of Holland, as is Johan de Vries, *The Netherlands Economy in the Twentieth Century: An Examination of the Most Characteristic Features in the Period 1900–1970* (Assen, Netherlands: Van Gorcum, 1978).

Information on the Dutch school system can be found in Loren S. Barritt, *An Elementary School in Holland: Experiment in Educational Practice* (Utrecht: Jan van Arkel International Books, 1996). The Web site <http://www.eur.nl/studeren/arsb/univned.html> of the Algemene Rotterdamse Studentenbond (General Rotterdam Union of Students) has links to the home pages of all the Dutch universities and colleges.

The history of Dutch literature from the twelfth to the twentieth century is found in Reinder Meijer, *Literature of the Low Countries: A Short History of Dutch Literature in the Netherlands and Belgium* (The Hague: Nijhoff, 1978), a revised and expanded version of the 1971 edition.

A survey of the history of Holland from prehistoric times to 1970 is found in Max Schuchart, *The Netherlands* (New York: Walker & Co., 1972).

The first part (pp. 10–109) of F. Gunther Eyck, *The Benelux Countries: An Historical Survey* (Princeton, NJ: Van Nostrand, 1959) is a short survey of Benelux history. J. Kossman-Putto and E. H. Kossman, *The Low Countries: A History of the Northern and Southern Netherlands, 1780–1940* (Rekkem, Flanders, Belgium: Flemish-Netherlands Foundation, 1987) takes a combined look at Dutch and Belgian history (1780–1940). The history of the Low Countries (Holland and Belgium) from the Middle Ages to the seventeenth century is presented in Herman van der Wee, *The Low Countries in the Early Modern World* (Brookfield, VT: Variorum, 1993).

The omnipresent, classic work on Dutch history to the nineteenth century is John Lothrop Motley, *The Rise of the Dutch Republic: A History in Four Volumes* (New York: Harper & Brothers, 1855). It is the story and drama of Dutch history, and Motley's persona shows through very clearly.

On the Roman Netherlands, see Tacitus, *Great Books of the Western World, Volume 15* (Chicago: Encyclopedia Britannica, 1952).

For the Burgundian Netherlands, see Walter Prevenier, *The Burgundian Netherlands* (Cambridge: Cambridge University Press, 1986).

On the Hapsburg Netherlands, see Charles W. Ingrao, *The Habsburg Monarchy, 1618–1815* (Cambridge: Cambridge University Press, 1994).

For an overview of the Eighty Years' War (Dutch War of Independence), see volume 1 (1609–1648) of Pieter Geyl, *The Netherlands in the Seventeenth Century*, 2 vols. (New York: Barnes & Noble, 1961–1964). Jonathan Irvine Israel, *The Dutch Republic: Its Rise, Greatness, and Fall, 1477–1806* (Oxford: Oxford University Press, 1995) places the War of Independence from Spain and the Golden Age in their historical context. He also explains the reasons for the split of the north and the south Netherlands into what became Belgium and Holland.

On the Reformation in Holland and Belgium, see Alastair C. Duke, *Reformation and Revolt in the Low Countries* (London: Hambledon Press, 1990). A biography of the Dutch philosopher Erasmus can be found in Albert Hyma, *The Life of Desiderius Erasmus* (Assen, Netherlands: Van Gorcum, 1972).

A look at the Golden Age from the point of view of the common man is found in Arie Theodorus van Deursen, *Plain Lives in a Golden Age: Popular Culture, Religion, and Society in Seventeenth-Century Holland* (Cambridge: Cambridge University Press, 1991). An interesting, if somewhat controversial, account of the Golden Age can be found in Simon Schama, *The Embarrassment of Riches: An Interpretation of Dutch Culture in the Golden Age* (New York: Alfred A. Knopf, 1987). See Johan Huizinga, *The*

Autumn of the Middle Ages: A Study of the Forms of Life, Thought, and Art in France and the Netherlands in the Fourteenth and Fifteenth Centuries (Chicago: University of Chicago Press, 1996) for the period of decline following the Golden Age.

On the Anglo-Dutch Wars, see James Rees Jones, *The Anglo-Dutch Wars of the Seventeenth Century* (New York: Longman, 1996).

Cornelis Christiaan Goslinga, *The Dutch in the Caribbean*, 3 vols.: vol. 1 —*and on the Wild Coast, 1580–1680*; vol. 2 —*and in the Guianas, 1680–1791*; vol. 3 —*and in Surinam, 1795–1942* (vol. 1: Gainesville: University of Florida Press, 1971; vols. 2 and 3: Assen, Netherlands: Van Gorcum, 1985 and 1990) is the source for information on the Dutch in Surinam. On Brazil, see Charles Ralph Boxer, *The Dutch in Brazil, 1624–54* (Oxford: Clarendon Press, 1957). On Brazil, Surinam, and the Antilles, see Johannes Postma, *The Dutch in the Atlantic Slave Trade, 1600–1815* (Cambridge: Cambridge University Press, 1990). Jean Gelman Taylor, *The Social World of Batavia: European and Eurasian in Dutch Asia* (Madison: University of Wisconsin Press, 1983) discusses social life in Dutch Asia. On the Dutch period in South African history, see Egidius Benedictus Watermeyer, *Selections of the Writings of the Late E. B. Watermeyer, with a Brief Sketch of His Life* (Cape Town: Juta, 1877). For the VOC and the WIC, see Pieter Geyl, *The Netherlands in the Seventeenth Century*, 2 vols. (New York: Barnes & Noble, 1961–1964). On the slave trade, see Johannes Postma, *The Dutch in the Atlantic Slave Trade, 1600–1815* (Cambridge: Cambridge University Press, 1990). Hendrik Riemens, *The Netherlands: Story of a Free People* (New York: Eagle Books, 1944) gives an interesting overview of the colonies from the perspective of the first half of the twentieth century, before decolonization.

For information on the Batavian Republic, the period of French domination, the Kingdom of the Netherlands, and the new constitution of 1848, see Simon Schama, *Patriots and Liberators: Revolution in the Netherlands, 1780–1813* (New York: Alfred A. Knopf, 1977); Jonathan Irvine Israel, *The Dutch Republic: Its Rise, Greatness, and Fall, 1477–1806* (Oxford: Oxford University Press, 1995) and volume five of Petrus Johannes Blok, *History of the People of the Netherlands*, 5 vols. (New York: AMS Press, 1970).

Hendrik Riemens, *The Netherlands: Story of a Free People* (New York: Eagle Books, 1944) offers an interesting, contemporary look at World War II, both in Europe and in the Pacific, from the Dutch point of view. The occupation of Holland during World War II is discussed in Louis de Jong, *The Netherlands and Nazi Germany* (Cambridge, MA: Harvard University

Press, 1990), and Werner Warmbrunn, *The Dutch under German Occupation 1940–1945* (Stanford, CA: Stanford University Press, 1963). On the battle to liberate Holland, see Henri A. van der Zee, *The Hunger Winter: Occupied Holland 1944–45* (London: J. Norman & Hobhouse, 1982).

For more information on Dutch drug policies, the Ministry of Health, Welfare, and Sport maintains a Web site at: <http://nederland.drugtext.nl/vws/drugnota/0/Default/htm>.

Gordon Langley Hall, *William, Father of the Netherlands* (New York: Rand McNally, 1969) is a biography of William the Silent. For all the stadholders (William I–V), see Herbert Harvey Rowen, *The Princes of Orange: The Stadholders in the Dutch Republic* (Cambridge: Cambridge University Press, 1988). The letters of Queen Sophie, consort of William III, are published in Sydney W. Jackman and Hella Haasse (eds.), *A Stranger in The Hague: The Letters of Queen Sophie of the Netherlands to Lady Malet, 1842–1877* (Durham, NC: Duke University Press, 1989). Information on the relationship between the Dutch and English royal houses during 1641–1672 is found in Pieter Geyl, *Orange and Stuart* (New York: Charles Scribner's Sons, 1969).

For general information on the Dutch military, see the Web site <http://www.mindef.nl/english/index.htm> maintained by the Dutch Ministry of Defense. Francis Vere, *Salt in Their Blood: The Lives of the Famous Dutch Admirals* (London: Cassell, 1955) is a collection of biographies of Dutch admirals.

A historical overview of Holland's foreign policy can be found in Amry J. Vandenbosch, *Dutch Foreign Policy since 1815: A Study in Small Power Politics* (The Hague: Nijhoff, 1959); J. H. Leurdijk, ed., *The Foreign Policy of the Netherlands* (Alphen aan den Rijn: Sijthoff & Noordhoff, 1978); and C. B. Wels, *Aloofness and Neutrality: Studies on Dutch Foreign Relations and Policy-Making Institutions* (Utrecht: H&S, 1982).

Pulitzer Prize–winning Barbara Tuchman, *The First Salute: A View of the American Revolution* (New York: Ballantine Books, 1988) places Dutch-American relations in the period of the American Revolution (1776–1781) in the historical context of England's conflicts with France and Holland. Her book demonstrates how French and Dutch aid made the American victory possible.

On Dutch immigration to North America, see Jacob van Hinte, *Netherlanders in America: A Study of Emigration and Settlement in the Nineteenth and Twentieth Centuries in the United States of America* (Grand Rapids, MI: Baker Book House, 1985) for a classic study based on firsthand interviews, first published in Dutch in 1928. A more modern treatment is found in Henry Stephen Lucas, *Netherlanders in America: Dutch Immigration to the United States and Canada, 1789–1950* (Grand Rapids, MI: W. B. Eerdmans, 1989). A collection of articles on Dutch immigration to the United States and Canada in the nineteenth and twentieth centuries is presented in Robert P. Swierenga, ed., *The Dutch in America: Immigration, Settlement, and Cultural Change* (New Brunswick, NJ: Rutgers University Press, 1985).

Bibliography of Translations of Works by Twentieth-Century Dutch Authors

Beckman, Thea. *Crusade in Jeans.* New York: Scribner, 1975.

Bloem, Marion. *Cockatoo's Lie.* Seattle, WA: Women in Translation, 1996.

Boon, Louis Paul. *Chapel Road.* New York: Macmillan, 1972.

Bordewijk, Ferdinand. *Character.* Franklin, NY: New Amsterdam Books, 1990.

Brouwers, Jeroen. *Sunken Red.* Franklin, NY: New Amsterdam Books, 1992.

Bruna, Dick. *Miffy at the Playground.* Handford: World International, 1996; reprinted in 1997.

———. *Miffy.* Handford: World International, 1997.

———. *Miffy at School.* New York: Kodansha International, 1997.

———. *Miffy at the Seaside.* Handford: World International, 1997.

———. *Miffy in the Snow.* Handford: World International, 1997.

Bussink, Gerrit, ed. *Bittersweet Pieces: Anthology of Short Stories.* Montreal: Guernica Editions, 1991.

———. *Nice People: Anthology of Short Stories.* Montreal: Guernica Editions, 1993.

Campert, Remco. *In the Year of the Strike.* Columbus: Ohio University Press, 1969.

———. "A Trip to Zwolle," in *The Library of Netherlandic Literature, Volume 2: Modern Stories from Holland and Flanders.* Egbert Krispyn (ed.). New York: Twayne Publishers, 1973.

———. "Pleasant Weeks in Paris," in *Nice People: Anthology of Short Stories.* Gerrit Bussink (ed.). Montreal: Guernica Editions, 1993.

————. "Property Is Theft," in *Nice People: Anthology of Short Stories.* Gerrit Bussink (ed.). Montreal: Guernica Editions, 1993.

————. "The Disappearance of Bertje S.," in *Dedalus Book of Dutch Fantasy: Anthology of Short Stories.* Richard Huijing (ed.). New York: Hippocrene Books, 1994.

————. *This Happened Everywhere.* San Francisco: Androgyne Books, 1997.

Claus, Hugo. *Sorrow of Belgium.* New York: Pantheon Books, 1990.

————. *Desire.* New York: Viking Penguin, 1997.

————. *The Swordfish.* Chester Springs, PA: Dufour Editions, 1997.

Couperus, L. *The Hidden Force.* Amherst: University of Massachusetts Press, 1990.

————. "Bluebeard's Daughter," in *Dedalus Book of Dutch Fantasy: Anthology of Short Stories.* Richard Huijing (ed.). New York: Hippocrene Books, 1994.

Dantzig, Rudi van. *For a Lost Soldier.* London: Bodley Head, 1996.

Dis, Adriaan van. *My Father's War.* New York: New Press, 1996.

Elsschot, Willem. *Villa des Roses.* New York: Viking Penguin, 1993.

————. *Three Tales from a Life.* Franklin, NY: New Amsterdam Books, 1999.

Frank, Anne. *The Diary of Anne Frank.* San Diego, CA: Harcourt Brace & Co., 1995.

Friedman, Carl. *Nightfather.* New York: Persea Books, 1995.

————. *The Shovel and the Loom.* New York: Persea Books, 1997.

————. *The Gray Lover.* New York: Persea Books, 1998.

Geeraerts, Jef. *Black Ulysses.* New York: Viking Penguin, 1978.

Grunberg, Arnon. *Blue Mondays.* New York: Farrar, Straus & Giroux, 1997.

Haasse, Hella S. *In a Dark Wood Wandering.* Chicago: Academy Chicago Publishers, 1994.

————. *Forever a Stranger and Other Stories.* New York: Oxford University Press, 1996.

————. *Threshold of Fire.* Chicago: Academy Chicago Publishers, Ltd., 1996.

————. *The Scarlet City.* Chicago: Academy Chicago Publishers, Ltd., 1997.

Half-a-Dozen Dutch: Six Writers-in-Residence at American Universities: Benno Barnard, Graa Boomsma, Renate Dorrestein, Thomas Rosenboom, Bert Schierbeek, Arie van den Berg. Ann Arbor, MI: Q.E.D. Press, 1989.

't Hart, Maarten. "Jaap Schaap," in *Bittersweet Pieces: Anthology of Short Stories.* Gerrit Bussink (ed.). Montreal: Guernica Editions, 1991.

Hartog, Jan de. *Captain Jan.* New York: White Lion, 1976.

Herzberg, Judith. *But What.* Oberlin, OH: Oberlin College Press, 1988.

Keuls, Yvonne. *The Mother of David S.* New York: St. Martin's Press, 1986.

Kopland, Rutger. *A World beyond Myself.* Chester Springs, PA: Dufour Editions, 1991.

Krabbé, Tim. "The Man Within the Cyclist," in *Nice People: Anthology of Short Stories.* Gerrit Bussink (ed.). Montreal, Guernica Editions, 1993.

————. *The Vanishing.* New York: Random House Value Publishing, 1995.

Minco, Marga. *Glass Bridge.* Chester Springs, PA: Dufour Editons, 1988.

————. *Empty House.* Chester Springs, PA: Dufour Editons, 1990.

————. *The Fall.* Chester Springs, PA: Dufour Editons, 1990.

————. *Bitter Herbs.* New York: Viking Penguin, 1991.

————. *The Other Side.* Chester Springs, PA: Dufour Editions, 1994.

Moor, Margriet de. *First Grey, Then White, Then Blue.* London: Picador, 1994.

Möring, Marcel. *The Great Longing.* New York: HarperCollins, 1996.

Mulisch, Harry. *The Stone Bridal Bed.* London and New York: Abelard-Schuman, 1962.

————. "The Horses' Jump and the Fresh Sea," in *The Library of Netherlandic Literature, Volume 2: Modern Stories from Holland and Flanders.* Egbert Krispyn (ed.). New York: Twayne Publishers, 1973.

————. *Two Women.* New York: Riverrun Press, Inc., 1981.

————. *What Poetry Is.* Merrick, NY: Cross-Cultural Communications, 1981.

————. *The Assault.* New York: Pantheon Books, 1986.

————. *Last Call.* New York: Viking Penguin, 1991.

————. "Decorated Man," in *Dedalus Book of Dutch Fantasy: Anthology of Short Stories.* Richard Huijing (ed.). New York: Hippocrene Books, 1994.

————. *The Discovery of Heaven.* New York: Viking Penguin, 1997.

New Writings and Writers, Volume 21: Alan Bold, John Wynne, Leonardo Schiascha, Philip O'Connor, Naomi May, Maarten 't Hart. New York: Riverrun Press, 1985.

Nine Dutch Poets: Rollins, Remco Campert, Bert Schierbeek, Simon Vinkenoog, J. Bernlef, Jules Deelder, Judith Herzberg, Karel Appel, Hans Plomp. San Francisco: City Lights Books, 1982.

Nooteboom, C. *Philip and the Others.* Baton Rouge: Louisiana State University Press, 1988.

————. *Knight Has Died.* Baton Rouge: Louisiana State University Press, 1990.

————. *A Song of Truth and Semblance.* New York: Viking Penguin, 1990.

————. *In the Dutch Mountains.* New York: Viking Penguin, 1991.

————. *The Following Story.* San Diego, CA: Harcourt Brace & Co., 1996.

————. *Rituals.* San Diego, CA: Harcourt Brace & Co., 1996.

————. *The Roads to Santiago.* San Diego, CA: Harcourt Brace & Co., 1996.

Ostaijen, Paul van. *Feasts of Fear and Agony.* New York: New Directions Pubishing, 1976.

————. *The First Book of Schmoll.* Los Angeles: Sun & Moon Press, 1996.

Palmen, Connie. *The Laws.* New York: George Braziller, 1993.

Poortvliet, Rien. *Gnomes.* London: New English Library, 1977; reprinted in New York: Harry N. Abrams, 1997.

————. *The Living Forest: A World of Animals.* New York: Harry N. Abrams, 1979.

————. *Secrets of the Gnomes.* New York: Harry N. Abrams, 1981; reprinted in 1982.

————. *Rien Poortvliet's Horses.* New York: Stewart, Tabori and Chang, 1995.

Reve, Gerard. "The Decline and Fall of the Boslowits Family," in *The Library of Netherlandic Literature, Volume 2: Modern Stories from Holland and Flanders.* Egbert Krispyn (ed.). New York: Twayne Publishers, 1973.

————. *Parents Worry.* North Pomfret, VT: Trafalgar Square, 1991.

————. "Werther Nieland," in *Dedalus Book of Dutch Fantasy: Anthology of Short Stories.* Richard Huijing (ed.). New York: Hippocrene Books, 1994.

Robinson, Tjalie. *The Hunt for the Heart.* Kuala Lumpur: Oxford University Press, 1997.

Ruyslinck, Ward. *Golden Ophelia.* London: Peter Owen, 1975.

Schmidt, Annie M. G. *Frizzlycurl.* Enschede, Holland: Tetem, 1966.

————. *Bob and Jilly.* London: Methuen, 1976.

————. *Bob and Jilly Are Friends.* London: Methuen, 1977.

————. *Dusty and Smudge and the Bride.* London: Methuen, 1977.

————. *Dusty and Smudge Keep Cool.* London: Methuen, 1977.

————. *Dusty and Smudge Spill the Paint.* London: Methuen, 1977.

————. *The Island of Nose.* London: Methuen, 1977.

————. *Dusty and Smudge and the Cake.* London: Methuen, 1979.

————. *Dusty and Smudge Splash the Soup.* London: Methuen, 1979.

————. *Bob and Jilly in Trouble.* London: Methuen, 1980.

————. *Pink Lemonade.* Grand Rapids, MI: Eerdmans, 1981; reprinted in 1992.

————. *Minnie.* Minneapolis, MN: Milkweed, 1994.

Vestdijk, Simon. *New Writers Two: Simon Vestdijk.* Atlantic Highlands, NJ: Humanities Press International, 1963.

————. *Red Dust Two: Alan Burns, Simon Vestdijk, Babette Sassoon.* New York: Red Dust, 1972.

————. *New Writers: Robert Pinget, Simon Vestdijk, Miodrag Bulatovic, Keith Johnstone.* New York: Riverrun Press, Inc., 1980.

————. *The Garden Where the Brass Band Played.* Franklin, NY: New Amsterdam Books, 1992.

————. "Affection," in *Dedalus Book of Dutch Fantasy: Anthology of Short Stories.* Richard Huijing (ed.). New York: Hippocrene Books, 1994.

Winter, Leon de. *The Day before Yesterday.* Ancram, NY: Vehicle Editions, 1985.

Wolkers, Jan. *A Rose of Flesh.* New York: George Braziller, 1963.

————. "Minister in a Straw Hat," in *The Library of Netherlandic Literature, Volume 2: Modern Stories from Holland and Flanders.* Egbert Krispyn (ed.). New York: Twayne Publishers, 1973.

————. *Turkish Delight.* London: Futura Publications, 1974; reprinted in 1976; reprinted in New York: Marion Boyars Publishing, 1983.

————. "Feathered Friends," in *Dedalus Book of Dutch Fantasy: Anthology of Short Stories.* Richard Huijing (ed.). New York: Hippocrene Books, 1994.

Index

About the Author

MARK T. HOOKER is a Visiting Scholar at Indiana University. He is the author of *The Military Uses of Literature* (Praeger 1996) and *Customs and Etiquette in Holland* (1997). His translation, with annotations, of *The Politically Correct Netherlands Since the Sixties* by Herman Vuijsje is forthcoming. He served as a linguist and foreign area specialist as a uniformed member of the U.S. Armed Forces and also as a Department of Defense civilian.